560-140

AGAINST THE TIDE

AGAINST THE TIDE

An Argument In Favor Of The American Soldier

LIEUTENANT COLONEL PETER B. PETERSEN

ARLINGTON HOUSE PUBLISHERS
NEW ROCHELLE, N. Y.

PRINTED IN THE UNITED STATES OF AMERICA

Library of Congress Cataloging in Publication Data

Petersen, Peter Barron.
    Against the tide: an argument in favor of the
American soldier.

    Bibliography: p.
    1. Soldiers--United States. 2. Vietnamese Con-
flict, 1961-   --Psychological aspects. 3. Sociology, Military. I. Title.
U22.3.P47   355.1   74-10970
ISBN 0-87000-270-8

To

my loving wife Jan and my three sons, John, Bill, and Jim. Their patience, assistance, and constant encouragement made completion of this book possible.

CONTENTS

TABLES

CHARTS

FIGURES

\

ACKNOWLEDGMENTS

I am deeply indebted to the many individuals and organizations that made completion of this book possible. Their continuing interest, efforts, and encouragement made the task easier, and the results more comprehensive and complete.

Professor Gordon L. Lippitt, as adviser of my research in its earlier stages, provided the essential and specific direction pertaining to behavioral science. He introduced the author to Professor Regis H. Walther, founder of the Job Analysis and Interest Measurement (JAIM). Professor Walther contributed hundreds of hours of his time in advising about the research design and the associated data processing. On many occasions he rolled up his sleeves at the Computer Center, working in the evenings and on weekends, and thus helped solve problems pertaining to computer operations. Both Professor Walther and Professor Lippitt provided continuing guidance on various parts of my research since 1966.

The author is especially grateful for the assistance received from Colonel Alfred E. McKenney, U.S. Army, Retired. His insight concerning the American soldier contributed substantially to the research project. His kindness and helpful advice are most appreciated

Mrs. Gwen O'Neill performed most of the programing and detailed data-processing operations. I am particularly appreciative of her patience and thoroughness in accomplishing these essential tasks. Key-punch operations during 1966–72 were performed superbly by the Key Punch Section, Data Management Branch, Operations Division, U.S. Army Management Systems Support Agency. Sincere thanks are expressed to Miss Roselia C. Burgin and the members of her section for their responsiveness and accurate work.

Miss Pauline C. Ramsey, chief of Army Studies Section, U.S. Army Library, contributed both time and effort in locating military studies relative to this project. Colonel Robert Leider, Lieutenant Colonel John W. Boyle, and Sergeant Major Betty L. Adams provided information pertaining to similar studies by nonmilitary sources. Their welcome assistance will be long remembered.

I am also deeply grateful to Mr. Nicholas A. LePore, a major innovator concerning personnel management procedures within the Office of Personnel Operations, U.S. Army, for his guidance and philosophy.

Dr. Shirley D. McCune, in 1967 a member of the Social Research Group,

13

George Washington University, furnished worthwhile advice and assistance.

Miss Carol McKenna was most helpful in sorting hundreds of essay-type responses to two questions asked in a biographical-data questionnaire. Her sensitivity to the attitudes of men in their early twenties provided a unique insight that otherwise might have been neglected.

The author is particularly indebted to Mrs. Helen B. Dawson for her constant and diligent work, as well as her devotion to the study. Her efficient management of many administrative details is directly responsible for the adequate control of data collection. Appreciation is also expressed to Mrs. Shirley A. Deely, Mrs. Ruth D. Dowden, Mrs. Ruth E. Kennedy, and Mrs. Diane J. Ramsey for their accurate assembling and addressing of over 2,100 questionnaire packets for mailing.

Appreciation is expressed to the Officer Candidate School authorities at Fort Belvoir, Virginia, for permitting this outsider to evaluate their program. Colonel Victor O. Wilson, who commanded the Engineer Officer Candidate Regiment in 1966 and 1967, was instrumental in the initiation of this study. His faculty board officer, Captain Kenneth D. Jobe, provided valuable assistance in the scheduling and coordination necessary for data collection. During 1970, the Engineer Officer Candidate School commander, Colonel Charles G. Olintine, and his faculty board officer, Captain Charles R. Edwards, were very helpful in conducting additional tests. Throughout the period 1966–70, Mrs. Mary Y. Payne and Mrs. Mary H. Jones, staff members of the faculty board, furnished reliable administrative data pertaining to officer candidates. Appreciation is also expressed to Colonel Piper, commander of the Infantry Officer Candidate School at Fort Benning, Georgia, for his assistance in data collection during 1968.

The author is grateful to Major General Franklin M. Davis, Jr., commandant of the U.S. Army War College, for his kind advice and professional thoughts on this subject. Members of his staff and faculty and their wives, as well as students attending the U.S. Army War College and their wives, have been very helpful. The contributions of the following were particularly noteworthy: Colonel George R. Allen, Jr., Colonel Donald W. Connelly, Colonel Robert E. Dingeman, Colonel Paul Goodman, Colonel Julius J. Jorgensen, Colonel William A. Rank, Colonel Roland H. Shamburek, Colonel Leroy Strong, Colonel John B. B. Trussell, Jr., Lieutenant Colonel Walter J. Bickston, Lieutenant Colonel Robert C. Gaskill, Colonel Dandridge M. Malone, Dr. Donald D. Penner, Mrs. Sharan Carbaugh, Miss Joyce M. Kovach, Mrs. Mary Lou Simmons, and Miss Shelby Wilkins.

Appreciation is expressed to Mr. Allen G. Fausnacht and his subordinates for their technical advice and welcome assistance. Mr. Jules Foreman is congratulated for his design and preparation of the charts used in this book. Mr. Richard D. Nale and Mr. William V. Caruso were most helpful in providing an insight regarding the use of photography to "liven up" a technical report. Sincere thanks are expressed to Mr. John C. Dupler for his help and professional advice. Thanks also to Mr. Daniel H. Bates and Mr. Roy E. Dively.

Appreciation is expressed to Colonel John P. M. Hughes, deputy commander, Strategic Studies Institute, U.S. Army Combat Developments Command, for his time and effort pertaining to research conducted concurrent with the writing of this book. The author is also grateful to the following members of the Medical Service Agency, U.S. Army Combat Developments Command: Colonel James K. Tillotson, Colonel John G. Morgan, and Colonel W. Rex Davis. Thanks also to Mr. L. David LeRoy for his professional guidance.

Appreciation is expressed to the thousands of individuals who completed questionnaires. Their response made this book possible.

Finally, the author is indebted particularly to Mrs. Janet March for her constant and diligent work connected with the final preparation and typing of this book.

Chapter 1

INTRODUCTION

The American soldier's beliefs have been described by many authors. At present, a somewhat popular concept is that the American soldier is inflexible and unimaginative, and that he readily conforms to regulations. The professional Army officer is viewed by Ward Just[1] as being "snobbish" and "strait-laced," and for the most part incapable of acting with human understanding. Today, many individuals regard the Army as being rigid, and its actions subordinate to doctrine. The following remarks by Ward Just tend to be typical of this criticism:

> Until the Army itself becomes more flexible, until it recognizes its priorities and places "doctrine" in the proper perspective, its troubles will multiply. The distinction between uniform and country will grow more apparent. And that will be tragic for everyone.

It is interesting to note that stereotypes held by the public view the soldier as being unlike their concept of the "typical" American. "Once the two-fisted hero of the silver screen, the American military man now suspects that Hollywood and television scriptwriters are trying to outdo one another in portraying him as venal, bumbling and brutal."[2] In contrast to much of the current rhetoric that portrays the American soldier unfairly, it is hoped that this volume will present a more objective analysis.

The soldier, above all other people, prays for peace, for he must suffer and bear the deepest wounds and scars of war.

GENERAL DOUGLAS MACARTHUR

PURPOSE

The purpose of this book is to describe objectively certain self-reported beliefs of the American soldier (other than aptitudes, training, or knowledge) that have an influence on his success or failure. Specific areas that will be

[1] Ward Just, *Military Men* (New York: Knopf, 1970).
[2] Tom Hamrick, "Coping with the Boob Image," *Army,* July 1970, pp. 26–30.

described are the individual's basic beliefs, activity preferences, personal values and behavioral styles. In this book, a realistic description of the American soldier of the Vietnam War will serve as an argument in favor of the American soldier. Commensurate with the findings of my research, developed over a six-year period, conclusions will be stated and specific recommendations will be made. It is hoped that the information provided in this book will be of value to military commanders, to staff officers, to the researchers who may conduct a more detailed and comprehensive study of the entire subject, and to the American people whom the soldier serves.

BACKGROUND

Prior research in the field of behavioral science indicated that many occupations have distinct subsets of occupations which, in turn, have their own typical self-reported beliefs. The overall occupation of being a soldier is no exception. An example of distinct subsets within the occupation of soldiering could be: senior officers, junior officers, and enlisted personnel. These three subsets probably have distinct differences in their beliefs. Within these three subsets there are numerous other subsets which probably also have distinct differences in their beliefs.

6,827 QUESTIONNAIRES ADMINISTERED TO 4,008 INDIVIDUALS DURING 1966–72

Category	Number of Individuals*	Number of Questionnaires Completed
Officer Candidates at Fort Belvoir (1966–67)	2,651	3,030
Officer Candidates at Fort Benning (1968)	271	271
Individuals Tested in Vietnam (1969)	534	543
Same Individuals Retested After Returning from Vietnam (1970)	n/a	177
Former Officer Candidates Retested (1970)	n/a	1,851
Officer Candidates at Fort Belvoir (1970)	329	509
Students Attending Army War College (1971–72)	223	446
TOTAL	4,008	6,827

* Many individuals were examined on several different occasions with the identical questionnaire, thus the number of persons examined is less than the number of questionnaires completed.

18

As well as investigating the differences in various groups of Army personnel, this study will also examine identical groups of individuals in different occupational settings. One such variance in occupational setting is found by studying the same group of individuals in various stages of completing an Officer Candidate School program. Another variance is found by examining a group of individuals in a combat setting and then examining them again after they return to the United States.

It is not intended to infer that the average American soldier of the Vietnam War period is typical of the subsets examined in this study. However, it is interesting to note that certain characteristics are typical for those individuals who decide to remain in the Service and for those who elect to depart. Further, it is interesting to find that certain self-reported beliefs are typical when groups of individuals interact with certain military occupational environments.

Although it presents interesting and basic factual information, it is recognized that the results of 6,827 questionnaires completed by 4,008 military personnel during the 1966–72 period do not constitute a detailed and accurate description of all the American soldiers of the Vietnam War, nor of an individual soldier. However, until a more extensive and comprehensive description is provided, it is hoped that this book will furnish some small measure of insight into the behavioral characteristics of the American soldier as he participated in the Vietnam conflict.

ARMY PROFESSIONALISM

A wide range of views are available concerning the subject of military professionalism. For example, a study conducted by the U.S. Army War College defines military professionalism as follows:

> Military professionalism is the attainment of excellence through education, experience and personal dedication. It is characterized by fidelity and selfless devotion to military service which presupposes self-discipline, great skill and extensive knowledge tempered by sound judgment, compassion and understanding. Professionalism implies lasting obligations and imposes a special trust which is inherent in the oath executed by every member of the Armed Forces of the United States.[3]

Another view is presented by Samuel P. Huntington, who considers Army officers a professional body. The fundamental thesis of his book *The Soldier and the State* is that the American Army officer is a professional man.

> A profession is a peculiar type of functional group with highly specialized characteristics. Sculptors, stenographers, entrepreneurs, and advertising copywriters all have distinct functions but no one of these functions is professional in nature. Professionalism, however, is characteristic of the modern officer in the same sense in which it is characteristic of the physician or lawyer.[4]

[3] Army War College Leadership Study, U.S. Army War College, June 30, 1970.
[4] Samuel P. Huntington, *The Soldier and the State: The Theory and Policies of Civil–Military Relations* (Cambridge, Mass.: Harvard University Press, 1967).

Huntington visualizes three distinguishing characteristics or criteria for military officership to be considered as a profession. These are expertise, responsibility, and corporateness.

> The professional man is an expert with specialized knowledge and skill in a significant field of human endeavor .... The responsibility to serve and devotion to his skill furnish the professional motive.[5]

With regard to corporateness, Huntington regards military men as sharing a sense of organic unity and consciousness of themselves as a group apart from laymen.

In contrast with the opinion of Huntington, many writers do not view the professionalism of Army officers in the same sense as they do that of lawyers, bankers, or doctors. To these individuals, the phrase "professional Army officer" is used to differentiate between "amateurs" and "careerists" rather than to denote trade or craft.

Morris Janowitz[6] believes that the civilian image of the professional soldier is securely rooted in the past. In his opinion, obsolete conceptions of the military remain because much of the public prefers to remain uninformed. In the United States, the military profession does not have great prestige. This view was not only intensively manifest during the period of the Vietnam War but was evident in periods before it. For example, a sampling[7] of national opinion in 1955 placed the prestige of the professional military officer below that of the physician, scientist, college professor, minister, and even public schoolteacher.

> A set of stereotyped assumptions has pervaded domestic politics with respect to the professional military .... It is typical to assert that the military establishment is the major source of thought or policy which overemphasizes the use of force in the resolution of conflict, whether domestic or international .... It is also typical to assert that the military professional is disciplined, inflexible, and, in a sense, unequipped for political compromise. In this view, since the perspectives of men are fashioned by their daily tasks, the life of the military professional produces a pattern of mental traits which are blunt, direct, and uncompromising.[8]

THE MILITARY MIND

Both Huntington and Janowitz indicate that the armed forces are eager to reduce civilian hostility toward the "military mind." "The 'military mind' has been charged with traditionalism and with a lack of inventiveness."[9] Much of the alleged contempt for the military mind is directed towards the officer as a disciplinarian.

[5] *Ibid.*, p. 8.
[6] Morris Janowitz, *The Professional Soldier* (New York: Free Press, 1971).
[7] Public Opinion Surveys, Inc., *Attitudes of Adult Civilians Toward the Military Services as a Career*, 1955.
[8] Janowitz, *op. cit.*, p. 4.
[9] *Ibid.*, p. 13.

Military and civilian writers generally seem to agree that the military mind is disciplined, rigid, logical, scientific; it is not flexible, tolerant, intuitive, emotional. The continuous performance of the military function may well give rise to these qualities. Intuitively one feels that these descriptions, also intuitive, come close to the mark. But until more knowledge is accumulated about the personality traits of military men and other politically significant groups and also about the relation between personality, values, and behavior in social situations, this approach will not be very useful in analyzing civil-military relations.[10]

The basis of some criticism of the military mind is cited by several historians in terms of the performance of American officers during World War II. A concern for the welfare of subordinates and a human approach to leadership are viewed incorrectly by many as modern phenomena. While it is recognized that the need for expediency during World War II often encouraged an authoritarian pattern of leadership, it nevertheless should be recognized that a more human side of leadership was also encouraged. Contrary to several popular views concerning the military mind during World War II, a 1942 edition of the U.S. Army's *Field Manual* 21–50: *Military Courtesy and Discipline* emphasized a concern for subordinates concurrent with accomplishing the mission.

> There is a tendency on the part of a few officers to think too much of the personal benefits which they might derive from their status as an officer. In the interests of good discipline, officers are required to wear distinctive uniforms, to live apart from their men in garrison, and to confine their social contacts to other officers. But do not make the mistake of thinking of yourself as a superior individual; rather regard yourself as one who has been accorded certain aids in order that he might best carry out the responsibilities of his office. In your relations with your men in the field never demand any bodily comforts for yourself which are denied to them. Think of yourself only after your men have been cared for. Through unselfish service, earn the respect and loyalty of your men, and they will cheerfully and willingly "take care of the old man"—that is the essence of the American system.[11]

QUESTIONNAIRE USED
IN RESEARCH PROJECT

Throughout this volume, my analysis is concerned with differences between groups of military personnel regarding certain self-reported beliefs. The test instrument I used is called the Job Analysis and Interest Measurement (JAIM).[12] JAIM is a 125-item questionnaire designed to measure certain self-reported beliefs of the individual (other than aptitudes, training, and knowledge) which have an influence on job success or failure. It provides 32 scales that measure self-reported beliefs. These scales pertain to basic beliefs, activity preferences, personal values, and behavioral styles. The differences in the specific scale averages, if statistically significant (determined

---

[10] Huntington, *op. cit.*, p. 60.

[11] U.S. Department of the Army, *Field Manual 21–50: Military Courtesy and Discipline,* June 15, 1942.

[12] The author is grateful to Professor Regis H. Walther, author of JAIM, for his personal guidance and assistance in accomplishing much of the work described in this book.

by using Fisher's t), will form the basis for further evaluation, explanation, and possible implications and speculation. In several instances, standard scores will be used in addition to t-tests in order to illustrate results on charts and tables.

It should be recognized that there are no right or wrong answers for this type of test. The instrument is based on the overall concept of the need to have a successful match between the professional requirements of an occupation and the qualities of the individual in that occupation. For example, it is obvious that the occupations of chief librarian and locomotive engineer require considerably different types of individuals; further, that most chief librarians would probably perform poorly as locomotive engineers and most locomotive engineers poorly as chief librarians.

An analysis of the results in this work will provide information relative to both the individual and the nature of his organization. The norms of the test instrument are intended only as a point of departure and are based on a wide variety of occupational groups. Listed below are the 32 JAIM scales in terms of their four major categories:

1. *Basic Beliefs*
    a. Extent of Optimism
    b. Degree of Self-Confidence
    c. Belief in Moral Absolutes
    d. Belief in Slow Change
2. *Activity Preferences*
    a. Prefers Problem Analysis
    b. Prefers Social Interaction
    c. Prefers Mechanical Activities
    d. Prefers Supervisory Activities
    e. Prefers Activity Frequent Change
3. *Personal Values*
    a. Values Status Attainment
    b. Values Social Service
    c. Values Approval from Others
    d. Values Intellectual Achievement
    e. Values Role Conformity
4. *Behavioral Styles*
    a. Degree of Perseverance
    b. Extent of Orderliness
    c. Prefers to Plan Ahead
    d. Influences by Persuasive Leadership
    e. Influences by Being Self-Assertive
    f. Move Toward Aggressor
    g. Move Away from Aggressor
    h. Move Against Aggressor
    i. Prefers Routine

j. Identifies with Authority
k. Prefers Independence
l. Prefers Directive Leadership Style
m. Prefers Participative Leadership Style
n. Prefers Delegative Leadership Style
o. Motivates by Knowledge of Results
p. Believes in External Controls
q. Prefers Being Systematic, Methodical
r. Prefers Group Participation

A brief description of each of the JAIM scales is presented below. Additional information pertaining to this questionnaire is presented in Appendix A.

1. *Basic Beliefs*

   a. Extent of Optimism—measures the degree to which the individual assumes that intentions of other people are benevolent and that satisfactions can be expected in the normal course of events.

   b. Degree of Self-Confidence—measures the degree to which the individual believes that he can influence his future.

   c. Belief in Moral Absolutes—measures the degree to which the individual believes in moral absolutes.

   d. Belief in Slow Change—measures the degree to which the individual believes that change should proceed slowly.

2. *Activity Preferences*

   a. Prefers Problem Analysis—measures the degree to which the individual likes to analyze situations and to develop ingenious solutions to problems.

   b. Prefers Social Interaction—measures the degree to which the individual likes work involving interaction with other people.

   c. Prefers Mechanical Activities—measures the degree to which the individual likes mechanical activities.

   d. Prefers Supervisory Activities—measures the degree to which the individual likes to plan and supervise the work of others.

   e. Prefers Activity Frequent Change—measures the degree to which the individual likes actively to engage in work providing excitement and a great deal of variety.

3. *Personal Values*

   a. Values Status Attainment—measures the degree to which the individual values himself by his achievement of status symbols established by the culture.

   b. Values Social Service—measures the degree to which the individual values himself by contributing to social improvement.

   c. Values Approval from Others—measures the degree to which the individual values himself by obtaining the approval of others.

   d. Values Intellectual Achievement—measures the degree to which the individual values himself by his intellectual attainments.

e. Values Role Conformity—measures the degree to which the individual values himself according to how successfully he can conform to the role requirements of society.

4. *Behavioral Styles*

a. Degree of Perseverance—measures the degree to which the individual continues at something even when he is not particularly interested in it.

b. Extent of Orderliness—measures the degree to which the individual has internal standards which are followed.

c. Prefers to Plan Ahead—measures the degree to which the individual is a self-starter and directs his own activity toward achievement of a goal.

d. Influences by Persuasive Leadership—measures the degree to which the individual exerts leadership in interpersonal relationships.

e. Influences by Being Self-Assertive—measures the degree to which the individual tends to pursue his own goals when they are in competition with the goals of others.

f. Move Toward Aggressor—measures the degree to which the individual tries to act diplomatically when someone acts toward him in a belligerent or aggressive manner.

g. Move Away from Aggressor—measures the degree to which the individual withdraws when someone acts toward him in a belligerent or aggressive manner.

h. Move Against Aggressor—measures the degree to which the individual counterattacks when someone acts toward him in a belligerent or aggressive manner.

i. Prefers Routine—measures the degree to which the individual likes to have definite procedures available which he can follow.

j. Identifies with Authority—measures the degree to which the individual identifies with his superior and tries to please him.

k. Prefers Independence—measures the degree to which the individual desires to act on his own.

l. Prefers Directive Leadership Style—measures the degree to which the individual believes that an executive gets best results by making decisions himself.

m. Prefers Participative Leadership Style—measures the degree to which the individual believes that executives get the best results by having their work groups participate in decisionmaking.

n. Prefers Delegative Leadership Style—measures the degree to which the individual believes that executives get the best results by delegating decisionmaking authority as much as possible to individual workers.

o. Motivates by Knowledge of Results—measures the degree to which the individual believes that people are motivated best by knowledge of results (intrinsic motivation).

p. Believes in External Controls—measures the degree to which

24

the individual believes that most people require external controls.

q. Prefers Being Systematic, Methodical—measures the degree to which the individual uses systematic methodical methods for processing information and for reaching his decisions.

r. Prefers Group Participation—measures the degree to which the individual identifies with a highly valued group.

ORGANIZATION OF BOOK

The next chapter will review literature on the American soldier of the Vietnam War. Then in Chapters 3 and 4, one form of U.S. Army leadership training will be described. During this leadership training specific changes in self-reported beliefs will be noted. Then, three years after training, the stability of these acquired beliefs will be measured.

Chapter 5 will concentrate on the effects of combat on the beliefs of infantrymen. Contrary to popular opinion, the sensitivity of infantrymen in combat to the needs of their friends is considerably higher than the norm of the test. It is interesting to note that the norm of the test is based on the norms of over 50 occupational groups tested in the United States. Contrary to another popular opinion, evidence does not emerge from my research that the Vietnam veteran finds it difficult to form close relationships with others.[13]

In Chapter 6, a comparison is made between a group of men on active duty in the Army and a similar group of individuals who recently departed from the Army. Major differences in many of their self-reported beliefs are analyzed. In addition, an analysis is made of the reasons why one group departed, and of the major goals in life for both of these groups combined.

Chapter 7 reports the findings of a study of certain self-reported beliefs of Army students attending the U.S. Army War College. Differences are then evident in a comparison of these individuals with five diverse groups of personnel associated with the Army.

In Chapter 8, the final chapter, the findings of this six-year study are summarized, conclusions stated, and recommendations offered.

---

[13] In a special article to the *New York Times* on May 3, 1972, "Delayed Trauma in Veterans Cited," Boyce Rensberger reports: "Perhaps the most commonly reported symptoms of what has been called the 'post-Vietnam syndrome' are a sense of shame and guilt for having participated in a war that the veteran now questions and the deeply felt anger and distrust of the government that the veterans believe duped and manipulated them.

In some cases, the doctors reported, the alienation and distrust engendered in the veterans extends to all those who have not served in Vietnam and who, the veteran believes, cannot understand his present feeling. Consequently, many veterans find it difficult to form close relationships with others."

Chapter 2

REVIEW OF CONTEMPORARY LITERATURE ON THE AMERICAN SOLDIER OF THE VIETNAM WAR

In reviewing the current literature about the American soldier of the Vietnam War, it seems the following five subjects are prevalent:

1. Characteristics of the American soldier.
2. Draft evasion.
3. Dissent by Service members.
4. Exiles.
5. Opinions concerning the U.S. military.

The purpose of this chapter is to represent clearly the views stated by various writers on this subject. It is the opinion of this writer that the majority of these views are incorrect. Therefore, my overall purpose is to "set the record straight" by eliminating certain misperceptions and by presenting the subject objectively. In reviewing the five subjects stated above, four misperceptions seem to play a substantial role:

1. *Training.* Training tends to change the individual from a "normal well-adjusted" person into a robot or perhaps even into a manipulating leader complete with a Machiavellian *modus operandi.* Many of the extreme views in contemporary writing are expressed in terms of a brainwashing system complete with the inoculation of a Dr. Strangelove vaccine.

2. *Effects of Combat.* Soldiers returning from Vietnam are disoriented and tend to be a detriment to society.

3. *Retention.* Those who make the Army a career are autocratic "hardheads" incapable of employment in a free society.

4. *Comparison of Various Subgroups.* There is in the current literature a tendency for critics of the Army to misjudge the characteristics of various subgroups within the Army. As a group, privates tend to be seen as oppressed pawns with a Beetle Bailey mentality. Junior officers, as a group, are often

viewed as naive; senior officers, as a group, tend to be looked on as manipulators of situations for the enhancement their own careers.

In the review that follows, the reader is encouraged to consider these four misperceptions. Then in subsequent chapters these misperceptions will be challenged.

CHARACTERISTICS OF THE AMERICAN SOLDIER

The following publications are representative of this broad subject:

1. *Military Men* by Ward Just (1970).
2. *The Sunshine Soldiers* by Peter Tauber (1971).
3. *No Victory Parades: The Return of the Vietnam Veteran* by Murray Polner (1971).
4. 365 *Days* by Ronald J. Glasser (1971).
5. *The American Military* ed. Martin Oppenheimer (1971).
6. *Pawns: The Plight of the Citizen-Soldier* by Peter Barnes (1972).
7. *The Role of the Military Professional in U.S. Foreign Policy* by Donald F. Bletz (1972).

Military Men[1] This book indicates considerable research and investigation. The greater part of Ward Just's account, however, seems affected by his delight in finding fault with the Army. In several instances in his overall argument, quotes from individuals, seemingly made during an unguarded moment, and perhaps in a minor portion of a statement, are exploited and expanded into major foundations. The otherwise uninformed reader might incorrectly assume that the following seven quotes featured by Mr. Just[2] accurately represent reality:

1. *A colonel:* The Army is the only goddam thing holding this country together.
2. *A West Point cadet:* There aren't any heroes any more.
3. *An officer's wife:* When my girls were growing up, I had to tell them that because their father was an officer that didn't make them different . . . . Now because of the war and what you read and hear, I have to defend who he is and what he does.
4. *A chaplain:* There are two boats which are sinking today, the military and the church, and I have a foot in both.
5. *A psywar colonel:* We are victimized. We are called upon to take abuse from the press and the public for decisions in which we have taken no part.
6. *A career sergeant:* These young guys can't seem to control their wives any more, and the wives don't seem to understand that a soldier's job is to fight.
7. *A general:* I will be damned if I will permit the U.S. Army, its institu-

[1] Ward Just, *Military Men* (New York: Knopf, 1970).
[2] *Ibid.*

tions, its doctrines, and its traditions, to be destroyed just to win this lousy war.

The Sunshine Soldiers[3] To avoid Vietnam, our hero in this pathetic description of basic training joined the Army Reserve. As a member of the Reserve he was called to active duty for training and was exposed briefly to Army life prior to returning to New York.

> It was four months of trying to pretend we were Americans, as good and bad as any others. Now we were merely weekend warriors, having bought life at a very cheap price, back for six years of probation, letting men with worn-out egos attempt to terrorize us; men who hope that there will always be a need for armies; so that they can feel some strength and frighten little boys.[4]

During his short stay in the Army, Peter Tauber managed to flex his self-proclaimed, liberal, middle-class, college-educated, New Yorker muscle. In feeding his own ego, one of his favorite delights was to ask a sergeant to define *eschaton*. In a series of self-reported adventures, our hero manages to fight the problem and seems to accomplish his mission of being a pest within legal limits. It's unfortunate that at the time the Army couldn't easily rid itself of individuals like Peter Tauber.

Perhaps in his former employment with the *New York Times* he should have asked his immediate supervisor to define *eschaton*. In any event, *The Sunshine Soldiers* lacks an objective view of soldiers; however, it is an entertaining story of how an individual can, in the United States, fight a large bureaucratic organization and accomplish his personal goal of making a worthless contribution.

No Victory Parades: The Return of the Vietnam Veteran[5] This book attempts to explore the meaning of the Vietnam War to our young servicemen. While the author interviewed over two hundred Vietnam veterans and their families and friends, he sifted out nine men and focused his investigation on them. It should be recognized that an investigation of nine other men would probably produce quite different results. In his analysis, these nine men were equally divided into three groups: the "hawks," the "doves," and the "haunted." However, in each case the analysis amounted to a hard-luck story of an individual from a lower-middle- or working-class family, who after returning from Vietnam was dissatisfied in varying degrees with the military establishment or with our society for sending him to Vietnam in the first place. The nine men, according to Polner, were somewhat ashamed of the war and had difficulty in explaining to their families why they should not have had to go, and why they were made to believe mistruths. A typical comment of a Vietnam veteran featured by Polner is:

---

[3] Peter Tauber, *The Sunshine Soldiers* (New York: Simon & Schuster, 1971).
[4] *Ibid.*, p. 259.
[5] Murray Polner, *No Victory Parades: The Return of the Vietnam Veteran* (New York: Holt, Rinehart and Winston, 1971).

Members of the 3rd Battalion, 60th Infantry welcomed home from Vietnam on July 10, 1969. Despite the prediction of Murray Polner in his book *No Victory Parades: The Return of the Vietnam Veteran,* these men received a very warm welcome from the people of Seattle, Washington, in spite of a rainy day. This parade may not have been a victory parade but it was the closest thing to it. Following the parade, the people of Seattle gave each soldier a salmon steak dinner with all the trimmings. It should be acknowledged, however, that several antiwar demonstrators were at the parade. Their antiwar sign is displayed left center, above.

I can't stand anyone who wasn't in combat telling me how we shoulda done this or that. They shoulda come to help out. I never wanted to be there; I only wanted to live and leave. So I can't help despising all those who were never in the paddies and would never allow their kids to become riflemen. The peace people confused me; the war people made it worse. They both mess up plain people's lives.[6]

Murray Polner's report lacks objective analysis. His detailed investigation of nine men emphasizes the "cruelty" they observed in combat. His report of three so-called hawks does not balance the series of atrocities, but rather reinforces his antimilitary argument. After reading his book, one might wrongly assume that there are very few soldiers who are both mature and not dissatisfied. The following is typical of his last chapter and of the overall impression conveyed by his book:

This time there will be no victory parades up Fifth Avenue. Despite the insistent superpatriotism of "hard-hat" construction workers who responded belligerently to antiwar students in 1970, the lower-middle and working-class combat veterans who gave so much for so little may well come to sympathize with what some of their deferred brothers were trying to tell them all along: that outside the bosom of military life and its mandated sacrifices there is an indifferent, insolent, and ruthless America.[7]

365 *Days*[8] This book gives an excellent account of the experiences of many servicemen in Vietnam. The author, a former major in the U.S. Army Medical Corps, interviewed hundreds of patients in an Army hospital in Japan during 1968 and 1969. His material is a result of a sincere and conscientious researcher reporting the human side of the horrors of combat. His interviews, however, are not limited to the subject of Vietnam, but include also the subject of training soldiers in the United States. His analysis of this instructional and socialization process is quite good and approaches the quality of several earlier studies reported by Morris Janowitz.

A major portion of the book reflects the emotions of seriously wounded men and their worries as they contemplate their future roles in society. In his description of events in a hospital in Japan, Glasser is both sensitive and perceptive. The reader, however, should not assume that the combat experiences of the patients interviewed by Glasser are representative of the experiences of all American soldiers in Vietnam. The individual perception of Vietnam combat events, as reported in Japan days later by men seriously wounded in battle, probably differs significantly from the individual perception of the same events by men who were not wounded. It is recognized in this case that objective reporting is difficult when events are reported in retrospect by individuals who had a traumatic experience in a particular battle.

The American Military[9] This book contains a number of essays by several

---

[6] *Ibid.*
[7] *Ibid.*, p. 159.
[8] Ronald J. Glasser, 365 *Days* (New York: George Braziller, 1971).
[9] Martin Oppenheimer, ed., *The American Military* (Chicago: Aldine, Transition Books, 1971).

authors about the American military. It is divided into two sections: (1) What the military is, and (2) What the military does to members in it and to the society in which it functions.

A particularly good essay is "Vietnam: Why Men Fight" by Charles C. Moskos. Moskos describes his observations of American soldiers in combat in Vietnam. Prior to presenting his view of why men fight, he described several popular notions:

1. Different armies perform according to the military spirit of their citizens. For example, Italians make poor soldiers while Germans tend to be good ones.

2. Combat performance is a consequence of the nature of the formal military organization. For example: discipline, training, *esprit de corps,* etc.

3. An effective military socialization process will give men the reason to fight. "Different premises by antimilitarists [are] concerned with the perversions that military life allegedly inflicts on men's minds."[10]

4. Combat performance depends on the soldier's belief in the purposes of the war. "Whether motivated by patriotism or a belief that he is fighting for a just cause, the effective soldier is ultimately an ideologically inspired soldier.[11]

5. The effectiveness of the soldier tends in part to depend on his solidarity and social intimacy with his peers at small group levels. (Stouffer *et al.,* and Janowitz have this view.)

Moskos, in describing why men fight in Vietnam, considers the following:

> My own research among American soldiers in Vietnam has led me to question the dominant influence of the primary group in combat motivation on at least two counts. First, the self-serving aspects of primary relations in combat units must be more fully appreciated. War is a Hobbesian World and, in combat, life is truly short, nasty and brutish. But, to carry Hobbes a step farther, primary group processes in combat are a kind of rudimentary social contract, a contract that is entered into because of its advantages to oneself. Second, although the American soldier has a deep aversion to overt political symbols and patriotic appeals, this fact should not obscure his even deeper commitments to other values that serve to maintain the soldier under dangerous conditions. These values—misguided or not—must be taken into account in explaining the generally creditable combat performance American soldiers have given. Put most formally, *I would argue that combat motivation arises out of the linkages between individual self-concern and the shared beliefs of soldiers as these are shaped by the immediate combat situation....*

> It is only in the immediate context of battle that one can grasp the nature of the group processes developed in combat squads. For within the network of his relations with fellow squad members, the combat soldier is also fighting a very private war, a war he desperately hopes to leave alive and unscathed.[12]

> I propose that primary groups maintain the soldier in his combat role only when he

10 Charles C. Moskos, "Vietnam: Why Men Fight," in *Ibid.,* pp. 16–36.
11 *Ibid.*
12 *Ibid.,* pp. 19–20.

has an underlying commitment to the worth of the larger social system for which he is fighting . . . .

Quite consistently, the American combat soldier displays a profound skepticism of political and ideological appeals. Somewhat paradoxically, then, anti-ideology itself is a recurrent and integral part of the soldier's belief system. They dismiss partiotic slogans or exhortations to defend democracy with "What a crock," "Be serious, man" or "Who's kidding who?"[13]

Pawns: The Plight of the Citizen-Soldier[14] It appears that the research conducted in connection with the preparation of this book is rather extensive. Peter Barnes is quite accurate in his quoting of the findings of many boards. He describes with glee many extraordinary instances that are unfavorable to the Army. However, Barnes falls short when he departs from his secondary sources of information and attempts to gain information from primary sources by interviewing the individuals who draw on their recollection to justify the conclusion reached by Barnes. His unrealistic indictment of the Army is probably caused, in part, by the fact that he has never been a member of the armed forces. Moreover, his argument rests mainly on a series of sensational news stories further developed into recommendations on how to develop a more democratic Army. It is interesting to note that a frequent reviewer of this book is Robert Sherrill, author of *Military Justice Is to Justice as Military Music Is to Music.*

Solutions, believe it or not, are something Barnes has plenty of. They're great solutions. Let an enlistee have, say, eight or ten days in uniform to change his mind about staying in (Britain allows four days). Give a GI the right to sue a drill instructor in civilian court for mistreatment. In noncombat areas, let a GI earn "free leave"—a certain number of days that he can just take off, the way a postman takes sick leave, by simply calling in and telling the sergeant he won't be back for a couple of days. Let soldiers organize into non-striking unions, to serve as gripe-channels and lobbies. Kick the military chaplains the hell out of uniform; it would be both a Constitutional and an aesthetic action. Fix it so that less-than-honorable discharges expire after five years.[15]

Robert Sherrill, like Barnes, feels that Barnes must be "on to something" in his expose and also supports a major part of Barnes' solution, the task of telling the brass how it is.

If we could just get Richard Nixon and Melvin Laird and the Joint Chiefs of Staff to take a dozen copies of *Pawns* and a couple of cases of beer down to the beach at San Clemente and spend the day reading and thinking about what Peter Barnes has to say, well, who knows, things might be done that would make young men actually proud to wear their country's uniform.[16]

[13] *Ibid.*, pp. 25–27.
[14] Peter Barnes, *Pawns: The Plight of the Citizen-Soldier* (New York: Knopf, 1972).
[15] Robert Sherrill, "Some Advice the Pentagon Should Heed," *Book World*, January 9, 1972, p. 1.
[16] Robert Sherrill, promotional endorsement of *Pawns: The Plight of the Citizen-Soldier.*

A recurring theme of Barnes is that training attempts to develop the civilian into a robot capable of being manipulated by autocratic leaders. A major assumption of Barnes is that soldiers don't want to fight for America and that it's not natural to expect that they should. Barnes is not correct when he assumes that patriotism is not applicable as a motivator today.

> Of the three prime objectives—discipline, motivation, and weapons skills—the simplest for the army to deal with is the last. Motivation and discipline are harder. They involve the spirit and the heart, the way men think and the way they behave.

> High motivation and good discipline are important in warfare for two rather obvious reasons: (1) it is not natural under ordinary circumstances for men to advance into a line of hostile and possibly lethal fire; (2) when men do advance or hold against an enemy, they have a much better chance of surviving, not to speak of winning, if they operate together. But the nature of America's role in the world today raises some important questions: *Should* motivation and discipline be imposed where they are voluntarily lacking? If so, *what kind* of motivation and discipline? And *how* should they be imposed?[17]

The Role of the Military Professional in U.S. Foreign Policy[18] This book identifies the extent to which the U.S. military has entered into the field of foreign affairs. It evaluates the changing role of the military professional in the formulation, coordination, and execution of U.S. foreign policy. In addition, this book conceptualizes major courses of action for the military profession as it concerns U.S. foreign policy. In his last chapter, Bletz presents a good summary of his book. His major points are covered in the following extracts:

> If the post-war era has indeed come to an end and we are in "an era of negotiations," it would seem, as one writer suggested, that the guiding principles of U.S. foreign policy will shift from the concept of "no more Munichs" to one of "no more Vietnams." The impact of such a shift in philosophical orientation will have a profound effect on the politico-military equation in the United States. A case has been made for the argument that military *factors* have played an extremely important part in construction of the politico-military since 1940. There is a real difference, from the point of view of military professionalism, between military factors and military men having a strong hand in balancing the equation. It follows, however, that if military factors are heavily weighted, the influence of the military professionals will likewise be felt either directly or indirectly. Extending this line of thinking into the next decade, it appears that there is a good chance that military factors will command less weight than has been the case. It would seem to follow that the role of the military professional in the foreign policymaking process will likewise be reduced.[19]

> ... As has been suggested several times in this study, the American military profession is a reflection of the nation it serves. If the nation wants a military

[17] Barnes, *op. cit.*, pp. 59–60.
[18] Donald F. Bletz, *The Role of the Military Professional in U.S. Foreign Policy* (New York: Praeger, 1972).
[19] *Ibid.*, p. 272.

establishment that is professional at the first (technical) level and possesses a "body count" mentality as a substitute for the second (politico-military) level of professionalism, that is what it will get. If, on the other hand, the United States wants its armed forces to be possessed of meaningful professionalism at both levels, that is what it will get. In a democracy the military profession does not and should not make the determination of what its role in that society should be. This is, and must always be, a domestic political decision made by the elected civilian leadership. From the preceding chapters, it is obvious that the author feels the United States needs the second, more inclusive and at the same time more demanding sort of military professionalism.[20]

DRAFT EVASION

A major portion of today's literature on the American soldier of the Vietnam War tends to focus on draft evasion. The following publications are considered representative of many others during this period:

1. *A Conflict of Loyalties* ed. James Finn (1968).
2. *Who Will Do the Fighting for Us?* by George Reedy (1969).
3. *If This Be Treason* by Franklin Stevens (1970).
4. *I Refuse* by J. K. Osborne (1971).
5. *Prophets Without Honor* by John Rohr (1971).
6. *The Draft and the Rest of Your Life* by Richard L. Killmer and Charles P. Lutz (1972).

A Conflict of Loyalties[21] This book is a collection of essays that argues in favor of selective conscientious objection. By selective conscientious objection the author is referring to objection to a particular war rather than to war in general. While the rights of a person who conscientiously objects to participating in all wars may be recognized, a person not generally opposed to war could not legally refuse to participate in the Vietnam War because he believed the Vietnam War unjust.

Who Will Do the Fighting for Us?[22] Mr. George E. Reedy was formerly a Presidential assistant and a member of the President's National Advisory Commission on Selective Service. In answering the question posed by the title of this book, he contrasts an Army raised by the draft with an all-volunteer professional Army.

> I do not relish either a conscript or a "volunteer" Army. But I believe that a democracy can live more easily with the conscripts than it can with the professionals. The former do not like what they are doing—and that is precisely the reason why they should be preferred.[23]

If This Be Treason[24] Franklin Stevens interviewed more than 50 draft

[20] *Ibid.*, pp. 283–284.
[21] James Finn, ed., *A Conflict of Loyalties: The Case for Selective Conscientious Objection* (New York: Western, 1968).
[22] George E. Reedy, *Who Will Do the Fighting for Us?* (New York: World, 1969).
[23] *Ibid.*, p. 14.
[24] Franklin Stevens, *If This Be Treason* (New York: Peter H. Wyden, 1970).

evaders in various regions of the country. The results of several of these tape-recorded interviews are presented in this book. It seems rather significant that evading the draft because of "reasons of conscience" appears to be disturbing the conscience of many of today's young draft evaders. The main thrust of many of their arguments is that draft evaders need a course of action available that will enable them to evade the draft with honor and not deceit. Current legal rules, according to one of the individuals interviewed by Stevens, do not offer an honorable choice. "My country presented me with a set of alternatives: to kill, to go to jail, or to be dishonest."[25]

In this account of several draft evaders, there seems to be a common process leading towards their actual decision. This process is interpreted by this reader as follows:

1. Prior to losing a deferment, individuals tend not to be particularly concerned about Vietnam or the possibility of being drafted. "The war should be fought, and there has to be a draft to get the soldiers to fight it, but that doesn't mean it has to be fought by me."[26]

2. After a deferment expires, the individual may be surprised to find himself eligible for the draft. At this point the issue may be whether or not to avoid the draft.

3. At this stage in the process, so-called ethical means may be attempted to avoid the draft. For example: immediate employment in a critical occupation. The individual may tend to feel guilty at this stage. He realizes his responsibility but has little or no concern about Vietnam. In a war in defense of the nation, his attitude might be quite different.

> The truth of the matter was that I felt lousy about it. I really felt guilty. On the other hand, I felt justified in not being willing to go, and this seemed to be the only avenue of escape.[27]

4. If the individual cannot avoid the draft by "ethical means," he will probably now have strong feelings against the morality of the Vietnam War and possibly against wars in general. At this stage, the issue is how to evade the draft.

5. Individual evades the draft.

6. Individual attempts to justify to himself his action as an honorable one.

I Refuse[28] This is the story of an individual who chose to disobey the law and subsequently selected prison instead of the Army. Mr. Osborne's diary started with his arrest by the FBI and concluded with his personal thoughts after being released from prison. His sad account reflects many changes during this period, including changes in his own personality, and changes in some of his own beliefs.

[25] *Ibid.*, p. 30.
[26] *Ibid.*, p. 5.
[27] *Ibid.*, p. 15.
[28] J. K. Osborne, *I Refuse* (Philadelphia: Westminster, 1971).

Prophets Without Honor[29] This is an adaptation of a dissertation previously submitted by the author to the Political Science Department of the University of Chicago. As a study of public policy, Dr. Rohr addresses selective conscientious objection with regards to whether or not it should be the law of the land. Two major parts of this book are concerned with:

1. Is there a constitutional right to selective conscientious objection?[30]
2. Despite the absence of a constitutional *mandate* for selective conscientious objection, are there sound theoretical and practical considerations that may prompt Congress to adopt such a measure anyway?[31]

It is interesting to note that typical of most books on this subject, the selective conscientious objector is referred to in heroic terms.

> They speak out boldly against the folly of those in power. They have also been treated in a manner consistent with that tradition. Jerusalem stoned her prophets, while we merely incarcerate ours. This may be "progress," but I am sure it will bring small comfort to those in prison for conscience sake.[32]

Although the argument made in these two parts of the book is well presented and easy to follow, the 3½-page conclusion is significantly unsubstantiated. This conclusion is not objective and overly emphasizes his personal opinion. His concluding sentence is rather surprising: "I would therefore invoke the principle of 'the lesser evil' to justify the painful course of stoning our prophets now and building our monuments in happier times."[33]

The Draft and the Rest of Your Life[34] This volume describes the operation of the Selective Service System and various courses that one might consider in order to escape the draft. It is a rather thin paperback and appears to be a well-written guide on the subject. It avoids much of the legal terminology associated with more sophisticated writings on the same subject.

> Basically there are three options: (1) serving in the military, (2) the legal alternative of conscientious objection, (3) the extralegal alternatives (various forms of refusing to cooperate with the draft).

> If you are a parent, pastor, guidance counselor, or other person related to draft-age men, the book is for you also. It will help you to understand the decision which must be made by draft-age men, and perhaps your role in facilitating the decision.[35]

It seems that the scope of this book is comparable to "Robbing a Bank and the Rest of Your Life." It's your decision to make, and here are the

[29] John A. Rohr, *Prophets Without Honor* (Nashville: Abingdon, 1971).
[30] *Ibid.*, p. 10.
[31] *Ibid.*
[32] *Ibid.*, p. 183.
[33] *Ibid.*, p. 184
[34] Richard L. Killmer and Charles P. Lutz, *The Draft and the Rest of Your Life* (Minneapolis: Augsburg, 1972).
[35] *Ibid.*, p. 5.

consequences if you are caught. Now, if you are still interested, here is how to rob a bank:

1. Security during operation.
2. Communication.
3. Antialarm device.
4. Antiphoto device.
5. Moving the money.
6. Early warning system.
7. Plan for immediate escape.
8. Long-range escape plan.

In a more serious vein, it seems rather extraordinary that there is such a high demand for books pertaining to draft evasion. Perhaps the demand stems from a desire to sidestep a call to Vietnam.

DISSENT BY SERVICE MEMBERS

A major subject pertaining to the American soldier of the Vietnam War is dissent by Service members. While the Army, because of its size and mission, tends to bear the brunt of the criticism, other Services are also represented. The following publications seem to be representative of contemporary material on this subject.

1. *GI Rights and Army Justice* by Robert Rivkin (1970).
2. *Military Justice Is to Justice as Military Music Is to Music* by Robert Sherrill (1970).
3. *Up Against the Brass* by Andy Stapp (1970).
4. *Turning the Guns Around* by Larry Waterhouse and Mariann Wizard (1971).
5. *Conscience and Command: Justice and Discipline in the Military* ed. James Finn (1971).
6. *Patriotism in America: A Study of Changing Devotions 1770–1970* by John Pullen (1971).
7. *The Lionheads* by Major Josiah Bunting (1972).

GI Rights and Army Justice[36] It seems that the guardhouse lawyer of yester-year has been resurrected as a coffeehouse lawyer. Robert Rivkin does a splendid job of describing the rights of today's soldier. However, the main thrust of his book is to elaborate discrepancies in the system where the rules conflict with actual practices.

This book about the Army's system of justice has two major weaknesses:

1. The author's indictment of the U.S. Army influences and destroys much of his analysis: "At the same time, any low-ranking soldier who asserts a right against authority can be deemed a 'troublemaker,' and to that extent this is a book about how to become exactly that."[37]

[36] Robert S. Rivkin, *GI Rights and Army Justice* (New York: Grove Press, 1970).
[37] *Ibid.*, p. xxi.

2. The book's objective, "the draftee's guide to military life and law," is not reached because the author overemphasized goldbrickmanship.

In the book the terms *Army* and *draftee* are often represented by the terms *oppressor* and *oppressed*. Much can be learned about misjudgments of the Army from Rivkin's startling evaluation.

> If the professional soldier who looks upon the movement for GI rights with utter dismay remembers that it is the defects in the system rather than the people who have tried to administer it with compassion and wisdom that are under attack, the pain of transition should not be that great. Our Army is where it is because morale can no longer be bought with movies and beer. Its court-martial system does what it does because justice can never be purchased by exhortations that commanders should behave. Men with power like to use it, and those with too much tend to abuse it. In a real sense, all the American people must unite to take back the power they have lost to the military. But it is the GI himself who must lead the struggle. As Dr. Martin Luther King wisely said, "Freedom is never voluntarily given by the oppressor; it must be demanded by the oppressed."[38]

Military Justice Is to Justice as Military Music Is to Music[39] In this work a collection of provocative cases is presented in terms of alleged mistakes in military justice. Emphasis is placed on analyzing the Presidio "mutiny" and the court-martial of Dr. Howard Levy. In his attack on both the military and the overall system of military justice, Sherrill projects the following:

1. Military commanders tend to view any form of dissent as a form of treason and act swiftly to find the accused guilty.
2. Command influence dominates the court-martial system and invalidates the possibility for achieving justice.
3. Military commanders maintain that they must have total domination over individual Service members or the armed forces will disintegrate.
4. Leaders of the military prefer to achieve total discipline with a minimum of blood and abuse; however, under the disguise of military justice they punish those individuals who threaten discipline in an organization.
5. There is panic in the military establishment in trying to repress antiwar dissent by members of the armed forces.
6. Military justice is prefabricated according to the wishes of the local commander, and trial is tantamount to a verdict of guilty.
7. There is a loss of all human rights when an individual is sent to a military prison.
8. The goal of military justice is not justice, but discipline. Discipline is achieved by any means, including debasement and vengeance.

Sherrill, in convicting the military, is quick to find fault with the military establishment, but is slow to find any fault with those individuals being tried.

In viewing servicemen's rights, Sherrill considered a statement made by

---

[38] *Ibid.*, p. 350.
[39] Robert Sherrill, *Military Justice Is to Justice as Military Music Is to Music* (New York: Harper & Row, 1970).

Judge George W. Latimer of the Court of Military Appeals over fifteen years ago pertaining to a freedom-of-speech case.

> Undoubtedly we should not deny servicemen any right that can be given reasonably. But in measuring reasonableness, we should bear in mind that military units have one major purpose justifying their existence: to prepare themselves for war and to wage it successfully .... If every member of the service was, during a time of conflict or preparation therefor, permitted to ridicule, deride, deprecate, and destroy the character of those chosen to lead the armed forces, and the cause for which this country was fighting, then the war effort would most assuredly fail .... If it is necessary for survival that this country maintain a sizable military establishment ... then I have a great deal of difficulty in following an argument that those who serve should be entitled to express their views, even though by so doing they may destroy the spirit and morale of others which are vital to military preparedness and success.

The above statement by Judge Latimer weakens many of the arguments concerning dissent made by Sherrill. However, Sherrill is true to form in stating his antimilitary beliefs by viewing Judge Latimer's statement as a device that can be used by military commanders to defend their so-called improper actions. In defense of the system convicted by Robert Sherrill, it seems that his analysis of military justice is to justice as banging garbage can lids is to music.

Up Against the Brass [40] This is an elaboration of the author's adventures as he opposed the U.S. Army. According to Stapp, he was forced to leave Pennsylvania State University because he burned his draft card. Later he joined the Army with the avowed purpose of organizing effective dissent against the war in Vietnam. "I reported for my induction physical in December 1965, believing I could be more effective if I joined the Army and organized from within ...." [41] "Even in May 1966, during the start of basic training at Fort Jackson, South Carolina, my thoughts centered solely on how I was going to organize effective dissent against the war in Vietnam." [42] It seems unfortunate that the Army wasted considerable time and effort in coping with this irresponsible individual. Stapp was eventually discharged as an undesirable during April 1969. Perhaps a better solution would have been not to have accepted him when he decided to join the Army.

Startling it is to note the lyrics of a song that was particularly enjoyed by Stapp and his pals.

> Come all you young soldiers,
> Good news to you I'll tell
> About a great new union
> That's really raising hell.
>
> The lifers are like bosses,

---

[40] Andy Stapp, *Up Against the Brass* (New York: Simon & Schuster, 1970).
[41] *Ibid.*, p. 16.
[42] *Ibid.*, p. 18.

They work us to the ground,
But we will have the last word
When we turn the guns around. [43]

According to Stapp, the following eight-point program became the corner-stone of the American Servicemen's Union:

1. An end to the saluting and sirring of officers . . .
2. Rank and file control over court martial boards . . .
3. An end to racism in the Armed Forces . . .
4. Federal minimum wages for all enlisted men . . .
5. The right of GI's to collective bargaining . . .
6. The right to free political association . . .
7. The election of officers by enlisted men . . .
8. The right to disobey illegal and immoral orders.[44]

After describing the so-called real heroes of history in terms of (for example) the defenders of Stalingrad, the Algerian rebels, the Viet Minh, and the Cuban rebels who died before Batista's guns, Stapp concludes that the real heroes of history also include members of the American Servicemen's Union "who have been sent to the stockade because they fought for what is right." [45]

Turning the Guns Around [46] Larry Waterhouse was involved in the Movement for a Democratic Military during his stay in the Army. Mariann Wizard has been active in radical politics in Texas since 1965. She is also an active partici-pant in the Women's Liberation Movement. The authors met while they were fellow members of the Students for a Democratic Society. This book is primarily concerned with the so-called GI Movement Within the Military. The authors believe that this movement is responsible for many of today's social changes within the military. Their bitter assaults include as targets the modern volunteer Army concept, and the motives of leaders within the Army.

Waterhouse tells of his reclassification to 1-A and his decision to go to Canada for good. It seems unfortunate for the Army that he decided to return after six weeks. "I found that I could not abandon my country so easily. I returned to Texas, joined the Students for a Democratic Society, and began to try to make a revolution." [47]

The list of demands by the Movement for a Democratic Military related in this book seems much like a warmed-over but expanded version of those previously listed by Andrew Stapp in the American Servicemen's Union. The book concludes with a description of behind-the-scenes activities of the Vietnam Veterans Against the War demonstration held in Washington, D.C., from April 19 to 23, 1971.

In retrospect, it seems counterproductive to force individuals like Larry

---

[43] *Ibid.*, p. 87.
[44] *Ibid.*, pp. 88–90.
[45] *Ibid.*, p. 192.
[46] Larry G. Waterhouse and Mariann G. Wizard, *Turning the Guns Around* (New York: Praeger, 1971).
[47] *Ibid.*, p. 5.

40

Waterhouse to participate in military service.

Conscience and Command; Justice and Discipline in the Military[48] This book contains a collection of papers edited by James Finn pertaining to justice and discipline in the military. All of the articles favor considerably less discipline and considerably greater individual rights. In this book, a paper by Dr. Peter G. Bourne concerning the military and the individual is well worth reading. Unlike the other papers and the personal testimony from antiwar celebrities such as Howard Levy and Roger Priest, the Bourne paper presents a rather convincing argument. He views the basic training process as a militarization process that molds attitudes and beliefs in a four-step system. His argument is so well presented it almost seems possible. However, the reality of how basic training is actually conducted today eliminates significantly much of the impact of his analysis.

> Does military service make an individual more mature, more responsible, and more psychologically stable, or does it destroy individual identity, warp idealism, and mutilate the minds of innocent young men? Does the draft result in better citizens with a fuller appreciation of a democratic society, or does it produce only subjugated, submissive conformists, brainwashed with the self-righteous ideologies of the military-industrial complex? While each viewpoint has its own strong body of adherents in our society, the truth probably contains elements of all of these positions. The effects of military service are by no means the same for every inductee. Personality characteristics, attitudes in the home, age at induction, political sophistication, educational level, and the prevailing political attitudes in the larger society are but a few of the factors that modify the experience for each individual. Yet there are certain sociological and psychological events that are common to the experience of all draftees, and provide a more valid understanding as to what are the short and long-term effects of the military on the individual and the implications which they have for his subsequent participation in a democratic society.[49]

Patriotism in America: A Study of Changing Devotions 1770–1970[50] John Pullen provided a rather good examination of the nature of patriotism in America spanning a 200-year period. However, his equating of today's rebels with the patriots of the American Revolution seems impossible to parallel. Conversely, his analysis of the impact of contemporary events on the frustration and anger of many Americans is quite helpful.

> In retrospect the Cambodian incursion was not a terribly serious widening of the war or encroachment upon international ethics—it was nothing to what the communists had been doing in that area of Southeast Asia for years. But in this country it was the trip-latch that loosed a flood of pent-up rage and frustration that had been accumulating for years and that now poured forth, inundating everything in its path. The President, the Pentagon, the ROTC, the draft boards, corporations,

---

[48] James Finn, ed., *Conscience and Command: Justice and Discipline in the Military* (New York: Random House, 1971).

[49] Peter G. Bourne, in *ibid.*, pp. 137–138.

[50] John J. Pullen, *Patriotism in America: A Study of Changing Devotions* 1770–1970 (New York: American Heritage, 1971).

universities—all were angrily attacked. Never before in America had there been such confusion, so much irrationality, so great a concern with symptoms and so little with disease, and no part of our society felt the weight of it quite so much as did the military.[51]

In his comparison of the patriotism of the American soldier of World War II with that of the American soldier of the Vietnam War, Pullen justifies exceptional acts of combat during the Vietnam War by a higher level of patriotism. This comparison is both provocative and an essential consideration in the further analysis of the nature of the American soldier during the Vietnam War.

> The soldier, sailor, or airman in Vietnam has found himself in quite a different position from that of World War II. He soon lost the support of the people back home. By and large he could not have had the feeling that he was fighting for a worthwhile cause, which was the mainstay of his father and uncles while they battled the Germans and Japanese. Without this support and this inner conviction, how have men managed to fight, and fight bravely, many of them, in Vietnam?
>
> Is this patriotism?
>
> If so, it is of a higher order than we have any right to expect. In Vietnam important elements of patriotism that otherwise would have sustained the fighting men had been sheared away. What remained, however, was at least one of the building blocks out of which patriotism is probably constructed—in the language of social psychology, loyalty to "the primary group." In the armed services this is, of course, the squad, crew, platoon, company, battery, or other unit with which the individual is associated; it is the little community of people whose standards he wishes to live up to, whose approval he desires, who reward him with various satisfactions, and upon whose survival his own may depend.
>
> The strength of this concept is borne out most dramatically by the following incident, which has been duplicated all too frequently in Vietnam.
>
> Five American soldiers are moving through the jungle on an October day in 1965. A live enemy grenade flies out of the brush and into their midst. There is no time to pick it up and hurl it back, no time to get away. One of the soldiers throws himself on the grenade, muffles the full force of the explosion with his body, and by giving his own life, saves those around him.
>
> His name is Milton L. Olive III.
> He is eighteen.
> He is black.
> He is awarded the Medal of Honor posthumously.
>
> An unusual act? It can certainly never be called common. But by the middle of May, 1970, Medals of Honor had been awarded to forty-six men who had absorbed the blasts of grenades, mines, or booby traps with their bodies in Vietnam or placed themselves between their comrades and an impending explosion. The deed was done so quickly in most cases that there could have been no time to think, nothing more

[51] *Ibid.*, p. 127.

than an impulse. And the psychologists who have told us that self-preservation is the No. 1 instinct might give this phenomenon some thought.[52]

While considerable portions of this book are concerned with dissent and a lack of patriotism during the Vietnam War, the author fairly portrays the emotions of many Americans who participated in Honor America Day in Washington, D.C., on July 4, 1970.

In viewing the changing devotions of patriotism in America during this span of 200 years, it is interesting to note the role of the flag.

> One characteristic of the flag, as the eminent divine Shailer Mathews once remarked, is that it is a symbol so charged with emotion that people cannot look at and judge, even, whether or not the design is aesthetically good or bad. It seems also that the flag blinds the individual who is looking at it with a dazzling reflection of his own ideas; hence, during the few weeks previous to Independence Day, 1970, the flag had been the center of more fist fights than it had of constructive discussion. It used to be that when the flag went by, you got a lump in your throat; during this period you were likely to have got one on your head.[53]

The Lionheads[54] Unlike many anti-Army and anti-Vietnam War books, this one hits skillfully at the Army's dirty linen. It seems refreshing to read a novel on the Vietnam War where the author has most of his military terminology straight. Unfortunately, Major Bunting's bias is evident in his overzealous disgust for the colonels, and hate for the commanding general. Much of his book focuses on the theme that the high-ranking brass are sacrificing low-ranking brass in order for them to get their tickets punched. It seems that the high-ranking brass are greener on the other side of the battlefield. In his novel, the low-ranking brass and their men are seen as the victims. It seems ironic that many of the other antimilitary books written by former enlisted men see the low-ranking brass as the ones who are trying to get their tickets punched. Perhaps the determination of who is trying to get his ticket punched is in the mind of the beholder and is also directly related to the beholder's rank.

EXILES

Our discussion of draft evaders and dissent by Service members would not be complete without a survey of the current writing pertaining to exiles. While numerous books have been published on this subject, the following seem typical.

1. *The New Exiles* by Roger Williams (1971).
2. *American Deserters in Sweden: The Men and Their Challenge* by Thomas Hayes (1971).
3. *They Can't Go Home Again* by Richard L. Killmer, Robert S. Lecky and Debrah S. Wiley (1971).

The New Exiles[55] This book pertains to American draft evaders and to

[52] *Ibid.*, pp. 171–172.
[53] *Ibid.*, pp. 184–185.
[54] Major Josiah Bunting, *The Lionheads* (New York: George Braziller, 1972).
[55] Roger N. Williams, *The New Exiles* (New York: Liveright, 1971).

American military deserters in Canada. The author claims that more Americans have emigrated to Canada because of the war in Vietnam than have died in Vietnam. His estimate of the size of the exile community in 1971 is from 40,000 to 100,000.

Roger Williams, in considering several problems that confront these individuals, views the impact of a lack of amnesty when returning to the United States as a major cause of their problems. William Sloane Coffin, Jr., in the foreword to this book, states:

> I am glad some exiles still want to return to America. I hope when this war is over we shall have the decency to pass legislation that will allow them their choice. It seems only right, a very small way for a country to make amends to citizens it offered the choice only of becoming killers or criminals.[56]

American Deserters in Sweden: The Men and Their Challenge[57] In this book considerable emphasis is placed on the justification of these men for deserting the armed forces of their country. In furnishing this justification, Hayes readily embraces the theory of "patriotic deserters," which is typified by the following statement by four servicemen presented during their press conference.

> You are looking at four deserters, four patriotic deserters from the United States armed forces. Throughout history, the name deserter has applied to cowards, traitors, and misfits. We are not concerned with categories or labels. We have reached the point where we must stand up for what we believe to be the truth.[58]

Similar to the book *They Can't Go Home Again,* this book discusses the nature of the individuals concerned, reasons why they emigrated, their life-styles, and their hopes. It should be recognized, however, that the proportion of American deserters in Sweden, according to Killmer *et al.*, is probably less than two percent of the American draft resisters and deserters who have fled to Canada. While the group in Sweden and the group in Canada may have similar characteristics, their problems in being assimilated into the local environment are considerably different.

They Can't Go Home Again[59] This book attempts to describe the attitudes of U.S. draft resisters and deserters who have fled to Canada. In many cases, their motives for leaving are defended in terms of a moral obligation not to fight in Vietnam, their individual conscience, and the recurring theme that it takes courage to be a draft resister or deserter. The authors do not use the term "cowardice" as a reason why even one of the approximately 30,000 American military age males emigrated to Canada since early 1965. Surely there must be at least one coward. It would be interesting to speculate the actions of these individuals in the event of a Canadian draft to support a

56 *Ibid.*, p. xiii.

57 Thomas Lee Hayes, *American Deserters in Sweden: The Men and Their Challenge* (New York: Association Press, 1971).

58 *Ibid.*, p. 17.

59 Richard L. Killmer, Robert S. Lecky, and Debrah S. Wiley, *They Can't Go Home Again* (Philadelphia: Pilgrim Press, 1971).

Canadian military mobilization.

The authors appear to be sincere in their attempt to remove the glamour often associated with the life of a draft resister or deserter emigrating to Canada.

> The deserter and the draft resister face many risks. There is the risk of getting caught, the risk of being rejected by family and friends, the risk of not being accepted by Canada, the risk of going to a new country where he has no friends, no place to stay, no promise of a job, and the risk of an open future where "making it" is up to the individual.[60]

OPINIONS CONCERNING THE U.S. MILITARY

It seems that the most popular subject in contemporary writing concerning the American soldier of the Vietnam War pertains to various opinions of the U.S. military. It is in this area that the four misperceptions elaborated in the beginning of this chapter are particularly evident. The following contemporary publications are typical of many others pertaining to opinions of the U.S. military.

1. *The Pentagon Watchers* by Leonard Rodberg *et al.* (1970).

2. *The Lonely Warriors: Case for the Military-Industrial Complex* by John Baumgartner (1970).

3. *Between Two Fires: The Unheard Voices of Vietnam* by Ly Qui Chung (1970).

4. *Attitudes and Motivations of Young Men Toward Enlisting in the U.S. Army* by the Opinion Research Corporation (1971).

5. *Young Men Look at Military Service* by Jerome Johnston and Jerald G. Bachman, Institute for Social Research, University of Michigan (1971).

6. *The Military Establishment: Its Impacts on American Society* by Adam Yarmolinsky (1971).

7. *Moral Argument and the War in Vietnam* by Paul Menzel (1971)

8. *Washington Plans an Aggressive War* by Ralph Stavins, Richard J. Barnet and Marcus G. Raskin (1971).

9. *International Dissent* by William O. Douglas (1971).

10. *The Military and American Society* by Martin Hickman (1971).

11. *Playing Soldier: A Diatribe* by Frank Getlein (1971).

12. *Soldiers, Scholars, and Society; The Social Impact of the American Military* by Bernard E. Glick (1971).

13. "Mutual Misperceptions: The Academic and the Soldier in Contemporary America" by Donald F. Bletz, *Parameters* (Fall 1971).

14. "Military Professionalism: A Conceptual Approach" by Donald F. Bletz, *Military Review* (May 1971).

15. "After Vietnam: A Professional Challenge" by Donald F. Bletz, *Military Review* (August 1971).

16. *Soldier* by Lt. Col. Anthony B. Herbert, U.S.A.—Ret., with James T. Wooten (1973).

---

[60] *Ibid.*, p. 91.

17. *Fire in the Lake: The Vietnamese and the Americans in Vietnam* by Frances FitzGerald (1972).

18. *Home from the War—Vietnam Veterans: Neither Victims nor Executioners* by Robert J. Lifton (1973).

The Pentagon Watchers[61] During the summer of 1969, a group of students researched various political-military subjects with the emphasis on activities within the Department of Defense. This book, edited by Leonard S. Rodberg and Derek Shearer, is primarily a report of their research findings. Other writers of papers in this book, such as Marcus Raskin, served as advisers to these students during the course of their investigation. The lack of objectivity in Mr. Raskin's paper, "The Kennedy Hawks Assume Power from the Eisenhower Vultures," serves as a pattern in the enthusiastic analysis and writing by many of these students.

> The idea for a student investigation of the national security establishment, especially the Pentagon, was suggested by the experience of the law students called "Nader's Raiders," who spent a summer looking closely at the Federal Trade Commission.[62]

The editors of this book believe that the United States has become the new imperial power and that their task is to elucidate the working of this so-called imperial system. Marc Kramer takes military research and development to task in his overdramatic "doom's day" paper, "Buck Rogers is alive and well — and doing R&D for the Pentagon." His major point is that complacency by the public will permit military research to increase indefinitely, which in turn, will provide dangerous consequences. "It is the hope of this paper to forewarn those who are complacent concerning the developments that will be upon us by 1980 if we fail to act."[63]

The overall theme of *The Pentagon Watchers* seems to be, "I hope I can find a mistake" or "I hope our military establishment loses." An appendix in this book describes how the reader can research the military.

> The Army Library, located on the first floor of the Pentagon, is open to the public and contains most of the periodicals, directories, manuals, etc., described above. (It is suggested that users of this library dress neatly.)[64]

The Lonely Warriors: Case for the Military-Industrial Complex[65] The argument presented by John Baumgartner tends to be too strong. For example, he infers on many occasions that the military-industrial complex, by itself, has deterred a general war for more than a quarter of a century.

People who have been in both the military establishment and the defense industry

---

[61] Leonard S. Rodberg and Derek Shearer, *The Pentagon Watchers* (New York: Doubleday, 1970).

[62] *Ibid.*, p. ix.

[63] *Ibid.*, p. 323.

[64] *Ibid.*, p. 397.

[65] John S. Baumgartner, *The Lonely Warriors: Case for the Military-Industrial Complex* (Los Angeles: Nash, 1970).

recognize the integrity, devotion, selflessness, and tremendous collective abilities of people in the military-industrial complex, the lonely warriors who provide the protective cover for us and for much of the free world. Theirs is a lonely war, just as this is a lonely book compared to the stacks of volumes and articles that would tear away this protective cover.[66]

While Stanley Baumgartner probably has good reason to react to the alleged "great abuse" received by the military-industrial complex, his argument is weakened by presenting his case too strongly. The central theme of this book is to describe, in layman's terms, the Department of Defense procurement process. His elaboration of this procurement process demonstrates effectively why much of the criticism of the military-industrial complex tends to be unfounded. Stanley Baumgartner's book is quite a contrast to Adam Yarmolinsky's *The Military Establishment*.

A more objective view could be achieved, perhaps, by integrating the arguments found in Baumgartner's book with those pertaining to the military-industrial complex found in Yarmolinsky's book.

Between Two Fires: The Unheard Voices of Vietnam[67] This book is a collection of nine stories about rural Vietnamese located in the Republic of Vietnam. Most of the cases describe individuals who are attempting to survive in a militarily contested rural area. Their determination to remain in the home of their ancestors placed them between massive American firepower, and Viet Cong bombardment and exploitation. Each article was written by a Vietnamese and was subsequently edited by Ly Qui Chung, the editor of the Saigon newspaper, *Tieng Noi Dan Toc*. These articles reflect the attitudes of American soldiers, as well as ARVN and Viet Cong soldiers, as perceived by rural Vietnamese. The article "The Refugee Hamlet" was written by Hoang Chau, a forty-two-year-old lady schoolteacher of Kien Hoa Province.

> Kien Hoa is where the second Indochina War really began. Here, in this land of canals and coconut groves, village and hamlet officials serving the government of President Ngo Dinh Diem began to fall victim to the assassin's knife in the 1957–58 period, long before anyone imagined that large areas of the province would be turned into free fire zones, where movement involved the double danger of American helicopters and Viet Cong booby traps.[68]

A particularly sensitive portion of the schoolteacher's story is an account of a rural Vietnamese woman killed by a Viet Cong booby trap.

> The moment she touched the banana tree with her knife a hand grenade set as a booby trap at the foot of the tree blew up. A long while later, those who were already in their boats got up courage to retrieve her body. They saw that she was lying face down on a board—er, what do you call it, Miss Nam?
>
> A death-warning signboard.

[66] *Ibid.*

[67] Ly Qui Chung, *Between Two Fires: The Unheard Voices of Vietnam* (New York: Praeger, 1970).

[68] *Ibid.*, p. 16.

Yes, the death-warning signboard. Because it had fallen down under the long grass, and so she did not see it.[69]

Attitudes and Motivations of Young Men Toward Enlisting in the U.S. Army[70]
In 1971, Opinion Research Corporation conducted a study of the attitudes and motivations of young men towards enlisting in the U.S. Army, including a special study among recent Army enlistees. Their sample consisted of 2,650 men who were considered representative of young men in the 17 through 21 age group with a tolerance limit of plus or minus two percent.

According to Opinion Research Corporation, a major problem concerning enlistments that needs to be overcome is the general hostile climate of opinion. The results of their survey indicate that:

> About four young men say they would definitely or probably not like to enter the Army, for every one who says he definitely or might like to enter (69% vs. 17%).

> The main basis for this hostility is the continuation of the Vietnam War. Some young men speak of disliking our foreign policy, and others speak of fear of being killed or wounded.

> The Army has definite strengths, in being or in the planning or experimental stage, that can help tip the balance for groups that are on the favorable side.

> These more favorable groups are the younger men (especially the 17-year-olds), non-college youths, those living in the South, and those in the middle- and lower-income groups.

> Whites and blacks do not differ greatly in their thinking, although the whites are slightly more favorable to the military than the blacks. The fact that blacks volunteer in disproportionately large numbers undoubtedly reflects economic and other pressures in their environment. The same can be said of all young men from poorer homes and with lower educational backgrounds.

> For many young men, especially the older and better educated, the Army just does not fit in with their plans. They would prefer to follow another career, and remain with their friends and family. To them Army duty is a period of wasted time. These people are the poorer prospects for enlistment.

> The Army has three principal attractions that warrant major promotional effort. These areas, which high proportions of young men rate both important to them and excellent in the Army, are listed below. The attractions are mentioned especially often by young men interested in joining the Armed Forces and by recent Army enlistees, and are made up of specific ingredients, as listed.

> *Self-fulfillment*
> Builds character
> Makes a man more mature
> Teaches discipline
> Develops self-reliance

[69] *Ibid.*, pp. 19–20.
[70] Opinion Research Corporation, *Attitudes and Motivations of Young Men Toward Enlisting in the U.S. Army*, a study prepared for N. W. Ayer & Son, Inc., and the U.S. Army, May 1971.

48

Helps one do something worthwhile with his life
Makes for a broader outlook on life
Builds self-respect
Helps one make new friends
Allows a man to start a new life

Training
Teaches a trade
Provides job training for civilian life
Offers educational opportunity, such as working toward a high school diploma

Economic benefits
Job security
Medical and dental care
Pension and retirement benefits

Other attractions, which are mentioned less often than the broad areas listed above, include the chance to serve one's country, travel, and opportunity for adventure and excitement.

Several factors that young men think are important but do not rate excellent in the Army represent targets for action:

Treating a man like an individual
Pay
Freedom of choice: duty station, work assignment

Other criticisms concern dislike of discipline, loss of identity and the lower status of enlisted men.

Many of the programs the Army is now considering or experimenting with, to build morale and make the Army more attractive, are in line with young men's thinking with regard to these various negative points. Thus, the new programs are highly justified [71]

Young Men Look at Military Service [72] This book describes the results of a study concerning young men's plans and attitudes toward military service. With regard to attitudes, several questions in a questionnaire focused on the following:

1. How strong is sentiment against the war in Vietnam?
2. How strong is the general antiwar or pacifist sentiment?
3. What do these individuals know about military service?
4. How is military service viewed as a job?
5. How would these individuals feel about being drafted?

The researchers concluded that most of the individuals sampled were not alienated from the nation, and that their views were consistent with U.S. policy in Vietnam, and with military matters in general. Data collected

[71] *Ibid*, pp.**vii–**ix.
[72] Jerome Johnston and Jerald G. Bachman, *Young Men Look at Military Service* (Ann Arbor, Mich.: University of Michigan, 1971).

indicated, however, that approximately 20 percent of those sampled dissented from the dominant position.

While most of the young men sampled were knowledgeable about the requirements of Selective Service, they tended not to be well-informed as to the conditions of military service.

The above conclusions pertained to a questionnaire completed during the spring of 1969. The results of the same questionnaire, when administered during the summer of 1970, were different in two major respects:

1. By mid-1970 the dominant position expressed by young men in our sample cannot be called "consistent with U.S. policy in Vietnam."
2. Young men and also adults are gradually losing trust and confidence in government.[73]

With respect to the post-high school plans of these young men, several questions in the questionnaire focused on the following:

1. What are your plans after high school?
2. How many will enter military service after high school?
3. How do background, ability, and career aspirations relate to post-high school plans?
4. Do antiwar attitudes differ according to post-high school plans?
5. Do most young men expect to serve sometime?
6. Do those expecting to serve differ from the average in background, ability, and career aspirations?
7. Do those expecting to serve differ from the average when it comes to antiwar attitudes?

The answers to the above seven questions seem to be closely related to attitudes toward the Vietnam War.

> The interpretation presented thus far may suggest that likelihood of serving is an important cause of attitudes toward the Vietnam War. That is probably true. But it seems equally true, if not more so, that attitudes toward the Vietnam War are influencing our respondents' intentions to enter the military. It is worth noting in this connection that those who expect not to serve because of *disqualification* show slightly less antiwar feeling than those who have other reasons for expecting not to serve .... And among those who do expect to serve, there are differences in antiwar attitudes that relate to *how* they expect to enter service. Vietnam dissent is highest among those expecting to be drafted and those thinking of enlisting in the Reserve or National Guard; dissent is lower for those planning to enlist; and the least dissent is found among those intending to enter service as officers. These differences are not very large, but they are in a direction that is quite consistent with our other findings. Taken together, these findings support a conclusion that seems both obvious and important: dissent over the U.S. Government's Vietnam policy is, for some young men, a major deterrent to military service.[74]

[73] *Ibid.*, pp. 17–18.
[74] *Ibid.*, pp. 33–34.

The Military Establishment: Its Impacts on American Society[75] The author, a former Deputy Assistant Secretary of Defense for International Security Affairs, is well-qualified to describe the impact of the military establishment on American society. His appraisal is based on a highly sophisticated elaboration of information bearing on many complex issues. In probing the complex issues, Adam Yarmolinsky tends to condemn the Department of Defense for many of the problems in the world today. While his book is not antimilitary, his findings that are favorable to the military tend to be obscure.

Major topics described by Yarmolinsky are as follows:

1. The size, scope, and cost of the defense establishment.
2. The military influence within the executive branch.
3. The military-congressional interdependence.
4. The military-industrial alliance.
5. The civilianized military command.
6. The military, the budget, and national priorities.
7. Nuclear equilibrium.
8. Military involvement in foreign policy.
9. Control of revolution and counterrevolution.
10. The traditional Federal role in domestic disorders.
11. Use of troops in recent domestic disorders.
12. Military public relations.
13. The Pentagon's handling of news.
14. Ideological education of the military and the public.
15. Military spending in the economy.
16. Weapons acquisitions and defense industry.
17. Military sponsorship of science and research.
18. Military research.
19. Military service and the social structure.
20. Military service and race.
21. Military justice and individual liberty.
22. Military management in a technological society.
23. The military establishment and social values.
24. "How Much Is Enough?"

Moral Argument and the War in Vietnam[76] This book is a collection of articles pertaining to the war in Vietnam. It appears that Paul Menzel selected and edited these articles objectively and that he presented fairly both sides of the question, "Should America be in Vietnam at all?" Major articles were written by: Richard M. Nixon, Noam Chomsky, Jean-Paul Sartre, Paul Ramsey, Henry A. Kissinger, Mary McCarthy, Theodore Draper, Jean Lacouture, David Schoenbrun, and Alfred Hassler. Mr. Menzel's selection of articles is divided into four major sections: (1) A Just War?, (2) Genocide?,

[75] Adam Yarmolinsky, *The Military Establishment: Its Impacts on American Society* (New York: Harper & Row, 1971).

[76] Paul Menzel, *Moral Argument and the War in Vietnam* (Nashville: Aurora, 1971).

(3) Solutions?, and (4) Can Ethics, Ideology and History Meet?

In the future this book should prove to be a valuable book of reference.

Washington Plans an Aggressive War[77] This book is extremely critical of the Vietnam War and those individuals who developed America's political-military strategy for Vietnam. Barnet and Raskin are quick to admit that they have been critics of the role of the United States in the Vietnam War for over a decade. A further consideration is that Stavins, according to their book, formerly headed a study team that made a critical investigation of the U.S. planning and decisionmaking process concerning the Vietnam War during the period prior to 1971. Early in their book, the authors acknowledge two explicit biases:

1. The Vietnam War was politically and morally wrong from the outset.

2. The lawlessness of the nation-state constitutes the greatest threat to peace and human survival. The only hope of subjecting the state to law is to hold individuals who act for the state responsible for their acts.

The book is divided into the three following major parts:

1. Washington determines the fate of Vietnam: 1954–1965.
2. The men who made the war.
3. From imperial warmaking to a code of personal responsibility.

Several of the authors' recommendations are frightening. A rather extreme portion of this book is Raskin's proposal to end America's Manichean approach to militarism. In this proposal, he recommends the use of two models for demilitarization of the armed forces and personal accountability of public officials. One model is based on the American occupation of Germany and the other model pertains to the American occupation of Japan. With respect to his proposed deactivation of the Department of Defense, he suggests the application of the following:

> Essential steps in the accomplishment of this objective are the elimination of Nazism and militarism in all their forms, the immediate apprehension of war criminals for punishment, the industrial disarmament and demilitarization of Germany, with continuing control over Germany's capacity to make war, and the preparation for an eventual reconstruction of German political life on a democratic basis.[78]

Raskin further proposes that exponents of militarism be removed and excluded from any position of public or substantial private responsibility. In using his occupation of Germany model, he defines *militarists* as follows:

> Militarists were those who "sought to bring the life of the German people into line with a policy of militaristic force." They included "anyone who advocated or is responsible for the domination of foreign peoples, their exploitation or displace-

[77] Ralph Stavins, Richard J. Barnet, and Marcus G. Raskin, *Washington Plans an Aggressive War* (New York: Random House, 1971).

[78] *Ibid.*, p. 301.

ment" as well as those who "promoted armament" for these purposes. They also include those who "disseminated militaristic programs ... serving the advancement of militaristic ideas." Profiteers who persecuted minorities or made "disproportionately high profits in armament or war transactions" were also viewed as offenders.[79]

International Dissent[80] Justice Douglas believes that there is an urgent need to find nonmilitary solutions for war. This belief is supported by a proposal of six steps toward world peace. These steps are as follows:

1. End all military alliances. "This is essential if we are to work toward the elimination of war as an instrument for the solution of international problems."[81]

2. Free all colonies and abolish all protectorates.

3. Recognize the Peoples' Republic of China and encourage her to enter the United Nations. (Since his book was written, the Peoples' Republic of China has in fact entered the United Nations.)

4. "An international regulatory body, or multinational corporation whose shares are owned by all the nations of the world, must be established to govern the control and use of the ocean floor."[82]

5. Help the developing nations enter the age of technology.

6. "Rules of law governing international relations must be agreed upon."[83]

While his views and steps towards world peace may have substantial value when considered in their abstract form, the actual implementation and application of several of these views and steps would be difficult, in some cases dangerous, and in several instances probably impossible even though desirable. His views pertaining to the size of the armed forces and his views concerning military alliances clearly indicate that he favors an extreme isolationist position. Many of the disadvantages of such an isolationist policy are not adequately presented in his book.

> That is why we must realize that it is not our destiny, nor that of any Great Power, to run the world. We have the blue-water zones protecting us; and we have this hemisphere as our immediate neighborhood. Our problem is to develop neighborhood values of the same intensity as we now express in military assaults on Asian armies and on Asian communities. That is why we must withdraw all our troops from Europe and Asia and turn our thoughts inward. As and when we do, we will find as great a sense of achievement in saving a sick child in a rat-ridden ghetto at home as we have in rescuing a GI in a hostile Asian jungle.[84]

[79] *Ibid.*, pp. 305–306.
[80] William O. Douglas, *International Dissent* (New York: Random House, 1971).
[81] *Ibid.*, p. 31.
[82] *Ibid.*, p. 65.
[83] *Ibid.*, p. 97.
[84] *Ibid.*, p. 47.

The Military and American Society[85] This book consists of a collection of papers edited by Martin B. Hickman. Three major sections of this collection are:

1. The military and society.
2. The military-industrial complex.
3. The military and the campus.

The author was objective in his selection of papers for each of the above three subjects and provided a balanced view of the many issues involved. His sources of essays range from the testimony of John Kenneth Galbraith before the Congressional Joint Economic Committee, to a speech given before a Defense and Contract Procurement Administration Conference by a former secretary of the Air Force.

Papers concerning the military-industrial complex range from Jack Raymond's discussion of the "Growing Threat of Our Military-Industrial Complex" to a discussion that appeared in *Navy* magazine pertaining to "What Eisenhower Really Said."

The case against "The Military-Industrial-Academic Complex" is vividly stated in the text of a speech by William F. Fulbright. In contrast, an article in *Army* magazine by Major William F. Muhlenfeld provides a different point of view. Martin B. Hickman accomplished an extraordinary feat by objectively introducing the many provocative issues facing both American society and the military.

Playing Soldier: A Diatribe[86] This book is a cleverly developed anti-Pentagon diatribe presented within a "games people play" framework. The main thrust of Getlein's argument is that America has become a military dictatorship. "Our country has become a military dictatorship in its own peculiar American way .... We operate in boardrooms and in balance sheets and it is in those quiet shelters that the change has taken place."[87]

Mr. Getlein frequently takes the opportunity to exaggerate as he mixes humor, the truth, and nonsense. This is quite evident in this appraisal of the role of veterans.

> But veterans, as veterans, know better than that. They have seen it all from the inside. They know that the military machine is a fraud, that the military mind is deliberately self-deluded most of the time, that the military capacity for incompetence is infinite. They know all these things and they have suffered because of them. And yet, if the military tomorrow asked for funds for a system to blow up the United States to save it from the Russians, the veterans' organizations would testify to Congress the day after tomorrow that what the country needs is to be blown up and at their next conventions would pass unanimous resolutions urging that Congress stop its temporizing and get on with the dynamite.[88]

[85] Martin B. Hickman, *The Military and American Society* (Beverly Hills, Calif.: Glencoe Press, 1971).

[86] Frank Getlein, *Playing Soldier* (New York: Holt, Rinehart and Winston, 1971).

[87] *Ibid.*, p. 166.

[88] *Ibid.*, p. 7.

Perhaps the most unobjective portion of this book is his discussion leading up to the theory that military leaders desire a situation of what Getlein calls "permawar." "The specter of Communism is stalking the Pentagon and never was a shade more welcome . . . . If it weren't for Communism, the place would have been out of business long ago."[89]

Soldiers, Scholars, and Society; The Social Impact of the American Military[90] The title of this book has little relation to the subject. The subject is what's wrong with the military; however, the framework for viewing military problems is through the eyes of students and a campus-based college professor. Glick acknowledges the limitations of his analysis and takes particular care in being objective. His arguments are well-developed and many of his concepts are truly innovative. The author discusses issues at random such as the following:

1. The black soldier.
2. Military conscription and nonmilitary national service.
3. Military training and education.
4. Military research.
5. ROTC.
6. Military academies.
7. Civic action.
8. Military-industrial complex.

The wide range of his topics seems to prohibit him from developing a detailed discussion. For example, in 16 pages he attempts to analyze the following:

> If one made a short list of some of the worst features of the military-industrial complex, especially as they relate to congressional actions and inactions, it might look something like this:
> 1. Too many defense installations.
> 2. Too much mismanagement and profiteering.
> 3. Too many retired officers in defense industry.
> 4. Too many pro-military congressmen.
> 5. Too much nonmilitary research by the military.
> 6. Too few congressmen who can understand the technical and economic complexities of defense requests.
> 7. Too much "public relations" by the military and their allies.

Let's examine the items on this list in some detail.[91] The major thrust of Glick's book is well-capsulized in his summary.

> Any reader who has come along with me this far realizes that my main aim has been to get some new ideas into the system. For example: a draft lottery that would be extended to women and to nonmilitary service, professors consulting to the military

[89] *Ibid.*, pp. 112–113.
[90] Edward Bernard Glick, *Soldiers, Scholars, and Society; The Social Impact of the American Military* (Pacific Palisades, Calif.: Goodyear, 1971).
[91] *Ibid.*, pp. 114–115.

for free, the possible retirement of military officers at 100 percent pay in return for iron-clad prohibitions against their working for the Defense Department or its contractors, the merging or elimination of our existing military academies, congressional mandating of a higher portion of promotions to general and flag officer ranks from among nonacademy graduates, and the end of the congressman-reservist.

In addition, any reader who has come along with me this far also knows of my belief that, unfortunately, military realities outside of the United States still require some American warriors, weapons, and weaponsmakers, and the money to pay for them. Hopefully, all of this will be at diminished levels and more for readiness than for use. He may have guessed that I am terribly worried that America's foreign policy pendulum is swinging from the one extreme of World Policemen to the other of Global Dropout. We have, in fact, already moved from an era of too many old and ill-conceived military commitments to perhaps an era of no new ones, regardless of the merits of the cases involved. In the end, this new extreme, if it persists, may prove as costly and as dangerous as the old one.

I have, of course, shown how unexpected, even unintended, benefits can and do flow from the military-industrial complex. But I do not want to be misunderstood. I do not want that complex to exist a moment longer than is necessary. I do not want it to do any nonmilitary things that other segments of our society and government can and *will* do faster and better, even if not more cheaply. And I certainly do not want it to be uncontrolled and uncriticized. But there is a world of difference between restraining and redirecting the military-industrial complex, and hobbling, humiliating, and prematurely destroying it altogether. To do the latter in today's unsettling world would be disastrous. Not to do the former in today's unsettling America would be unconscionable.[92]

"Mutual Misperceptions: The Academic and the Soldier in Contemporary America" [93] After discussing the mutual misperceptions held by the American academic profession and the American military profession, the author proposes how these misperceptions might be reduced.

A reasonable place to begin, and it is a shallow beginning at best, is to understand the basic similarities and differences. Both can then at least understand why the other thinks as he does. For example, I doubt seriously if the military profession as a whole understands the intellectual's perception of his role as a critic of society, and I doubt equally seriously if the intellectual community really understands why it is difficult for the soldier to criticize in a similar way. It is important for the academic to understand why the soldier may feel he was deserted in Vietnam by the academic community.[94]

It is recognized that the understanding of differences will not necessarily develop agreement but will, at least, provide the basis for meaningful discussion. The increasing tendency in the military to encourage its officers to participate in graduate programs is advantageous to both professions. However, the

[92] *Ibid.*, pp. 127–128.
[93] Donald F. Bletz, "Mutual Misperceptions: The Academic and the Soldier in Contemporary America," *Parameters* 1, no. 2 (Fall 1971).
[94] *Ibid.*, p. 12.

concurrent reduction in participation in military-related research by the academic profession should be reversed. A disturbing aspect of the tendency of the academic profession's withdrawal from military-related research is that there will be a resulting loss to both the academic and military professions.

> The United States will be ill-served by a military profession turned "academic" and by an academic profession turned "soldier." On this there should be little disagreement. The nation does, however, need a military profession with the intellectual competence to understand and work with the academic profession, just as it needs an academic profession which maintains a scholarly interest in military affairs so as to provide rational, positive criticism. The separation between the "doer" and the "thinker" is valid and must remain, but the two must converse on a mutually understandable level. [95]

"Military Professionalism: A Conceptual Approach"[96] This article adds a conceptual dimension to the argument that today's military leader should be well-grounded in political-military affairs as well as the traditional requirements of technical-military expertise. The argument posed by Bletz is that professional military officers must be more than narrow military technicians. In a normal career pattern, the young officer would focus his professional development mainly on achieving technical-military expertise. Then, as he advances during his career, his professional development would focus towards achieving political-military expertise. This pattern is illustrated by the following model.

> The chart shows this balance in the broadest terms. The vertical axis (technical military) represents the nation's demands on the professional officer to be technically competent in his particular field. The horizontal axis (politico-military) represents the country's expectation that the professional officer broaden his professional base

[95] *Ibid.*, p. 13.
[96] Donald F. Bletz, "Military Professionalism: A Conceptual Approach," *Military Review* (May 1971): 9–17.

well beyond pure military technology. The dotted diagonal line represents the midpoint—a balance—between the two conflicting demands. Finally, the solid curved line (C-R) represents what the United States may logically demand of an officer along the way from point C (commissioning) to R (retirement).

Following the demand line (C-R), it is seen that, in his early years, the officer is concerned with the technical aspects of his profession. As he progresses along in his career and is subject to staff and command assignments which place broad demands on him, his professional base is expected to broaden and he moves away from the technical military axis . . . .

The levels which have been suggested here can be identified on the chart in broad terms by a horizontal line, or preferably the wider shaded belt, through the point at which the diagonal line and the C-R line intersect. The first level is below that divider; the second above it. A precise division between these two levels is neither possible nor desirable. An understanding is essential, however, on the part of military professionals that "levels," by whatever name one wishes to identify them, do exist and that the professional demands differ significantly in each.[97]

"After Vietnam: A Professional Challenge"[98] The author believes that a major challenge facing the Army following the Vietnam War will be the Army's reaction towards forces of isolationism and major reductions in defense spending.

Three approaches available to the Army for meeting this challenge are:

1. Withdraw into some form of social isolation and accept the consequences.

2. Dismiss the possibility of the public having a substantial antimilitary feeling. However, if such a feeling becomes evident, assume that civilian leaders will solve the problem.

3. "The remaining broad alternative, in the face of an antimilitary reaction, is for the military profession to face the problem squarely."[99]

In selecting the third alternative as a course of action for meeting the challenge, Bletz elaborates the following:

Recognition of the problem and expression of concern at the highest level is not enough. The "subjective" challenges of the post-Vietnam period should be as much a subject of professional military shoptalk as hardware, organization, and doctrine.

These problems are legitimate subjects for research papers at the staff colleges and war colleges, and should prove as valuable to the national security as any paper on "The Strategic Implication of NATO," "The Role of the Joint Chiefs of Staff," "An Indian Ocean Strategy," or other equally popular topics. Several of the individual research papers at the National War College in 1970 did address some of these problems. Hopefully, this trend is present elsewhere in the military educational system.

[97] *Ibid.*, pp. 12–15.
[98] Donald F. Bletz, "After Vietnam: A Professional Challenge," *Military Review* (August 1971): 11–15.
[99] *Ibid.*, p. 15.

58

We must realize that the world in which we live is not the same as it was 20 years ago, or even one year ago. It is essential that we take on these new challenges in light of today's—not yesterday's—international and domestic conditions.

This is the professional challenge of the post-Vietnam era.[100]

Soldier[101] Tony Herbert's views of the American soldier of the Vietnam War received widespread notoriety. His many generalizations and simplex conclusions were well-suited for interviews on television. The following is a typical generalization by Herbert: "The major leadership problem in Vietnam was the generals, and the rest of the senior officers' corps—the colonels, the lieutenant colonels, and the majors. The captains, lieutenants, and enlisted men weren't to blame."[102] Probably Herbert's zeal for excitement prompted him to convert his job as Inspector General into being a tropical Ralph Nader, dashing about coaching small unit leaders under fire. The account of his experiences as a battalion commander reads like a reclaimer to a devastating efficiency report. Herbert's book is interesting and exciting, but not quite believable.

Fire in the Lake—The Vietnamese and the Americans in Vietnam[103] This 1972 award-winning book is comparable to Bernard Fall's *Street Without Joy* published in 1961. Had he lived, I believe Fall would have readily endorsed the views of FitzGerald. While I admire the detailed reporting in FitzGerald's book, I strongly disagree with her unfavorable evaluation of the American soldier in Vietnam.

Home From the War—Vietnam Veterans—Neither Victims nor Executioners[104] Lifton concludes that Vietnam veterans feel guilty about their participation in the Vietnam War and feel that they were duped by the U.S. government. His many conclusions seem to be affected by his own antiwar bias. He gathered his data from an extended rap session with a group of the Vietnam Veterans Against the War. Certainly such a source of information cannot be considered typical or unbiased.

With the conclusion of the Vietnam War, it is only natural that young American soldiers will want to return to their normal environment, which means living in the United States with all the comforts, conveniences, and opportunities that the nation has to offer. The average young veteran tends to see nothing ahead for him in the U.S. Army at this time of extended demobilization. At best, the soldier comes home from this war not as a hero, but as one who has done his duty and carried out his obligation as an American citizen. Many of these young men are not sure what they want to do. In fact, it will be several years before they are settled into a permanent channel; whether it be as a salesman, a mechanic, or a member of a profession to include serving in

[100] *Ibid.,* p. 3.

[101] Lt Col., U.S.A.—Ret. Anthony B. Herbert with James T. Wooten, *Soldier* (New York: Holt, Rinehart and Winston, 1973).

[102] *Ibid.,* p. 240.

[103] Frances FitzGerald, *Fire in the Lake—The Vietnamese and the Americans in Vietnam* (Boston: Little, Brown, 1972).

[104] Robert J. Lifton, *Home From the War—Vietnam Veterans—Neither Victims nor Executioners* (New York: Simon & Schuster, 1973).

the U.S. Army. The U.S. Army, as a profession, no more appeals to all young Americans than does that of becoming a farmer appeal to all. The trend at the end of every war has been a swing away from the military but future circumstances have always caused a readjustment.

CLOSING REMARKS

The American soldier of the Vietnam War was described unfairly in much of the contemporary literature during the Vietnam War. The majority of the literature reviewed in this chapter substantiates this conclusion. There are, however, several exceptions which are also included.

Many of the unfair comments focus on issues that tend to be either irrelevant or extraordinary. Many unfair arguments are also based on the following four misperceptions:

1. *Training.* Training tends to change the individual from a "normal well-adjusted" person into a robot or perhaps even into a manipulating leader complete with a Machiavellian *modus operandi.*

2. *Effects of Combat.* Soldiers returning from Vietnam are disoriented and tend to be a detriment to society.

3. *Retention.* Those who make the Army a career are autocratic "hardheads" incapable of employment in a free society.

4. *Comparison of Various Subgroups.* There is a tendency in the current literature for critics of the Army to misjudge the characteristics of various subgroups within the Army. A factual study will indicate entirely different results.

An argument in favor of the American soldier is presented in the chapters that follow. Subjects relative to each of the four misperceptions listed above will be investigated in detail.

In chapters 3 and 4 an investigation of the impact of training will focus on a specific training situation that exerts a strong influence on the molding of behavior and beliefs. The effect and stability of Officer Candidate School training will be analyzed in terms of individual responses to thousands of copies of a questionnaire administered over a period of several years. The findings of this research differ substantially from many of the views that are critical of the American soldier of the Vietnam War.

Chapter 5 challenges the view that soldiers returning from Vietnam are disoriented and tend to be a detriment to society. Unlike much of the speculation in this area, the discussion focuses on the responses of individuals questioned in combat, and then again back home.

The retention of well-qualified individuals in the Army continues to be a problem. Many critics of the American soldier of the Vietnam War maintain that men leave the Army because of their ideological dissatisfaction with the role of the United States in Vietnam and because of widespread corruption throughout the Army establishment. These reasons, given by many critics of the Army, are not the correct reasons why these men are departing from the Army. It is imperative to note the facts. In chapter 6, reasons for departure are provided by 919 men. In addition, there is a comparison of certain beliefs between a group of 358 men who remained in the Army with a group of 919 men who departed from the Army. An analysis is also made of the major goals in life of both groups combined.

In viewing a complex world it is often convenient to categorize various groups of individuals by their ethnic group, occupation, age, education, and so forth. As a result, there is a tendency to create a perceptual distortion when discussing, for example, the nature and characteristics of college students, Army officers, or construction workers. It would be interesting to reduce these perceptual generalizations and determine the facts. Chapter 7 attempts to accomplish this by describing the self-reported beliefs of Army field grade officers attending the U.S. Army War College. Then this group of 183 individuals is compared with other subgroups associated with the U.S. Army. Many of the results found by comparing these groups are in complete disagreement with views critical of the American soldier of the Vietnam War.

This argument in favor of the American soldier of the Vietnam War does not claim that all is well within the Army. On the contrary, there is much to be done within the system to turn the tide of unfavorable sentiment that is provided by many observers. Part of an overall solution for turning the tide is described in Chapter 8, the last chapter.

Chapter 3

COMPARISON OF SELECTED BELIEFS BETWEEN ENTERING AND GRADUATING STUDENTS IN OFFICER CANDIDATE SCHOOL

One of the Army's major sources of junior officers is the Army's Officer Candidate Schools.

> At Fort Benning alone more than 100,000 candidates were enrolled in 448 officer candidate classes from July 1941 to May 1947. Over 67,000, some 67 percent, completed the course and were commissioned. It was by far the biggest and fastest "commissioning job" ever attempted by an army.[1]

During the Vietnam War, officer candidate training was conducted for 13 of the Army's branches such as Infantry, Artillery, Engineer, and Signal Corps. This training was conducted at six locations. "The system is designed to place the candidate under physical, mental and emotional stress to simulate, as closely as possible, the stress and fatigue of combat."[2] A major advantage of this method is that it can rapidly provide large numbers of new officers essential for an expanding Army. Since the start of the withdrawal of U.S. forces from Vietnam in 1969, many of these schools have been discontinued. Engineer Officer Candidate School, located at Fort Belvoir, Virginia, is the specific school described in this study. It was organized during the end of 1965 to help fill a shortage of engineer lieutenants caused by a major increase in U.S. troops in Vietnam. The school operated for five years during the Vietnam War and graduated its last class towards the end of 1970. When it operated at its fullest capacity, the school was a regimental size organization with four battalions of four companies each. A permanent cadre of 620 men conducted the training which lasted 23 weeks for each group of students.

Although I observed training at this school during most of the five-year period, this chapter will pertain only to that training observed during 1966.

---

[1] U.S. Department of the Army, *Department of the Army Pamphlet 601–1: The OCS Story*, June 1, 1966, p. 2.
[2] *Ibid.*, p. 4.

At that time, approximately 2,600 students were enrolled and the annual output of officers from this newly formed Officer Candidate School was expected to be approximately 4,000. During this period, approximately 77 percent of the newly-commissioned officers in the Corps of Engineers were provided by this school, while 22 percent were from college ROTC programs. Approximately one percent were graduates of the United States Military Academy. The high percentage of newly-commissioned officers provided by this training source indicated a need for this, and similar, studies.

As a field grade officer and as a former officer candidate, I was often impressed by the fact that some officer candidates have a propensity to complete successfully Officer Candidate School while others are quite ready to resign after they are in the course for only a short time, some for only a few hours. An initial thought was that students with a favorable degree of certain beliefs might be more likely to successfully complete Officer Candidate School. A start in making such an idea fruitful might be a comparison of certain self-reported beliefs between entering and graduating students in Officer Candidate School. This chapter will attempt to describe such a comparison pertaining to four specific self-reported beliefs.

Groups of students, rather than individuals, will be analyzed. A group of entering students will be compared with a different group of graduating students. Self-reported beliefs will be analyzed in terms of the significant difference between the average self-reported beliefs of the two groups. A weakness in comparing groups rather than individuals is the inability to determine whether the difference in group scores is caused by:

1. Students actually changing their beliefs during the time considered.

2. Students with certain beliefs resigning from the course and subsequently not being sampled as graduating students.

3. Students with certain beliefs failing from the course and subsequently not being sampled as graduating students.

Probably undetermined varying amounts of the above three situations will account for the differences in the average beliefs between entering and graduating students. With these limitations in mind, the structure of the predictions (presented later in this chapter) will be related in terms of groups of students.

The predictions will reflect directly the purpose of this research, which is to compare four specific self-reported beliefs between entering and graduating students in Officer Candidate School.

REVIEW OF RELATIVE LITERATURE

The review of the literature reported in this section will focus on five areas:

1. Identification of the individual characteristics of potential officers.

2. Evaluation of training.

3. Changes in an individual's perception of others and self-perception.

4. Interaction between changes in an individual's perception of others and changes in self-perception.

5. Influencing students to change their beliefs.

Initially the review will concentrate on previous studies conducted within a military setting that help identify the individual characteristics of potential officers. Then a review of the literature concerning the evaluation of training will be presented. Inasmuch as the perception of each person in answering a questionnaire plays a major part in how the questions are answered, two subject areas dealing with perception will be covered. Differences in the two groups of men may, in part, be caused by changes in the beliefs of the group of graduating students. To assist in analyzing this factor, the last area in the literature reviewed is "influencing individuals to change their beliefs."

IDENTIFICATION OF THE INDIVIDUAL CHARACTERISTICS OF POTENTIAL OFFICERS

The following studies were conducted within the Departments of the Army, Navy, and Air Force. They represent a small fraction of the research performed by these departments relative to identifying the individual characteristics of potential officers. These studies were selected based on their relevance to the study reported in this chapter.

Gordon and Medland conducted research within an Army setting to help develop measures of leadership which might identify men who are capable of becoming effective combat leaders. Their specific requirement was "to evaluate measures of an individual's value system as predictors of career motivation."[3] Gordon and Medland concluded that:

> Three values were found to be predictive of career motivation. Officers who desired to remain in service as a group tended to score higher on Conformity and Benevolence and lower on Independence than those electing to leave the Army. Enlisted men desiring to remain scored higher on Benevolence and lower on Independence and Support.[4]

Holmen, Katter, Jones, and Richardson conducted a study of an assessment program for Army Officer Candidate School applicants. They concluded that:

> Use of the assessment procedures as a screening device could be expected to reduce attrition at the OCS's, provided the schools applied the same standards to the assessment-screened candidates as they now employ. If the OCS standards remained constant and there were three applicants available for every OCS graduate desired, assessment screening could result in an appreciable saving.

> The most important component of the OCS criterial judgment appears from the study to be concerned with what might be called minimum requisites of good junior leadership—ability to direct drills and command exercised in small groups, effective speaking, and personal impressiveness in the eyes of associates. The criteria do not appear to be heavily concerned with measurable personality differences.[5]

[3] Leonard V. Gordon and Francis F. Medland, *Values Associated with Military Career Motivation* (Washington, D.C.: U.S. Dept. of the Army, 1964), p. iii.

[4] *Ibid.*

[5] Milton G. Holmen, *et al., An Assessment Program for OCS Applicants* (Washington, D.C.: George Washington Univ., 1956), p. iii.

64

Medland and Olans evaluated the use of peer ratings within an Army setting as predictors of leadership potential. In addition, they assessed the effectiveness of several methods of employing peer ratings. They found that:

> Peer ratings of leadership potential in groups of 12 to 16 men had substantial reliability over 4 to 16 weeks.

> The reliability held whether individuals were in stable groups and rated by the same men a second time, or in changing groups and rated by different men.

> Peer ratings were more reliable than cadre ratings obtained under comparable circumstances.[6]

Nelson conducted a study in the Navy to assess similarities and differences in personality characteristics among four types of individuals.

1. Liked leaders
2. Less-liked leaders
3. Liked followers
4. Less-liked followers

> A total of 72 men who had wintered-over at four Antarctic scientific stations served as subjects. Based upon a year's experience with the men at their stations, two supervisors at each station independently evaluated all station members on several attitudinal and behavioral characteristics, one of which was a leadership-follower-ship scale and another of which was a likability scale. By dichotomizing the members of each station on both the leadership and the likability scales, four experimental groups of liked and less-liked leaders and followers were obtained for comparison on other personal characteristics.

> Both liked and less-liked leaders were more self-confident, alert, job motivated, and aggressive than the follower groups of comparable likability. On the other hand, liked leaders and liked followers, in contrast to the less-liked leaders and followers, were more satisfied with the assignment, emotionally controlled, accepting of authority, and motivated to be efficient group members. In terms of their overall profile of attitudes and behavior, the liked leaders and the liked followers were found to be most similar—more so than liked leaders with less-liked leaders, liked followers with less-liked followers, or less-liked leaders with less-liked followers. It was suggested that the underlying orientation in common to liked leaders and followers was an attitude of teamwork, and respect for various forms and sources of authority.[7]

Miller and Creager conducted an experiment in which they attempted to predict the achievement of cadets at the Air Force Academy.

> Results of these tests and previously administered selection tests were correlated with final academic grades and Cadet Effectiveness Ratings earned in the fourth class year .... Thirteen predictors had significant validity coefficients for the prediction

[6]F. F. Medland and J. L. Olans *Peer Rating Stability in Changing Groups,* U.S. Army Technical Research Note 142, April 1964, p. iii.

[7]Paul D. Nelson, "Similarities and Differences Among Leaders and Followers," *Journal of Social Psychology* 63 (1964): 167.

of Cadet Effectiveness Ratings. The best single predictor of this leadership criterion was the experimental Peer Status scale of the Life Experience Inventory.[8]

These studies tend to indicate that the characteristics of potential leaders can be identified to some extent. However, it seems that the actual use of these characteristics for the selection of potential officers is considerably more difficult.

EVALUATION OF TRAINING

In comparing the response of individuals before and after training, it is usually assumed that learning or a change in beliefs is related to the training program. The evaluation of individuals who complete training and a subsequent analysis of this evaluation, as compared with their previous response, may be a good measure of the effectiveness of the training. The following review is concerned with the evaluation of training.

Kirkpatrick, in describing procedures, methods, and techniques for evaluating training programs, emphasizes that the future of a training program depends, to a large extent, on its evaluation and the subsequent use of the evaluation results. Kirkpatrick visualizes the evaluation process as consisting of four steps which evaluate:

1. The trainee's reaction to the course.
2. What was learned.
3. Desired changes in the trainee's behavior.
4. Results back on the job.

The first step in the evaluation process is to measure the reactions to training programs. It is important to determine how people feel about the programs they attend.

. . . . Several guideposts should be used in establishing a procedure for measuring the amount of learning that takes place.

1. The learning of each conferee should be measured so that quantitative results can be determined.
2. A before-and-after approach should be used so that any learning can be related to the program.
3. As far as possible, the learning should be measured on an objective basis.
4. Where possible, a control group (not receiving the training) should be used to compare with the experimental group which receives the training.
5. Where possible, the evaluation results should be analyzed statistically so that learning can be proven in terms of correlation or level of confidence.[9]

The third step visualized by Kirkpatrick evaluates training in terms of to what extent an individual's self-reported beliefs change as desired by the trainers. In this step the trainee's self-reported beliefs before and after training

[8]Robert E. Miller and John A. Creager, *Predicting Achievement of Cadets in Their First Year at the Air Force Academy, Class of* 1962 (Texas: Lackland Air Force Base, 1960), p. ii.
[9]D. L. Kirkpatrick, "Techniques for Evaluating Training Programs," *Journal of American Society for Training and Development,* a series of four articles, November 1960–February 1961.

are measured, compared, and analyzed.

Kirkpatrick's fourth step evaluates training by using results back on the job as criteria.

> These results could be classified as: reduction of costs; reduction of turnover and absenteeism; reduction of grievances; increase in quality and quantity of production; or improved morale.[10]

Lippitt, McCune, and Church conducted a study of the most common methods of evaluating training. Seventy-five completed questionnaires returned by members of the American Society of Training Directors revealed some of the methods and purposes used by these members in evaluating training.

> The most common methods of evaluating training include use of questionnaires, interviews, supervisor's reports and efficiency reports. The primary purpose of the evaluations is to improve the present program and establish guidelines for the development of future programs.[11]

Mayeske, Harmon, and Glickman, in conducting research at the U.S. Department of Agriculture, utilized a workable information-reporting technique that may be applicable in determining the relevance of training. Their technique operates in terms of effective or ineffective "critical incidents."

> Critical incidents involve specific actions or behavior that have actually been observed. They do not involve personality labels or lists of traits. An effective critical incident leads to significantly better than average accomplishment of a particular aspect of a job, assignment, mission or responsibility. An ineffective incident leads to significant delay, mistakes, omissions, lack of accomplishment, or obstacles to achievement of work.[12]

According to Mayeske, Harmon, and Glickman, this technique can be used to assess and validate existing training. Critical incidents are sampled in the job environment after the trainees are back on the job for a specified period of time following training.

Miles visualizes training evaluation as a continuous process conducted by the persons responsible for establishing and carrying out training activities. He proposes that:

> Absolute standards of rigor in evaluating are undesirable, but it is important to make evaluation procedures more and more systematic. Evaluation is needed for immediate steering purposes, and for longer-term assessment purposes. Many instruments can be used to contribute to both ends. The basic step in evaluation planning is clear specification of the learning outcomes which the training is being set up to produce. After that come instrumentation, data collection, analysis and

[10] *Ibid.*, pp. 1–12.

[11] G. L. Lippitt, S. D. McCune, and L. D. Church, "Attitudes of Training Directors Toward the Application of Research to Training Programs," *Training Director's Journal* 18, no. 3 (March 1964): 20.

[12] G. W. Mayeske, F. L. Harmon, and A. S. Glickman, "What Can Critical Incidents Tell Management?" *Training and Development Journal* 20, no. 4 (April 1966): 21.

interpretation, and new program planning.[13]

Murdick concludes that training programs in industry should be subjected to careful scrutiny and evaluation just as any other business expense. The problem described by Murdick is how to develop an effective training program that will provide a favorable return on a long-run basis. To help provide this favorable return, he feels that a sound training evaluation program should be employed.[14]

Sterner found that the training needs required to perform a job should be evaluated concurrent with an evaluation of the persons trained. The purpose, according to Sterner, in reviewing training needs and priorities is to:

> (1) develop a program which teaches the skills required on the job, (2) provide an environment which fosters development of proper attitudes and motivations for the work, and (3) make available other information about the work of an organization which may lead to improvement in job performance.[15]

These studies tend to indicate that a worthwhile evaluation of training can be conducted by evaluating groups of trainees before and after they are trained. The extent trainees learn or change their self-reported beliefs may be related to the program. Environmental factors, other than the training, may cause a change in beliefs and should also be considered.

CHANGES IN AN INDIVIDUAL'S PERCEPTION OF OTHERS AND SELF-PERCEPTION

Bossom and Maslow conclude that the individual's personal characteristics affect the characteristics he will most likely see in others.

> From a larger group of judges, a secure and an insecure group were selected. All judges were exposed to a series of 200 photographs. Judges were required to indicate whether the person in the photograph was Very Warm, Warm, Cold, or Very Cold. The percentage of judges reporting Warm impressions more often than Cold impressions tended to be greater in the secure group than in the insecure group.[16]

Cantril observed that our perception depends for the most part on the assumptions that we bring to any particular situation.

> The meanings and significances we assign to things, to symbols, to people, and to events are the meanings and significances we have built up through our past experience, and are not inherent or intrinsic in the stimulus itself.[17]

---

[13] Matthew B. Miles, *Learning to Work in Groups* (New York: Columbia Univ., 1959), p. 251.

[14] R. G. Murdick, "Measuring the Profit in Industry Training Programs," *Journal of the American Society of Training Directors* 14, no. 4 (April 1960): 34.

[15] F. M. Sterner, "Determining Training Needs: A Method," *Training Director's Journal* 19, no. 9 (September 1965): 45.

[16] J. Bossom and A. H. Maslow, "Security of Judges as a Factor in Impressions of Warmth in Others," *Journal of Abnormal and Social Psychology* 55 (1957): 148.

[17] Hadley Cantril, "Perception and Interpersonal Relations," *American Journal of Psychiatry* 114, no. 2 (1957): 119.

Dearborn and Simon studied the perceptions of 23 executives who participated in an executive training program. The executives were directed to employ a company-wide viewpoint in solving a standard business school case study problem. The results of the study indicated that each executive perceived those aspects of the case study that were most related to the activities and objectives of his particular department. Dearborn and Simon concluded that executives' perceptions will often be limited to those components of a situation that relate specifically to their own positions despite an attempt to influence them to adopt a wider perspective. [18]

Kelley studied the effects of assigning a personality label to a person to see if it influences the impression others have of him. The personality label used was whether the person was "warm" or "cold." Several undergraduate classes at M.I.T. were asked to evaluate a substitute instructor. Biographical notes of the substitute instructor were read by the students before they came in contact with him. The notes were identical except that one form described the substitute as being rather "cold" while another described him as being very "warm." The results indicated that the substitute was consistently rated more favorably by those students who were told he was "warm" than by those who were told he was "cold." A larger proportion of the students who had been told that the instructor was very "warm" participated in class discussions than those students who had been told that the instructor was rather "cold." Kelley concluded that perception guides the individual's behavior in his social environment and that an unfavorable perception can reduce corresponding interaction.[19]

Lieberman concluded from an experiment conducted in an industrial setting that employee attitudes are affected by changes in their respective work roles. These changes are shown when some employees get the new role of foreman and others become shop stewards.[20]

Stephenson, Erickson, and Lehner found that the self-perception of 47 members of four sensitivity training groups changed with training (as measured immediately following training), and that there was a tendency for these self-perception changes to diminish over a period of time. However, the training groups, as compared with a control group, had lasting significant positive change in self-perceived intelligence and self-assurance. "Individual changes in a negative direction ... occurred with less frequency among those who received sensitivity training than would be expected on the basis of the control group distributions."[21]

Tannenbaum, Weschler, and Massarik, in evaluating human relations training, recognize the following about changes in the self-perception of trainees.

[18] D. C. Dearborn and H. A. Simon, "Selective Perception: A Note on the Departmental Identifications of Executives," *Sociometry* 21 (1958): 140–144.

[19] H. H. Kelley, "The Warm-Cold Variable in First Impressions of Persons," *Journal of Personality* 18 (1950): 431–439.

[20] Seymour Lieberman, "The Effects of Changes in Roles on the Attitudes of Role Occupants," *Human Relations* 9 (1956): 385–402.

[21] R. W. Stephenson, C. E. Erickson, and G. F. J. Lehner, *Self-Perception Changes in a Sensitivity Training Laboratory* (Washington, D.C.: National Education Assoc., 1965), p. 27.

Experience shows that if participation in the training process has "taken," the first impact will probably occur in the trainee's own perception about himself and others. His new self-assessment may lead to more confidence and security and to less anxiety in his day-to-day relations on the job. Next, the repercussions of such insights will probably be felt by those with whom he deals. He may "blow up" less often, turn an attentive rather than a deaf ear to suggestions, or play a more constructive role in staff meetings. As he begins to feel his way, he may discard old attitudes and behavior and become comfortable in more spontaneous, creative, and mature patterns for productive living. [22]

Zajonc and Wolfe studied the communication contacts of 42 employees of an industrial company in terms of their effects on the employee's cognitions of the company. It was found that cognitive structure differed as a function of formal communication.

Employees who have wide formal communication contacts showed more differentiated, more complex, less segmented, and more highly organized cognitive structures than employees with narrow formal communication contacts.[23]

Cognitive differences also were found to be related to the employee's position in the company.

These studies tend to indicate that perception is affected by many factors such as those associated with past experiences, present interactions, and other environmental forces. In some cases, perceptions are changed because the subjects are acting on the basis of assumptions that prove "wrong." Perceptions may also be changed because of changes in the individual's role. A central theme seems to be that perceptions are changed by experience. It will be interesting to note the effect of the experience of attending Officer Candidate School on possible changes in perception of graduating students.

INTERACTION BETWEEN CHANGES IN AN INDIVIDUAL'S PERCEPTION
OF OTHERS AND CHANGES IN SELF-PERCEPTION

Another area of research concerning perception which has a bearing on the predictions contained in the study reported in this chapter is the interaction between changes in perception of others and changes in self-perception.

Bieri in an experiment predicted that one's perception of another person will change in the direction of increased similarity to oneself.

The findings of the study are construed as supporting the hypothesis that in a constructive group interaction situation in which mutual agreement on experiences and preferred activities is emphasized, members come to perceive their partners as more similar to themselves.[24]

[22] R. Tannenbaum, I. R. Weschler, and F. Massarik, *Leadership and Organization,* (New York: McGraw–Hill, 1961), pp. 232–233.

[23] Robert B. Zajonc and Donald M. Wolfe, "Cognitive Consequences of a Person's Position in a Formal Organization," *Human Relations* 19, no. 2 (1966): 149.

[24] J. Bieri, "Changes in Interpersonal Perceptions Following Social Interaction," *Journal of Abnormal and Social Psychology* 48 (1953): 66.

Burke and Bennis examined changes in perception of self and others during human relations training at the National Training Laboratory in Group Development at Bethel, Maine.

> The results of this study are of two kinds. First, perceptions by members of self and others, at the second testing, were factor analyzed, and three factors were found, accounting for 86 percent of the total variance. The first factor is called friendliness evaluation, the second dominance-potency, and the third participation-activity. Second, significant changes over time were found in the perception of group members, as follows: profile similarity between perceived actual self and perceived ideal self increased; changes in perceived actual self were greater than changes in perceived ideal self; profile similarity between the individual's perceived actual self and mean perception of him by others increased; changes in the perception of the individual by others were greater than changes in the individual's perception of actual self; variance between members, in their perception of individuals on the participation-activity dimension, decreased.[25]

Deutsch and Solomon, in observing the reactions of subjects to evaluations by others, indicate the value of self-evaluation. They found that:

> An individual will tend to regard favorably those whose evaluations of him are favorable and tend to regard unfavorably those whose evaluations are negative. Implicit in such a prediction is the hidden assumption that the individual evaluates himself positively. If the opposite assumption is made, namely that the individual evaluates himself negatively, one would predict that he would tend to view negatively another who esteems him and tend to esteem those who view him negatively.[26]

Lehner conducted an investigation to determine the relationship of the self-rating of personal adjustment and its relation to self-scores and projected average scores. He found that:

> College men and women have higher self-ratings than actual self-scores on a personality test, and both self-ratings and self-scores are considerably higher than their projected adjustment scores for the "average" person .... It appears from this and related research done by the author that one might be dealing here with a "I-high, you–low" phenomenon of self-up-manship in interpersonal perceptions.[27]

In summary, these studies on the interaction between changes in an individual's perception of others and changes in self-perception indicate that many complex dynamic forces are involved. These studies tend to show that one's perception of others changes in the direction of increased similarity to one's self-perception.

[25]R. L. Burke and W. G. Bennis, "Changes in Perception of Self and Others During Human Relations Training," *Human Relations* 2 (1961): 181.

[26]M. Deutsch and L. Solomon, "Reactions to Evaluations by Others as Influenced by Self-Evaluation," *Sociometry* 22 (1959): 110.

[27]G. F. J. Lehner, "Some Relationships Among Personal Adjustment Self-Ratings, Self-Scores, and Assigned 'Average' Scores," *Journal of Psychology* 50 (1960): 337.

Inasmuch as differences in the scores of the two officer candidate groups may be caused by changes that occurred to the graduating students, the process of influencing individuals to change their beliefs is reviewed.

Bennis describes how planned change is distinguished from other forms of human change.

> Planned change entails mutual goal setting by one or both parties, an equal power-ratio, and deliberateness, eventually at least, on the part of both sides.

> Indoctrination involves mutual goal setting and is deliberate, but involves an imbalanced power ratio. Many schools, prisons, and mental hospitals or other "total institutions" would fall into this category.

> Coercive change is characterized by nonmutual goal setting (or goals set only by one side), an imbalanced power-ratio, and one-sided deliberateness. Coercive change, as we are using the term, may be exemplified by the thought-control and brainwashing practices of the Communists. Here there is no opportunity to engage in mutual goal setting.[28]

Schein's amplification of several of these views will be described later in this section.

Festinger, Gerard, Hymovitch, Kelley, and Raven found that:

> The relative strength of the tendency to redefine the boundaries of the group in response to pressure toward uniformity increases for a member as the discrepancy between his opinion and the modal opinion in the group increases.[29]

Lippitt, in a study of the effects of information about group desire for change on group members, determined that: "A feedback interview during the life of a T-Group on how group members desire change does affect change in the individual to whom this data is presented."[30]

Miles, in a study of the process and outcome of human relations training, found that:

> Personality inputs seem important mainly as facilitating factors during training: what counts is the person's actual transaction with the experiences of the laboratory. This transaction seems not to have "bite" until the second week, when fuller engagement with the situation may be under way; certainly initial desire for change is no indicator at all of what learnings will emerge for the person. Finally, back-home organizational factors, for this sample, exerted some—but less than expected—impact.[31]

---

[28] Warren G. Bennis, Kenneth D. Benne, and Robert Chin, *The Planning of Change: Readings in the Applied Behavioral Sciences* (New York: Holt, Rinehart and Winston, 1964), p. 154.

[29] L. Festinger, *et al.*, "The Influence Process in the Presence of Extreme Deviates," *Human Relations* 5 (1952): 345.

[30] G. L. Lippitt, "Effects of Information About Group Desire for Change on Members of a Group," Doctoral Dissertation (Washington, D.C.: American Univ., 1959), p. 128.

[31] M. B. Miles, "Human Relations Training: Processes and Outcomes," *Journal of Counseling Psychology* 7 (1960): 306.

Schein, with Schneier and Barker, studied the effects and techniques used in the "brainwashing" of American civilian prisoners by the Chinese Communists. Then, this method was compared with methods common to the American environment. When the individual is "unfrozen," "he becomes a number, a nonentity; his former self ceases officially to exist."[32] With respect to "changing," there is a parallel between the importance of the cellmate in influencing prisoners in Chinese Communist prisons and the use of the "big brother" or "buddy" system in Alcoholics Anonymous. In Chinese Communist prisons, "the cellmate often becomes a model of how to behave .... In A.A. the key change agent is the person who becomes responsible for and closest to the new member."[33]

With regard to "refreezing," the use of social support and reinforcement of changed attitudes is also common in the non-Communist settings. "In religious orders the support and reinforcement for a new self-conception comes from a whole series of role perceptions, rituals, and general social expectations."[34]

Schein considered that the process of management development is within the Lewin classical framework for developing change. Schein's model of influence and change suggests that coercive persuasion (reflected above) is employed in some management development programs. Schein feels that managers need to be "unfrozen" initially in a management development program because they are psychologically unprepared to change certain beliefs in favor of untried new ones.[35]

Whyte concludes that some members of a company are so company-oriented that they are willing to conform to all company standards. "When a young man says that to make a living these days you must do what somebody else wants you to do, he states not only a fact of life but a good proposition."[36]

These studies tend to indicate that an individual's beliefs can be changed in a variety of ways. The differences, for the most part, seem to center on the degree of influence exercised by the person being changed. This influence can range from "planned change" to "coercive change." Planned change employs mutual goal-setting by both parties and a near equal power ratio between both instructor and student. Coercive change in contrast has nonmutual goal-setting and a one-sided power ratio in favor of one party. Results vary with the environment, type of change process used, purpose of change, and parties involved. It will be interesting to note the specific effects of training in the possible difference in response between the groups of entering and graduating students.

---

[32] Edgar H. Schein, Inga Schneier, and Curtis H. Barker, *Coercive Persuasion* (New York: W. W. Norton, 1961), p. 271.

[33] *Ibid.*, p. 279.

[34] *Ibid.*, p. 281.

[35] Edgar H. Schein, "Management Development as a Process of Influence," *Industrial Management Review of the School of Industrial Management, MIT* (May 1961), pp. 59–77.

[36] William H. Whyte, *The Organization Man* (New York: Simon and Schuster, 1956), p. 5.

This section reviewed pertinent literature relative to: identification of the individual characteristics of potential officers, evaluation of training, changes in perception, and varying methods of influencing students to change their beliefs.

Several studies conducted within the Departments of the Army, Navy, and Air Force tend to indicate that the individual characteristics of potential officers can, to some extent, be identified and measured.

The evaluation of individuals who complete training may form, to a large degree, the basis of measuring the effectiveness of a training program.

The perception of the person answering a questionnaire may play a major role in determining how questions are answered. Perception of others and self-perception are affected by many factors. In some cases, perceptions are changed because the subjects are acting on the basis of assumptions that prove wrong. Role changes may cause changes in perception. The interaction between changes in an individual's perception of others and changes in self-perception will normally cause one's perception of others to change in the direction of increased similarity to one's self-perception.

Students may be influenced to change their beliefs in a variety of ways. The main difference in these ways seems to center on the degree of influence exercised by the person being changed. With "planned change," goals are established mutually by both parties, and a near equal power ratio exists. In contrast, coercive change uses nonmutual goal-setting and thus provides a one-sided power ratio in favor of one party. It would seem from the review of the literature in this area that the process of change may take various means from nondirective to rather directive in terms of the role of the change agent influencing the client system.

THEORETICAL FRAMEWORK

The literature review presented in the previous section indicated that to some extent the characteristics of potential officers can be identified. This study will attempt to make such an idea fruitful by comparing the beliefs between a group of entering and graduating students in Officer Candidate School. First, the theoretical framework of the study reported in this chapter will be examined. Conceptual ideas rather than research methods will be explored. Research methods will, however, be described in a later section. Factors that influence officer candidates to change their beliefs will also be presented. Then four factors deemed especially pertinent in influencing these students will be more fully considered.

FACTORS INFLUENCING THE BELIEFS OF OFFICER CANDIDATES

Entering students in Officer Candidate School probably undergo a socialization process in which they adjust to their new environment. If their behavior, such as neatness and posture, for example, is similar to their upperclassmen and tactical officers, they are rewarded by not being corrected. If, however, their behavior is noticably dissimilar from the standards that are desired, they run the risk of receiving one or more reprimands; and if dissimilarities continue, of failing the course. A student who desires to complete the course finds that it is in his best interest to adjust as quickly and accurately as possible to the requirements and standards of his new environment. For many, the role of being a candidate demands a change in behavior. Some of these behavioral changes may become part of the individual's self-concept. The beliefs of some of these candidates may change due to this socialization process, caused in part not only by their new environment, but also by the standards set for the individual as a result of inspections and the example of their leaders.

> All roles organize behavior, but some roles are so important that they serve to integrate the personality. They become part of the individual's self-conception, which is built around the behavior and the attitudes that go with a role. The individual sees the world from a point of view of a particular role and may find it difficult to take on other roles or to behave in ways alien to his critical role.[37]

There are a number of factors that tend to influence the beliefs of officer candidates during training. Four of these factors are especially pertinent to this study. Their pertinence is judged on the basis of their role in determining the culture that characterizes Officer Candidate School, the social situation of the candidate within Officer Candidate School, and the relationship between the candidate's social and academic experience. These four factors are:

1. The goal and standards of Officer Candidate School.
2. The course of instruction.
3. The tactical officer.
4. The system of voluntary resignation.

It is recognized that many other factors may influence the beliefs of these individuals. Other factors will not be developed in detail but their existence will be recognized and considered. Some of these other factors that may influence the beliefs of officer candidates during training are as follows:

1. The prior experience and training of the student.
2. The role of the student within the formal and informal organization associated with his platoon.
3. The student's age and physical fitness.
4. The changing amounts of power, authority, and influence exercised by the student.
5. The expectations of the student and his current responsibilities outside of the Army environment.

The four factors stated as being especially pertinent in influencing the beliefs of officer candidates during training are:

1. *The Goal and Standards of Officer Candidate School.* The goal of

---

[37] Leonard Broom and Phillip Selznick, *Sociology* (New York: Row Petersen, 1958), p. 98.

Officer Candidate School is to develop combat leaders. A further function is to instill, within the time available, military knowledge essential for Army officers. A 1966 publication describes the mission as follows:

> The mission of ... Officer Candidate Schools is to develop combat leaders. These schools emphasize the development of practical leadership, physical stamina, and the mastery of tactics and weapons.[38]

The standards of Officer Candidate School require that a candidate have the potential ability to become a leader in combat.

> The rigorous program of training and discipline furnishes the means of confirming whether a candidate possesses the potential ability to become a combat leader. The school's further function is to develop this ability, once it is recognized, by teaching the professional knowledge needed for successful leadership in combat.[39]

2. *The Course of Instruction.* In Officer Candidate School, the major emphasis is placed on the development of the student's leadership ability.

> The twenty-three week course of instruction ... revolved around the development of leadership ability. The candidate must be able to stand on his own two feet and direct the operations of small units. In order to develop leadership, the candidates are given an intensive course in the theory of leadership plus considerable practical work .... Candidates are rotated through various command positions .... In addition, candidates are required to hold instruction periods and present talks on various military subjects such as dismounted drill, physical training, Army information, and military history.[40]

Physical fitness is maintained and improved by a scheduled program as well as by off-duty workouts. Physical fitness tests administered during the course provide an incentive as well as a measure of the improvement of the student's physical fitness. The potential officer also learns how to conduct physical fitness training.

To provide the military knowledge necessary to function as a platoon leader, the students receive an intensive program of military subjects deemed most necessary for a platoon leader in combat. For example, at the Infantry Officer Candidate School the program of military subjects as described in a 1966 Department of the Army pamphlet is as follows:

> An extensive program of military subjects is presented. These subjects fall into three basic groups; weapons, tactics and general subjects. The weapons instruction includes all weapons found in the Infantry Battalion, from the pistol to the 106-mm recoilless rifle. Tactics instruction is given at the platoon and company level, with emphasis placed on platoon offensive tactics. The general subject training covers nuclear warfare, communications, vehicles, mapreading, leadership, and similar military subjects.[41]

[38] U.S. Department of the Army, *Department of the Army Pamphlet 601–1: The OCS Story,* June 1, 1966, p. 2.
[39] *Ibid.*
[40] *Ibid.*, p. 5.
[41] *Ibid.*

The course emphasizes the development of the candidate's leadership ability. Also stressed is physical fitness and the development of professional military knowledge necessary to become an effective platoon leader.

   3. *The Tactical Officer.* The tactical officer plays an important role in shaping the behavior of each candidate. The tactical officer's function is to assist candidates in successfully completing the course. Unlike the instructors who meet with the platoon for specific formal instruction, such as mapreading, the tactical officer is in contact with the same platoon throughout the six months of training. Thus, the tactical officer becomes familiar with the characteristics and behavioral style of each member of his platoon of 20 to 45 students.

> The performance of each candidate is observed continuously by the tactical officer assigned to his platoon. The tactical officer's principal duty is to assist candidates in successfully completing the course. This is done by advising candidates on their deficiencies and of ways to overcome them. It is not uncommon for candidates to spend long hours of their "free" time working to overcome deficiencies which otherwise would detract from leadership ability after graduation.[42]

   4. *The System of Voluntary Resignation.* Following World War II, a system of voluntary resignation was initiated in Officer Candidate School. During the Vietnam War, students were permitted to resign from the course after a limited period of training. This technique probably eliminates many whose beliefs differ from the required standards. In some cases, students who are not meeting the standards realize it, and resign, rather than fail later in the course. Others change, work harder, and meet the standards. Historically, the attrition rate for officer candidates has been high. The following statement made at the end of the Korean War acknowledges this fact.

> In a typical training battalion of 1000 men, about 300 would be eligible to apply for OCS, and about 100 would usually apply. Of the 100 applicants, 65 would be accepted for officer training, and about 35 would finally receive commissions. Of the men who began OCS training, approximately 55 percent receive commissions, 25 percent are failed by the schools, and 20 percent resign. Lack of motivation and lack of leadership each account for a little more than one-third of all OCS attrition, the remaining losses are about equally divided among academic, physical and other deficiencies.[43]

   Some students claim that the possibility of being able to resign from Officer Candidate School has helped them to endure some of the more difficult portions of the course. Others feel that being able to resign is too great a temptation for some and causes many who would normally stay to leave the course.

RESEARCH METHOD AND DESCRIPTION OF SAMPLE

   In the previous section, conceptual ideas rather than the research method

[42] *Ibid.,* p. 5.
[43] Milton G. Holmen and Robert V. Katter, *Attitude and Information Patterns of OCS Eligibles* (Washington, D.C.: George Washington Univ., 1953), p. 1.

were explored. This section will be concerned, initially, with the research method. Then the section will conclude with a description of the sample.

RESEARCH METHOD

This study attempts to compare systematically several variables in self-reported beliefs between entering and graduating students in Officer Candidate School. The difference is revealed by comparing the average scores of a sample from each of these two groups. The predictions of this study are concerned with the difference in four specific scales represented in the test instrument used. The instrument, called the Job Analysis and Interest Measurement (JAIM), provides measures for 32 scales relating to (a) Basic beliefs, (b) Activity preferences, (c) Personal values, and (d) Behavioral styles. A description of the JAIM was presented in Chapter 1 and a more detailed explanation of the JAIM can be found in Appendix A.

During the early spring of 1966, arrangements were made for the administration of the JAIM instrument to officer candidates. I accomplished this by personally contacting and subsequently coordinating with the commander of the Officer Candidate School. In addition to administering the JAIM, observations were made of various phases of candidate life. Many candidates were interviewed, starting with the school's first class which graduated in June 1966. Entering students sampled were administered the JAIM during their first week of training in Officer Candidate School while graduating students were sampled in their 20th to 22nd week. Students in their last week of training (23rd) were not usually found to be psychologically typical of the group called graduating students in this study. They were normally concerned with graduation, their new assignment, and leave. The 20th week tended to be the optimum time for examining students from a psychological and scheduling point of view. A total of 1,111 JAIM questionnaires were administered to officer candidates during the period from June 21, 1966 through October 21, 1966. Of this group, 671 were entering students, 87 were in their 12th week (midway in the course), and 353 were graduating students. The schedule of sampling is described in Table 1, while a summary of the respondents and classes sampled is provided in Table 2. All JAIM questionnaires were administered to the candidates by the author. The conditions of the testing facilities were reasonably equal in all cases. Starting October 7, 1966, an administrative data questionnaire was also completed by each person administered the JAIM. The analysis of the data was accomplished by a 1620 IBM computer.[44]

The method of evaluating the JAIM results is to determine if there is a significant [45] difference between the average scores on a specific JAIM scale between 561 entering students and 319 graduating students. The significance in the difference of averages is tested by conducting a t-test of the two averages.

[44] Computer operations were conducted by David Reimer, Staff Associate in the Social Research Group of the George Washington University.
[45] The term significant is reserved for the meaning statistically significant.

78

TABLE 1

SCHEDULE OF SAMPLING

Date		Number of Students	Week of Training
June	21, 1966	34*	22
June	23, 1966	53	1
June	23, 1966	56*	1
July	5, 1966	24	21
July	5, 1966	33	21
July	8, 1966	45	1
July	8, 1966	47	1
July	16, 1966	40	12
July	16, 1966	47	12
July	21, 1966	51	1
July	21, 1966	56	1
August	25, 1966	39	22
August	25, 1966	56	1
August	25, 1966	59	1
September	15, 1966	37	21
September	15, 1966	34	21
September	15, 1966	50	1
September	15, 1966	47	1
October	7, 1966	38	20
October	7, 1966	40	20
October	7, 1966	35	1
October	7, 1966	35	1
October	14, 1966	41	1
October	14, 1966	40	1
October	21, 1966	35	20
October	21, 1966	39	20

* Pilot Study.

In this study, a positive t-value indicates that graduating students are higher in a particular scale, while a negative t-value indicates that entering students are higher as pertains to this particular scale. In the evaluation of the two experimental groups, significance will be required at the .01 confidence level.[46]

DESCRIPTION OF SAMPLE

The students in the population sampled were homogeneous as to their age, sex (male), state of health, and general educational level. Exclusive of these homogeneous factors, the students represented a substantial cross-section of

[46] Confidence level refers to probability theory. A confidence level of .01 would indicate that this finding could only happen by chance one time out of a hundred.

TABLE 2

SUMMARY OF RESPONDENTS AND CLASSES SAMPLED

A. Number of Respondents

Entering Students

Pilot Study	56	
Experimental Group	561	
Questionnaire Not Completed	1	
Sample of One Class Rejected*	53	

Total Entering Students 671

Students Midway in Course (12th Week of Training) 87

Graduating Students

Pilot Study	33	
Experimental Group	319	
Questionnaire Not Completed	1	

Total Graduating Students 353

Total Respondents 1,111

B. Number of Classes

Entering Classes

Pilot Study	1	
Experimental Group	12	
Sample of One Class Rejected*	1	

Total Entering Classes 14

Classes Midway in Course (12th Week of Training) 2

Graduating Classes

Pilot Study	1	
Experimental Group	9	

Total Graduating Classes 10

Total Classes 26

*Sample of class consisting of 53 students was rejected because 25 men did not complete the questionnaire. Students were fatigued physically and kept falling asleep.

the American population. A few black students were present, but the proportion of blacks in Officer Candidate School was much less than the proportion of blacks in the enlisted ranks.

Examinations administered to all enlisted personnel when they initially enter military service screen out approximately 75 percent of all enlisted personnel for further consideration to attend Officer Candidate School. The selection system for Officer Candidate School is:

> Essentially a successive hurdles system, inasmuch as only those who qualify on initial mental screening tests are eligible to apply for OCS. Physical, educational and moral requirements must also be met. Applicants who meet these general requirements are selected competitively on the basis of a leadership selection battery— evaluation report, personal inventory, and board interview. These instruments provide a standard and convenient basis for determining objectively the relative leadership potential of OCS applicants.[47]

The results of an Administrative Data questionnaire completed by entering and graduating students are shown in Table 3. This questionnaire was designed to help describe the sample. It reflects the aggregate of individual characteristics for a group containing 151 entering students, and a group containing 152 graduating students. The results from the Administrative Data questionnaire have, in my opinion, considerably less validity than the JAIM results, inasmuch as the Administrative Data questionnaire was completed by approximately 31 percent of the classes that were administered the JAIM, or of only approximately 27 percent of the students administered the JAIM. An additional weak point of the Administrative Data questionnaire is that it was administered during a two-week period in October 1966, while the JAIM was administered during the four-month period, June 21 to October 21, 1966.

DEVELOPMENT OF PREDICTIONS

This section will describe the development of the predictions concerning the study. The results of a pilot study will be presented. Then, this section will conclude with the predictions.

PILOT STUDY

In the development of the predictions of this study, an initial thought was that students who score high in the JAIM scale "Degree of Perseverance" would have a high propensity to graduate, and that those low in the JAIM scale "Degree of Perseverance" would be likely to fail or resign from the course. A pilot study was conducted in June 1966 in which the average self-reported beliefs of 56 entering students were compared with the average self-reported beliefs of 33 graduating students. The results of this pilot study are shown in

---

[47] Leo J. Kotula and Helen R. Haggerty, *Research on the Selection of Officer Candidates and Cadets*, U.S. Army Technical Research Report 1146 (1966), p. 7.

TABLE 3

COMPARISON OF SEVERAL CHARACTERISTICS OF 151
ENTERING STUDENTS WITH 152 GRADUATING STUDENTS

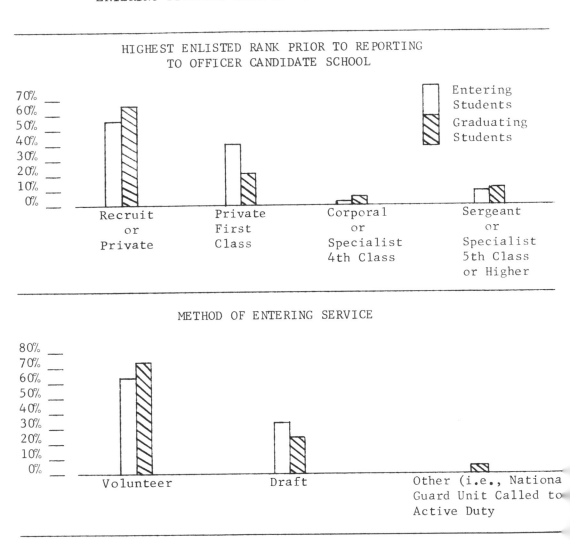

82

TABLE 3 - CONTINUED

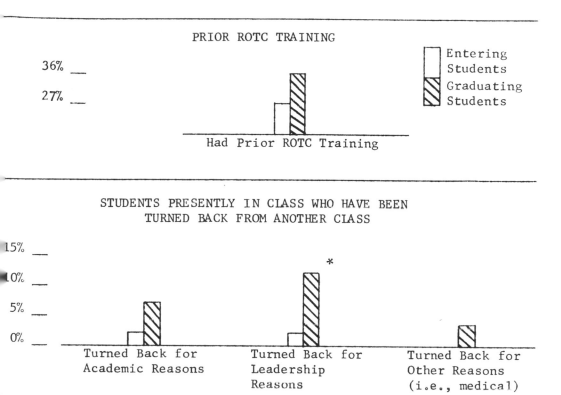

PRIOR ROTC TRAINING

36% —

27% —

Had Prior ROTC Training

☐ Entering Students
▨ Graduating Students

STUDENTS PRESENTLY IN CLASS WHO HAVE BEEN
TURNED BACK FROM ANOTHER CLASS

15% —

10% —

5% —

0% —

Turned Back for
Academic Reasons

Turned Back for
Leadership
Reasons

Turned Back for
Other Reasons
(i.e., medical)

* This may indicate that for this particular study difficulties in meeting leadership proficiency standards have a higher propensity of being corrected than difficulties in meeting academic proficiency standards. This is probubly indicated by the higher percentage of students graduating that have been previously turned back for leadership reasons than those previously turned back for academic reasons. It may also indicate that judgments on leadership proficiency are more subjective and, therefore, less reliable than judgments on academic proficiency.

TABLE 3 - CONTINUED

EDUCATIONAL LEVEL

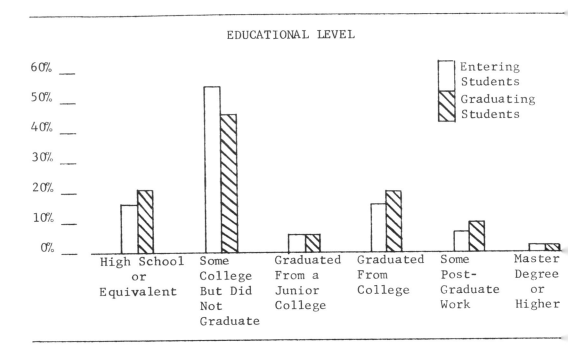

AGE

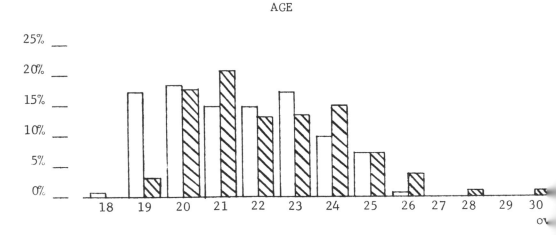

Age in Whole Years as of Date Administered

JAIM INSTRUMENT

84

TABLE 3 - CONTINUED

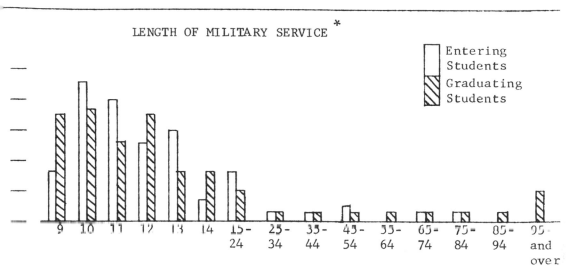

LENGTH OF MILITARY SERVICE *

Length of Military Service in Whole Months

* The entering student's length of service is adjusted so that a comparison can be made while both groups are in their 20th week of training.

TABLE 4

RESULTS OF PILOT STUDY

Scales	Difference Between the Average of 56 Entering Students and 33 Graduating Students*
1. BASIC BELIEFS	
a. Extent of Optimism	.08
b. Degree of Self-Confidence	.75
c. Belief in Moral Absolutes	.31
d. Belief in Slow Change	— .52
2. ACTIVITY PREFERENCES	
a. Prefers Problem Analysis	1.06
b. Prefers Social Interaction	−2.46**
c. Prefers Mechanical Activities	— .11
d. Prefers Supervisory Activities	3.16***
e. Prefers Activity Frequent Change	2.57**
3. PERSONAL VALUES	
a. Values Status Attainment	— .91
b. Values Social Service	— .50
c. Values Approval from Others	−6.02***
d. Values Intellectual Achievement	1.26
e. Values Role Conformity	1.15
4. BEHAVIORAL STYLES	
a. Degree of Perseverance	.82
b. Extent of Orderliness	1.21
c. Prefers to Plan Ahead	— .61
d. Influences by Persuasive Leadership	3.67***
e. Influences by Being Self-Assertive	3.91
f. Move toward Aggressor	−4.80***
g. Move away from Aggressor	.34
h. Move against Aggressor	.17
i. Prefers Routines	−2.45**
j. Identifies with Authority	— .45
k. Prefers Independence	1.42
l. Prefers Directive Leadership Style	1.52
m. Prefers Participative Leadership Style	−2.81***
n. Prefers Delegative Leadership Style	1.58
o. Motivates by Knowledge of Results	.64
p. Believes in External Controls	1.26
q. Prefers Being Systematic, Methodical	.25
r. Prefers Group Participation	−1.12

* A positive t-value indicates graduating students are higher in this particular scale while a negative t-value indicates that entering students are higher as pertains to this particular scale.
    ** $p < .05$
    *** $p < .01$

Table 4. Results of the pilot study indicated little difference in the average JAIM scale "Degree of Perseverance" between entering students and graduating students. Other scales, however, emerged as being significant and were further analyzed for their relevance as the basis for predictions in this study. The nature of candidate life eliminated scales related to current social activities. Therefore, answers to a question pertaining to the frequency of attending parties or social gatherings were considered distorted and its respective scale was eliminated subsequently from further consideration as the basis of a potential prediction. Four of the 32 scales in the Job Analysis and Interest Measurement were considered to have the strongest potential for a meaningful significant difference between groups of entering and graduating students. The following four scales are the basis of the four predictions of this study:

1. Values Approval from Others.
2. Influences by Being Self-Assertive.
3. Influences by Persuasive Leadership.
4. Prefers Supervisory Activities.

PREDICTIONS

This study was designed to test four predictions relating to the self-reported beliefs of officer candidate students. Each prediction is concerned with comparing the average self-reported belief of a group of entering officer candidates with a group of graduating officer candidates. The following underlying assumptions are applicable to the four predictions described in this chapter:

1. The sample of entering students selected represents the entering student population.
2. The sample of graduating students selected represents the graduating student population.
3. The standards and techniques of evaluating students remained constant during the sampling period.
4. The system of rewards and punishments for students remained constant during the sampling period.
5. The Job Analysis and Interest Measurement instrument is reliable and valid.

The predictions of this study are:

1. *First Prediction.* Entering students compared with graduating students tend to place a higher value on the approval from others and, therefore, entering students will score significantly higher on the JAIM scale "Values Approval from Others."
2. *Second Prediction.* Compared with entering students, the graduating students in Officer Candidate School tend to be more self-assertive and, therefore, graduating students will score significantly higher on the JAIM scale "Influences by Being Self-Assertive."

3. *Third Prediction.* Compared with entering students, the graduating students in Officer Candidate School are more likely to be persuasive leaders and, therefore, graduating students will score significantly higher on the JAIM scale "Influences by Persuasive Leadership."

4. *Fourth Prediction.* Compared with entering students, the graduating students in Officer Candidate School are more prone to like supervisory activities, and, therefore, graduating students will score significantly higher on the JAIM scale "Prefers Supervisory Activities."

RESULTS

Results presented in this section pertain to the four predictions of the study. Each prediction is tested by determining if there is a significant [48] difference between the average scores on a JAIM scale between a group of 561 entering students and a group of 319 graduating students. A t-test of the two averages is conducted. A positive t-value indicates that graduating students are higher in a particular scale, while a negative t-value indicates that entering students are higher. A significance of at least the .01 confidence level will affirm the prediction.

The four predictions of this study which were stated in the previous section will guide the organization of the reporting of the results. Results of the four predictions are presented in Table 5.

VALUES APPROVAL FROM OTHERS

The first prediction explored the area in which the individual values himself by the degree to which he obtains approval from others. It was stated as follows:

> Entering students compared with graduating students tend to place a higher value on the approval from others and, therefore, entering students will score significantly higher on the JAIM scale Values Approval from Others.

This prediction was tested by comparing the average score on the JAIM scale "Values Approval from Others" between a group of 561 entering students and a group of 319 graduating students. The difference between the averages was significant at the .01 confidence level. Inasmuch as there is a significant difference in the average JAIM scores between entering and graduating students, the first prediction is affirmed. The first prediction is therefore accepted within the structure of earlier assumptions.

INFLUENCES BY BEING SELF-ASSERTIVE

The second prediction is concerned with the degree to which the individual tends to pursue his own goals when they are in competition with the goals of others. It was stated as follows:

---

[48] The term significant is reserved for the meaning statistically significant.

TABLE 5

RESULTS OF PREDICTIONS

Scales	t-Value*	Prediction Affirmed**
561 *Entering Students Higher:*		
Values Approval from Others	−7.40	Yes
319 *Graduating Students Higher:*		
Influences by Being Self-Assertive	5.61	Yes
Influences by Persuasive Leadership	4.15	Yes
Prefers Supervisory Activities	2.58	Yes

* A positive t-value indicates graduating students are higher in this particular scale, while a negative t-value indicates that entering students are higher as pertains to this particular scale.
** At the .01 level of significance.

> Compared with entering students the graduating students in Officer Candidate School tend to be more self-assertive and, therefore, graduating students will score significantly higher on the JAIM scale "Influences by Being Self-Assertive."

This prediction was tested by comparing the average score on the specific JAIM scale "Influences by Being Self-Assertive" between entering students and graduating students. The significance in the difference of the averages was tested by conducting a t-test of the averages. The difference between averages was significant at the .01 level of confidence. Inasmuch as there is a significant difference in the average JAIM scores between entering and graduating students, the second prediction is affirmed. The second prediction is therefore accepted within the structure of earlier assumptions.

INFLUENCES BY PERSUASIVE LEADERSHIP

The third prediction explored the area that measures the degree to which the individual exerts leadership in interpersonal situations. It was stated as follows:

> Compared with entering students the graduating students in Officer Candidate School are more likely to be persuasive leaders and, therefore, graduating students will score significantly higher on the JAIM scale "Influences by Persuasive Leadership."

This prediction was tested by comparing the average score on the specific JAIM scale "Influences by Persuasive Leadership" between entering students and graduating students. The significance in the difference of the averages was tested by conducting a t-test of the averages. The difference between averages

89

was significant at the .01 level of confidence. Inasmuch as there is a significant difference between the average JAIM scores of entering and graduating students, the third prediction is affirmed. The third prediction is therefore accepted within the confines of earlier assumptions.

Prefers Supervisory Activities

The fourth prediction is concerned with the degree to which the individual likes to plan and supervise the work of other people. This prediction, the last, was stated as follows:

> Compared with entering students the graduating students in Officer Candidate School are more prone to like supervisory activities and, therefore, graduating students will score significantly higher on the JAIM scale "Prefers Supervisory Activities."

This prediction was tested by comparing the average score on the specific JAIM scale "Prefers Supervisory Activities" between entering students and graduating students. The significance in the difference of the averages was tested by conducting a t-test of the averages. The difference between averages was significant at the .01 level of confidence. Inasmuch as there is a significant difference in the average JAIM scores between entering and graduating students, the fourth prediction is affirmed. The fourth prediction is therefore accepted within the confines of earlier assumptions.

Inasmuch as 13 entering classes and 10 graduating classes were sampled, it seemed advisable to determine the variance among different classes. The statistical test selected for this comparison of classes was the analysis of variance which provides a method of testing for significant differences between averages among and between groups. Each of the four JAIM scales was evaluated in terms of the stability of the entering classes set of 13 averages and the stability of the graduating classes set of 10 averages.

The results of the analysis of variance tests for entering and graduating classes are given in Table 6. Among the entering classes, one significant difference was found on the "Values Approval from Others" scale. The fact that one out of eight comparisons shows a significant difference among groups indicates that different classes vary more than would be expected due to chance. This should be considered when interpreting the data.

Summary

The results of the measurement of two experimental groups relative to four specific JAIM scales were revealed. One experimental group consisted of 561 entering students, while the other consisted of 319 graduating students. All four reported scales were confirmed at the .01 level of confidence. Entering students, compared with graduating students, tend to place a higher value on the approval from others. In the other three scales, the graduating students were higher, which indicated the following:

90

TABLE 6

ANALYSIS OF VARIANCE AMONG ENTERING
AND GRADUATING CLASSES

Scales	F Ratio	Confidence Level
Values Approval from Others		
13 Entering Classes	1.967	.05
10 Graduating Classes	1.880	—
Influences by Persuasive Leadership		
13 Entering Classes	.945	—
10 Graduating Classes	1.552	—
Influences by Being Self-Assertive		
13 Entering Classes	.798	—
10 Graduating Classes	1.065	—
Prefers Supervisory Activities		
13 Entering Classes	.908	—
10 Graduating Classes	1.026	—

13 Entering Classes:
  $p < .05$ with $F = 1.77$ for 12 degrees of freedom.
  $p < .01$ with $F = 2.19$ for 12 degrees of freedom.

10 Graduating Classes:
  $p < .05$ with $F = 1.91$ for 9 degrees of freedom.
  $p < .01$ with $F = 2.48$ for 9 degrees of freedom.

1. Compared with entering students, the graduating students in Officer Candidate School tend to be more self-assertive.

2. Compared with entering students, the graduating students in Officer Candidate School are more likely to be persuasive leaders.

3. Compared with entering students, the graduating students in Officer Candidate School are more prone to like supervisory activities.

There is a significant difference in the average JAIM scores between groups of entering and graduating students in the four prechosen comparisons established by the four predictions. Within the structure of the restraints established by earlier assumptions, the four predictions were affirmed and accepted.

DISCUSSION OF FINDINGS

The comparison of self-reported beliefs between a group of entering and a group of graduating students in Officer Candidate School was described in the previous section. The difference was revealed by comparing the average of a sample from each of these two populations. The predictions, which are concerned with the differences in four specific self-reported beliefs, were affirmed by the results stated in the previous section. Following an explanation of these results, their implications and the causes of the differences in self-reported beliefs will be considered in this section. Based on these results, speculations will be made. Speculations will include the interacting causes pertaining to the significant differences between entering and graduating students in the scales "Values Approval from Others" and "Prefers Participative Leadership Style."

EXPLANATION OF RESULTS

It has been established that there is a significant difference in the average JAIM scores between entering and graduating students in the four prechosen comparisons.

The scale "Values Approval from Others" measures the degree to which the individual values himself by obtaining the approval of others.

> Persons scoring high consider it most important to have congenial co-workers; to be well liked; and like to please others through their work; and to be considered gracious, attractive and pleasant. It is correlated positively with the Edwards affiliation scale (.54) and the Kuder Clerical (.46) and the Social Service (—.43) scales, and negatively with the Kuder Outdoor (—.50), Scientific (—.44), and Mechanical (—.43) scales, and the Edwards Achievement scale (—.44). High school counselors and social workers scored high on this scale and engineers scored low.[49]

The JAIM scale "Values Approval from Others" is a part of the category of JAIM scales called, "Personal Values." The originator of the Job Analysis and Interest Measurement, Dr. Regis H. Walther, considers personal values as the criteria against which an individual judges the "goodness" or "badness" of work.

> Each of us has a set of standards or values about what is worthwhile and what is not, what we would like to be and what we would not. We use our standards to judge ourselves and our activities. These values are an essential component of our self-concepts and are reflected in the meaning work has for us.[50]

The results of this study indicate that the "Values Approval from Others" scale located within the "Personal Values" category of scales has the most

[49] Regis H. Walther, Shirley D. McCune, and Peter B. Petersen, *The Shaping of Professional Subcultures: A Study of Student Groups from Five Professions,* (Washington, D.C.: George Washington Univ., 1968), p. 52.

[50] Regis H. Walther, *The Psychological Dimensions of Work: A Research Approach Through Use of a Self-Report Inventory* (Washington, D.C.: George Washington Univ., 1972).

TABLE 7

DIFFERENCES BETWEEN ENTERING STUDENTS AND GRADUATING STUDENTS

Scales	Difference Between the Averages of 561 Entering Students and 319 Graduating Students*
1. BASIC BELIEFS	
a. Extent of Optimism	3.09***
b. Degree of Self-Confidence	5.18***
c. Belief in Moral Absolutes	—1.99**
d. Belief in Slow Change	.85
2. ACTIVITY PREFERENCES	
a. Prefers Problem Analysis	1.65
b. Prefers Social Interaction	—1.21
c. Prefers Mechanical Activities	.32
d. Prefers Supervisory Activities	2.58***
e. Prefers Activity Frequent Change	2.86***
3. PERSONAL VALUES	
a. Values Status Attainment	1.58
b. Values Social Service	—1.61
c. Values Approval from Others	—7.40***
d. Values Intellectual Achievement	1.71
e. Values Role Conformity	1.88
4. BEHAVIORAL STYLES	
a. Degree of Perseverance	3.05***
b. Extent of Orderliness	2.54**
c. Prefers to Plan Ahead	— .79
d. Influences by Persuasive Leadership	4.15***
e. Influences by Being Self-Assertive	5.61***
f. Move Toward Aggressor	—3.77***
g. Move Away from Aggressor	—1.83
h. Move Against Aggressor	2.74***
i. Prefers Routine	—3.01***
j. Identifies with Authority	—1.97**
k. Prefers Independence	3.29***
l. Prefers Directive Leadership Style	3.44***
m. Prefers Participative Leadership Style	—5.43***
n. Prefers Delegative Leadership Style	3.30***
o. Motivates by Knowledge of Results	6.15***
p. Believes in External Controls	4.34***
q. Prefers Being Systematic, Methodical	—1.32
r. Prefers Group Participation	—1.19

* A positive t-value indicates graduating students are higher in this particular scale, while a negative t-value indicates that entering student are higher as pertains to this particular scale.

** $p < .05$

*** $p < .01$

significant t-value among any of the 32 JAIM scales for research reported in this chapter. (See Table 7.)

The results of the research conducted in this study indicate that none of the other "Personal Values" category scales differed at a significant level between entering and graduating students.

The comparison of the "Values Approval from Others" scale with the scale "Prefers Participative Leadership Style" is worthy of study. These two scales appear to have a definite and positive relationship. The survey results indicate that the "Prefers Participative Leadership Style" scale had the second highest negative score, which indicates that entering students placed a higher value on participative leadership than graduating students. Since this scale was not predicted, no conclusions will be drawn relative to it. However, later in this study, implications and speculations will be made concerning this scale.

The JAIM scale "Influences by Being Self-Assertive" measures the degree the individual tends to pursue his own goals when they are in competition with the goals of others.

> Persons scoring high say that it is important to avoid being diverted from doing what is right in order to please someone; that they do better under competition or stress; and that they are proficient in athletic games. It correlated positively with the Kuder Outdoors (.41) and the MMPI Hypomania (.37) scales, and negatively with MMPI Masculine-Feminine scale (−.47). Presidents of business corporations were very high on this scale.[51]

The JAIM scale "Influences by Being Self-Assertive" is a part of the category of JAIM scales called "Behavioral Styles." Dr. Regis H. Walther describes this category as follows:

> Individuals necessarily develop standard ways for dealing with recurring situations and reserve conscious information processing and decision-making for more significant occasions. This organization gives rise to characteristic types of performance or behavioral styles, conscious and unconscious, in various life situations.[52]

The study results indicate that the "Influences by Being Self-Assertive" scale has the next to highest score among the other scales in this category. It relates that graduating students are more self-assertive than entering students.

The JAIM scale "Influences by Persuasive Leadership" measures the degree the individual exerts leadership in interpersonal situations.

> Persons scoring high report that they have no difficulty giving a speech or reciting before a large group; that they often take the leadership in groups; and that they like best in a job the opportunity to get results through persuasion or negotiation. It correlated positively with the Edwards Dominance (.59) and the MMPI Hypomania (.44) scales and negatively with the MMPI Social Isolation (−.43) and

---

[51] Walther, McCune, and Petersen, *op. cit.,* p. 46.
[52] Walther, *op. cit.*

the Edwards Abasement ($-.42$) scales. Presidents of business corporations, juvenile court judges and Foreign Service Officers scored high on this scale and Foreign Service code clerks and police patrolmen scored low.[53]

Like the scale "Influences by Being Self-Assertive," the scale "Influences by Persuasive Leadership" is also within the JAIM category "Behavioral Styles." The results from these two scales in this study are quite similar. Both indicate that graduating students place a higher value on each of these two scales. Both are significant at the .01 level of confidence.

The JAIM scale "Prefers Supervisory Activities" measures the degree to which an individual likes to plan and supervise the work of other people.

> Persons scoring high on this scale find that they get along best when they know what they want and work for it; they are generally striving to reach some goal they have established for themselves and like to supervise others in the carrying out of difficult assignments. Business executives scored high on this scale and Foreign Service Officers low.[54]

The "Prefers Supervisory Activities" scale is a part of the category of JAIM scales called "Activity Preferences." This category is defined as follows:

> Activity preferences involve the anticipation of intrinsic satisfaction from the performance of certain types of tasks. Some people derive their greatest satisfaction from jobs that involve a challenge; some from jobs that emphasize working with people; and some from jobs that require the competent manipulation of tools and materials. Individuals also appear to differ in the amount of environmental stimulation they require without which boredom influences their satisfaction and perhaps also their performance.[55]

The actual difference in the four predicted scales may, in part, be caused by the individuals in the group actually changing their self-reported beliefs between the time they enter Officer Candidate School and when they graduate. Another possibility is that failure to comply with the standards required for graduation may eliminate students by their failure or resignation. Thus, elimination of a student with certain beliefs from a group containing graduating students probably will affect the average of the scales involved. An evident weakness in my research is that it cannot be determined what portion of the difference in self-reported beliefs is caused by attrition (due to failing or resigning) and what portion is caused by students actually changing. From the research results, however, it is evident that there is a significant difference in self-reported beliefs and that this difference is in the direction that is desired.

One difference observed between entering and graduating students is their perception of the approval from others. Graduating students appear to be mission-oriented. Some express the philosophy of "not being overly concerned with what my buddies think; it's the mission that counts." In contrast, entering

---

[53] Walther, McCune, and Petersen, *op. cit.,* p. 46.
[54] *Ibid.,* p. 51.
[55] Walther, *op. cit.*

students tend to "worry too much about what their buddies think." Mission orientation becomes paramount during training, while the approval from others seems to be secondary. An example of the emphasis placed on accomplishing the mission is as follows: "There is no substitute for victory, that if you lose, the nation will be destroyed, that the very obsession of your public service must be duty, honor, country."[56]

With regard to self-assertiveness, candidates are placed in a training environment where they pursue their own goals in competition with the goals of others. Peer ratings also contribute to the competitive environment even when they are not actively participating in formal training. A strong degree of self-assertiveness seems to be compatible with the importance of a mission orientation over the value of the approval from others.

The view that it is important to avoid being diverted from doing what is right in order to please someone was evident in the behavior of the graduating students observed. The standards of Officer Candidate School are clear, particularly concerning self-assertiveness. "The candidate must be able to stand on his own two feet and direct the operations of small units."[57] The degree of perseverance exhibited by graduating students seems to be compatible with their competitive nature. To "survive" as a candidate until graduation the student needs the psychological stamina to continue competing. The importance of perseverance is indicated in a portion of a 1966 publication quoted below:

> Those of you who do not have an intense desire to become an officer should forget about applying. Primarily it is this desire that will carry you through your 6 months of training. There will be times when you will feel that you have been subjected to seemingly impossible hardships. Unless you have made up your mind to complete the course before you arrive at OCS, the chances are great that you will not be able to take it.[58]

The "Degree of Perseverance" scale was not prechosen as a prediction and is mentioned here only as it relates to the scale "Influences by Being Self-Assertive."

The development of a persuasive style of leadership is evident in the training. Candidates are placed constantly in interpersonal situations where they are required to exert leadership. In such situations, their actions are reflected in ratings by their peers as well as from their instructors and from their tactical officers. The standards require that graduating students have little difficulty in appearing before an audience and presenting a speech or leading a discussion. Each candidate has the opportunity to further develop his attributes regarding this particular scale.

[56] General Douglas MacArthur, May 12, 1962, on the occasion of his farewell address to the men of West Point.
[57] U.S. Department of the Army, *Department of the Army Pamphlet* 601–1: *The OCS* Story, June 1, 1966, p. 5.
[58] *Ibid.*, p. 12.

Candidates are required to hold instruction periods and present talks on various military subjects such as dismounted drill, physical training, Army information and military history.[59]

Most entering students want to be leaders, inasmuch as they volunteered to attend Officer Candidate School. It was observed that the degree to which candidates actually enjoy the supervising of others seems to increase with their experience in leading others as well as participating in leadership training.

> In order to develop leadership, the candidates are given an intensive course in the theory of leadership plus considerable practical work. Each class is organized as a company and candidates are rotated through the various command positions.[60]

IMPLICATIONS OF RESULTS

The implications of the results found in this study are that differences in certain self-reported beliefs may be attributed to a combination of three major implied causes. One of these causes is that graduating students may have had certain of their beliefs changed during the time considered. Two other causes are that candidates exhibiting undesired beliefs may have been eliminated from the course by failing or resigning. These implied causes, in varying proportions, play a role in shaping the difference between entering and graduating students.

An implication that may be drawn from these findings is that the beliefs of candidates are being molded into that form required for them to become successful as junior officers. The graduating student is action-oriented with a greater concern for the mission than the welfare of his subordinates. However, this does not imply that he is not concerned with their welfare. It does imply that concern for subordinates is second only to the accomplishment of the mission. The graduating student has a set of beliefs that are probably best suited to accomplish the short range goals of his vocation such as leading a platoon or commanding a company in combat.

While I was primarily interested in four selected self-reported beliefs, the entire JAIM instrument was administered. The reader may be interested in the findings of the other scales which are presented in Table 7.

At Officer Candidate School the student learns how to become a junior officer. Other schools within the military establishment will, hopefully, train him for more advanced assignments as his years of service increase. The implication is that different grades require different sets of beliefs. The commanding general of an Infantry Division would not have a set of self-reported beliefs comparable with a graduating student at Officer Candidate School. Instead, he probably would have a set of self-reported beliefs which would enable him to accomplish the following:

1. Get positive results without alienating others in the process.
2. Get the most out of people by effectively influencing their actions.

[59] *Ibid.*, p. 5.
[60] *Ibid.*

3. Be able to adjust to each new situation and to bear up and be resolute and logical under pressure.

4. Welcome additional and more important responsibility.

5. Think logically and make sound and practical decisions.

6. Have the desire to continue learning.

7. Have the desire to succeed in his present position and the ambition to advance to a higher and more responsible position.

8. Have the capability to establish realistic objectives and work intelligently to accomplish them.

9. Have the ability to evaluate his accomplishments and failures.

10. Be intrinsically motivated.

11. Control his resources wisely.[61]

According to Field Marshall Sir William Slim, Chief of the Imperial General Staff, British Army, in a speech to American officers at Fort Leavenworth, Kansas:

> There are many qualities that an American infantry division commanding general should have to be successful ... but there are certain ones that are basic, and without which he will never be a commander at all:
>
> a. Willpower (determination)
> b. Judgment
> c. Flexibility of mind
> d. Knowledge
> e. Integrity
>
> All of the really great commanders control their men because of their own personal integrity. The only foundations which will stand under great stress are the moral ones. I'm a hell of a general when I'm winning, anybody is, but it's when you're not winning, and I have not always been winning ... that the real test of leadership is made. I can remember when the situation was just as bad as it could be .... I walked up to a group of subordinate commanders waiting for me and those chaps just looked at me and I didn't know what to say. So I put the best face I could on it; I tried to look cheerful, and said, "Well, Gentlemen, it might be worse." And one of those unspeakable fellows said, "How?" The only thing I could think of saying was, "Well it might be raining." And in two hours it was .... The way to survive ... is by having the confidence of your men which you will get by honesty and integrity.[62]

The above comments by Field Marshall Slim reinforce my opinion that a set of beliefs required to lead successfully vary with military grade. An extreme example might be the difference in a set of beliefs between a lieutenant and a general. If this is correct, the beliefs of lieutenants may need to be changed again prior to these men being assigned to the duties of a higher grade.

---

[61] A composite response of several interviewed senior Army officers to the question, "What must an infantry division commanding general do personally to successfully accomplish his job?"

[62] U.S. Army Command and General Staff College, *Leadership-RB* 22-1 (Fort Leavenworth, Kans.: U.S. Department of the Army, 1952), pp. 8–1 to 8–11.

SPECULATION BASED ON RESULTS

From a speculative standpoint, a possible explanation for entering students receiving such a high score for the scale "Values Approval from Others" may be because entering students are introduced to a peer rating environment three or four days prior to being administered the JAIM. The peer rating system of Officer Candidate School may be new to many of the entering students. At this early stage of training, their value of the approval from others may be distorted because of a sudden need to make a favorable impression on their peers. Another possibility for the significant difference in the scale "Values Approval from Others" is that an orientation towards various combinations of other scales may cause a subsequent loss in the graduating students' need for the approval from others. Scales in this particular study which may be negatively related to the "Values Approval from Others" scale are:

1. "Motivates by Knowledge of Results."
2. "Influences by Being Self-Assertive."
3. "Degree of Self-Confidence."
4. "Believes in External Controls."
5. "Influences by Persuasive Leadership."
6. "Prefers Directive Leadership Style."
7. "Prefers Independence."
8. "Move Against Aggressor."

Speculation may also be made concerning the significant difference in the scale "Prefers Participative Leadership Style" (second highest score received by entering students). This difference may be caused by the student's experience and training during the course. A series of experiences requiring apt and suitable action, as similar as possible to those of a lieutenant in combat, may require the student to exercise a high degree of control without giving much freedom to subordinates or allowing them to participate in group decisions. An orientation towards various combinations of other scales may cause a subsequent loss in the degree to which the graduating student believes that leaders get the best results by having their subordinates participate in making decisions. The same eight scales listed as possibly being negatively related to the "Values Approval from Others" scale may also be, for this particular study, negatively related to the "Prefers Participative Leadership Style" scale. Some situations may require expedient action. In these cases, a set of beliefs more autocratic[63] than democratic[64] may be necessary for achieving a short range success. People-oriented beliefs in cases such as the following are secondary to an orientation toward the mission.

---

[63]"Autocracy here implies a high degree of control by the leader without much freedom by the members or participation by them in group decisions." R. K. White and R. O. Lippitt, *Autocracy and Democracy; An Experimental Inquiry* (New York: Harper, 1960), p. 135.

[64] According to R. K. White and R. O. Lippitt, democratic leadership should convey four meanings: people's rule, freedom, responsibility to cooperate, and concern for the *individual. Ibid.*

"Bob," said General MacArthur in a grim voice, "I'm putting you in command at Buna. Relieve Harding .... I want you to remove all officers who won't fight. Relieve regimental and battalion commanders; if necessary, put sergeants in charge of battalions and corporals in charge of companies. Time is of the essence; the Japs may land reinforcements any night." "Bob," he said, "I want you to take Buna, or not come back alive ... and that goes for your chief of staff too. Do you understand?"[65]

Beliefs contrasting to those indicated above would be required to achieve long range success involving perpetual change.

Democracy ... is not an idealistic conception but a hard necessity in those areas in which change is ever present .... For democracy is the only system of organization which is compatible with perpetual change.[66]

When the sole objective is to reach a decision, democratic leadership will probably take longer. But if implementation of the decision is desired, the entire process will take less time if democratic leadership procedures are used.

Studies show that (democratic) leadership can be more effective even from the time point of view if we consider the total time elapsed from the emergence of a problem to its implementation.[67]

It is conjectured that the set of beliefs of the typical graduating student is best suited for leading a platoon in combat. This set of beliefs is needed to manage violence and to make correct decisions quickly in time of crisis. Subsequent duties following about eight years of company grade assignments probably will require another set of beliefs. Prior to that time, these men will receive additional training and become more experienced.

During the past two decades, a trend in behavioral styles in the military seems to have been emerging. This trend is reflected in the following quotation from a U.S. Army field manual dealing with field service regulations. It suggests that concern for the individual may, at times, nearly equal the priority that must be given to the accomplishment of the mission.

Despite advance in technology, success in war depends on man. Man remains the essential element on the battlefield. The commander must be acutely sensitive to the physical and mental condition of his troops, and his plans must take account of their strengths and weaknesses. He must make allowances for the frailties to which the stresses and strains of combat subject the human mind and body. His actions must inspire and motivate his command with the will to succeed under the most adverse conditions, and must also assure his troops that hardship and sacrifice will not be needlessly imposed and that their well being is of primary concern.[68]

[65] Robert L. Eichelberger, *Our Jungle Road to Tokyo* (New York: Viking Press, 1950).

[66] P. E. Slater and W. G. Bennis, "Democracy is Inevitable," *Harvard Business Review* 42, no. 2 (March/April 1964): 54.

[67] Gordon L. Lippitt, "What Do We Know About Leadership?" *National Education Association Journal* (December 1955): 557.

[68] U.S. Department of the Army, *Field Manual No. 100–5: Field Service Regulations–Operations*, February 19, 1962, p. 19.

This philosophy seems to indicate a trend in giving greater consideration to the human resources required to accomplish a mission.

SUMMARY AND CONCLUSIONS

SUMMARY

The study reported in this chapter was a comparison of the average self-reported beliefs between a group of entering and graduating students in one Officer Candidate School. Engineer Officer Candidate School was the specific school used and it was representative of others in operation at that time. The duration of the training was 23 weeks. Self-reported beliefs refer to the consistent ways in which a person organizes his physical, emotional and energy resources. The instrument used in this study was the Job Analysis and Interest Measurement which contains 125 multiple-choice items pertaining to 32 scales.

There was a significant difference in the average JAIM scores between entering and graduating students in four prechosen comparisons established by four predictions. Entering students, compared with graduating students, placed a higher value on the approval from others as determined by the Job Analysis and Interest Measurement. In the three other scales considered by the other predictions, the average graduating students' scores were higher than the entering students' scores. This indicated that:

1. Graduating students, compared with entering students, are more self-assertive.
2. Graduating students, as compared with entering students, are more likely to be persuasive leaders.
3. Graduating students, as compared with entering students are more prone to like supervisory activities.

The actual difference in the four predicted scales may, in part, be caused by the individual changing his self-reported beliefs between the time he enters Officer Candidate School and the time he graduates. Another possibility is that the standards for graduation may eliminate students by failure or resignation. The elimination of a student with certain self-reported beliefs from a group containing graduating students probably will affect the average of the scales involved. From the research results, however, it is evident that there is a significant difference in self-reported beliefs and that this difference is in the direction desired by the school.

An implication that may be drawn from these findings is that the beliefs of candidates are being molded into a configuration required for these men to become successful junior officers. The graduating student seems to place concern for others second only to the accomplishment of the mission. Another possible explanation for the difference in the approval from others between entering and graduating students is that entering students are introduced to a peer rating environment three or four days prior to being administered the JAIM. At this early stage of training, their score on the "Values Approval from Others" scale may be distorted because of a sudden need to make a favorable impression on their peers. Speculation was made concerning the significant difference in the scale "Prefers Participative Leadership Style" (second highest score received by entering students). A series of experiences requiring expedient action similar to combat may require the student to exercise a high degree of control without giving much freedom to subordinates, or allowing them to make group decisions. In these cases a set of beliefs more autocratic than democratic may be necessary for achieving short range success. A contrasting set of beliefs would be required to achieve long range success involving perpetual change.

It is speculated that the beliefs of graduating students are best suited for leading a platoon in combat. Subsequent duties following approximately eight years of company grade assignments probably will require another set of beliefs. During this time, these men will receive additional training and become more experienced. A trend in behavioral styles in the military, as speculated by the author, is that concern for the individual is increasing and may, at times, nearly equal in priority the accomplishment of any given mission.

Further research could correct the current weakness in this study relative to determining the cause of the actual change in beliefs. The difference is now explained as an unknown combination of both attrition and change. A continued study of the same individuals could determine to what extent they change their beliefs due to experience, age, new roles, changes in their leadership philosophy, and other factors not recognized at this time. It would be interesting to measure, in twenty to thirty years from now, the self-reported beliefs of the few students from the 1,111 tested who become general officers. Then, follow this by comparing their scores with the average of the class during the period they were lieutenants, captains, majors, lieutenant colonels, and colonels.

CONCLUSIONS

1. Evidence has been presented to show that there is a difference in the self-reported beliefs between entering and graduating students.

2. Entering students, compared with graduating students, tend to place a higher value on the approval from others as determined by entering students scoring significantly higher on the JAIM scale "Values Approval from Others."

3. Compared with entering students, the graduating students in Officer Candidate School tend to be more self-assertive as determined by graduating students scoring significantly higher on the JAIM scale "Influences by Being Self-Assertive."

4. Compared with entering students, the graduating students in Officer Candidate School are more likely to be persuasive leaders as determined by graduating students scoring significantly higher on the JAIM scale "Influences by Persuasive Leadership."

5. Compared with entering students, the graduating students in Officer Candidate School are more prone to like supervisory activities as determined by graduating students scoring significantly higher on the JAIM scale "Prefers Supervisory Activities."

Chapter 4

A MORE DETAILED INVESTIGATION OF THE EFFECT AND STABILITY OF OFFICER CANDIDATE SCHOOL TRAINING

The purpose of the study reported in this chapter was to conduct a more detailed investigation of the immediate effects of training and the stability of these effects. The research described in Chapter 3 was conducted in relation to a master's thesis at George Washington University, while the research project described in Chapter 4 pertains to a doctoral dissertation accepted by George Washington University on February 15, 1971. Although the identical Officer Candidate School was studied in both projects, the second project pertained to different individuals who were in training a year later and then retested three years after completing training.

This chapter is organized to provide: first, a review of related research; then, an elaboration of the overall research design, which includes methodology, theoretical framework of study, predictions, and method for evaluation of predictions. The research design is followed by pertinent findings and their analyses. The chapter ends with conclusions and recommendations for further research.

NATURE OF PROBLEM

I have been interested for several years in determining the actual value of Officer Candidate School training. Many hours of spirited discussion with infantry officer colleagues served to increase this genuine curiosity. If the characteristics needed to become a competent officer can be developed for an individual who initially does not possess them, it seems that the novice should either: modify his behavior, or perhaps acquire a new set of beliefs; or develop a combination of modified behavior and a newly acquired set of beliefs.

In the previous chapter, a comparison was conducted of the average self-reported beliefs as measured by the JAIM between a group of 561 entering students and a group of 319 graduating students attending the U.S. Army Engineer Officer Candidate School at Fort Belvoir, Virginia. The JAIM scales of each of these two groups were significantly different; however, the effect of training could not be measured because the same individuals were not tested as both entering and graduating students. In the normal course of events, most of the individuals who failed to graduate actually resigned from the program rather than wait to be selected for relief by the school authorities. There was a possibility that this self-selection departure process would further prevent an accurate analysis between entering and graduating students. If individuals with certain self-reported beliefs were selected to fail, it could be possible that instead of training men to become officers, the school was selecting men to become officers. A more likely possibility to account for the difference between groups of entering and graduating students was a combination of training and selection.

In the study reported in this chapter, the same individuals will be observed as entering and graduating students. It should be possible, when observing these individuals, to determine specific differences in self-reported beliefs that can be attributed to their association with Officer Candidate School.

The results of an investigation of the effect of training several years after depature from Officer Candidate School should be a beneficial consideration in the development of future training programs. In this study, a comparison will also be made of the same individuals, initially as students, and then again years after departure from Officer Candidate School.

The mission of Officer Candidate School is to develop competent second lieutenants for the U.S. Army. Since the beginning of the program immediately prior to World War II, there have been various numbers of such schools corresponding to branches such as Infantry, Quartermaster, Ordnance, and Military Police. However, during August 1967, there were only four Officer Candidate Schools. These were: Infantry Officer Candidate School at Fort Benning, Georgia; Artillery Officer Candidate School at Fort Sill, Oklahoma; Engineer Officer Candidate School in Fort Belvoir, Virginia; and WAC Officer Candidate School at Fort McClellan, Alabama.

One of the four Officer Candidate Schools in operation during 1967 (Engineer Officer Candidate School) is included in this study. The majority of graduates from Engineer Officer Candidate School are commissioned in the Corps of Engineers; some, however, are commissioned in other branches and receive additional training at the appropriate branch school prior to their initial assignment.

> Basically the schools are conducted as they were in 1941. However, the subject matter presented has been changed considerably to keep pace with the changes in organization and tactics employed by our modern Army.[1]

The 23-week program at Engineer Officer Candidate School consists mainly of field engineering subjects, tactics, weapons, and other general subjects applicable to all branches of the Army.

[1] U.S. Department of the Army, *Department of the Army Pamphlet* 601–1: *The OCS Story,* October 1969, p. 5.

Student members of the U.S. Army Engineer Officer Candidate Regiment construct a timber trestle bridge during training at Fort Belvoir in 1967. (Photo by Sp 5 William D. Riley, Post Photographic Facility, Fort Belvoir, Virginia.)

Training at the Engineer Officer Candidate School, Fort Belvoir, Virginia is designed to produce thoroughly competent, highly motivated second lieutenants .... The course is challenging and demanding. Its goal is to train each candidate to the limit of his aptitude in the time available.[2]

Three other sources used for providing commissioned officers are "... Reserve Officer Training Corps (ROTC) and other in-college programs, service academies, and direct appointments."[3] While the largest source of newly commissioned officers is ROTC, the six-month Officer Candidate Program has the advantage of being more responsive to changing manpower needs.

While officer candidate programs were originally established to train officers recruited from the enlisted ranks, they have increasingly been used in recent years to supplement the flow of new college graduates into the officer corps. The large demand for new officers created by the Vietnam buildup, however, required the Army in particular to allow significant numbers of non–college graduates to enter its OCS program.[4]

Findings reported in this chapter strongly indicate that Officer Candidate School training changes certain of the self-reported beliefs of individuals attending. These changes are beneficial to both the individual and the Army.

REVIEW OF RELATED RESEARCH

This section is designed to report the findings of a review of related research that should be beneficial in the development of this study. The purpose of reviewing the literature is to develop a summary of pertinent prior and current concepts, then build on these concepts to formulate a worthwhile addition to present knowledge in this specific field. In attempting to accomplish this goal, four major areas relevant to this chapter were determined to be as follows:

1. The learning process.
2. Impact of the organization on the individual.
3. Military studies relative to this study.
4. JAIM research related to this study.

Inasmuch as the subject of the study pertains to the learning process in an organizational setting, the review first considers the broad subject of the learning process, then focuses on the impact of the organization on the individual. Then, as an extension of these two subjects, specific military studies relative to this study are presented. The review of the relevant literature concludes by further narrowing its scope concerning specific JAIM research related to this study.

The Learning Process

As an initial point of reference, the literature will focus on the learning

2 *Ibid.,* p. 11.
3 *The President's Commission on an All-Volunteer Armed Force,* February 1970, pp. 70–71.
4 *Ibid.,* p. 77.

process. In examining the various aspects of the learning process, the following major areas appear to be essential: learning theory; application of feedback; relationship of training to the overall function of the organization; and development of effective leadership.

In conceptualizing the process of learning, it is necessary to consider several allied factors such as the purpose of learning a specific subject, objective in terms of individual change or proficiency, a method for learning, and an evaluation of both the learning process and of what was learned. Once the purpose of learning is determined, specific objectives can be established. Then, related to these objectives, a program of instruction can be designed to meet the objectives. An instructional objective, according to Mager,[5] should be stated in concrete terms. It should indicate "... what a student would be doing when demonstrating his achievement of the objective, suggest conditions relevant to desired performance, and suggest how to tell when the objective has been achieved."[6] With regard to evaluation, there are two evaluations considered by Mager. "One is the evaluation of results and the other is the evaluation of process. Results evaluation tells us something about how well we are doing; process evaluation tells us how we might do better."[7]

In an overview of "Learning Theories and Training," Leslie E. This and Gordon L. Lippitt generalize how learning occurs. "Learning occurs when a stimulus is associated with a response."[8] An analysis of the various theories of learning grouped these theories into the following six general schools:

1. The first school is known as the *Behaviorist School.* Primarily, these theories hold that the learning results from the reward or punishment that follows a response to a stimulus. These are the so-called S-R Theories ....

2. The second grouping is the *Gestalt School.* These theorists believe that learning is not a simple matter of stimulus and response. They hold that learning is cognitive and involves the whole personality. To them, learning is infinitely more complex than the S-R Theories would indicate .... Kurt Lewin, Wolfgang Kohler, E. C. Tolman and Max Wertheimer are typical theorists in this school .... To them, "the whole is more than the sum of the parts" ....

3. A third school is the *Freudian School.* ... Freud was interested in individual development and the kind of re-education that goes on in psychotherapy .... Psychoanalytic theory is too complex and, at least at the present time, too little formalized for it to be presented as a set of propositions subject to experimental testing ....

4. A fourth school is the *Functionalists.* These seem to take parts of all the theories and view learning as a very complex phenomenon that is not explained by either the Gestalt or the Behavioral Theories. Some of the leaders in this school are John Dewey, J. R. Angell, and R. S. Woodworth ....

5. A fifth so-called school is those who subscribe to *Mathematical Models.* To

[5] Robert F. Mager, *Developing Attitude Toward Learning* (Palo Alto, Calif.: Feardon, 1968).
[6] *Ibid.,* p. 13.
[7] *Ibid.,* p. 69.
[8] Leslie E. This and Gordon L. Lippitt, "Learning Theories and Training," *Training and Development Journal* (April–May 1966).

these researchers, learning theories must be stated in mathematical form. Some of these proponents come from different learning theory schools but tend to focus on mathematical models such as the Feedback Model, Information-Theory Model, Gaming Model, Differential Calculus Model, Stochastic Model, and the Statistical Association Model . . . .

6. A sixth school is more general in nature and can be characterized by calling it *Current Learning Theory Schools*. These are quite difficult to classify and seem to run the range of modifying Gestalt Theories, modifying Behavioral Theories, accommodating two pieces of both theories, assuming that training involves the whole man—psychological, physiological, biological, and neurophysiological. Some of these are the Postulate System of MacCorquodale and Meehl and the Social Learning Theory of Rotter. [9]

Learning theory applied to individuals in an organization can provide an insight in terms of individual performance. James N. Mosel believes that the effective application of feedback is essential for training to be successful.

Feeding back to employees the results of their work embodies what psychologists call the "principle of knowledge of performance." This principle is one of the most thoroughly validated principles of learning. It is also one of the most neglected in industrial training. It may be stated as follows: *as knowledge of performance increases, learning increases both in rate and level.* [10]

If training is to contribute to the total organization, it should have a direct relationship to the overall function of the organization. In a discussion of the logic of training, Edgar H. Schein[11] identified three major problems.

1. The outcome is often not clearly specifiable, not because of insufficient study of the job for which a person is to be trained, but because the trainee sometimes is expected to grow and develop in terms of his general attitudes, his basic capacities, and general knowledge *in order to prepare him for an uncertain future.*
2. The training itself unleashes some forces within the organization which produce pressures toward change in other parts of the organization, changes which those parts may not be prepared to cope with.
3. The training effort interacts with recruitment, selection, and job design [12]

Bernard J. Bienvenu[13] believes that training must keep current and, in fact, ahead of needed changes in employee performance requirements. Training goals are therefore, according to Bienvenu, established by specific performance requirements. In contrast to training new members of the firm, older members may, in some cases, require additional training or retraining. Training that is an extension of current work skills may be presented as a reward or as a means to generate potential for further advancement. Retraining of the same current

[9] *Ibid.*

[10] James N. Mosel, "How to Feed Back Performance Results to Trainees," A paper read before the Employee Training Institute at the annual conference of Public Personnel Administration of the Civil Service Assembly (Washington, D.C.: October 9, 1966).

[11] Edgar H. Schein, *Organizational Psychology* (Englewood Cliffs, N.J.: Prentice-Hall, 1965).

[12] *Ibid.*, p. 40.

[13] Bernard J. Bienvenu, *New Priorities in Training* (American Management Assoc.: 1969).

skills, however, may be looked on by the employee as boring or even as punishment.

> Retraining should be recognized for what it is, a very difficult, specialized, and expensive practice .... It should also be recognized that a retraining project cannot really be termed successful unless it conditions the individual being retrained to take advantage of the concepts of continuous and total training.[14]

Chris Argyris, in an investigation of a leadership pattern, concludes that a specific leader "... is, by his superior's own evaluation, a successful executive."[15] Argyris then considers the price the company must pay for this particular leadership pattern. In this case, junior leaders depend on the leader for most of their authority, rewards, and penalties. Thus, the junior leaders become leader-centered with the following results:

> 1. They ... spend much of their time competing against each other for tne leader's praise and favor.
> 2. .... They hide things that may imply that they are not a "cooperative team." .... They also hide their own feelings, especially the negative ones.
> 3. .... They spend many hours trying to find out what the leader desires.
> 4. .... They depend on the leader to define their goals and the way to achieve these goals.
> 5. Their insecurity ... is increased by their inability to predict the leader's daily behavior.
> 6. .... They are continually in interdepartmental conflicts ....
> 7. This interdepartmental hostility is kept hidden from the leader.
> 8. .... They depend upon the leader for a sense of group cohesiveness.
> 9. .... Their informal behavior is characterized by expression of their pent-up feelings that arise from conflict, tension, and frustration.
> 10. They begin to hide their conflict, frustration, and tension not only from the leader, but from themselves.[16]

Prior to recommending ways to evolve a new and more effective philosophy of leadership, Argyris is quick to point out that "there have been no successful substitutes offered for the basically authoritarian type of organization that exists today. ... It is this type of organization that has helped make American industry what it is today."[17] Argyris further suggests that a more effective leadership philosophy would concentrate on continuing successful leadership, demonstrated in this case, while reducing the cost the organization must pay for this successful leadership. Argyris proposes that the leader be re-educated to develop a new pattern of leadership that would generally follow the guideposts listed below:

> 1. In the final analysis people are basically responsible to themselves. They can

---

[14] *Ibid.*, p. 141.

[15] Chris Argyris, *Executive Leadership: An Appraisal of a Manager in Action* (New York: Harper & Row, 1953), p. 107.

[16] *Ibid.*, pp. 108–110.

[17] *Ibid.*, p. 111.

only tell themselves what to do. A leader should be willing to permit people to keep this responsibility.

2. Most people have a desire to be mature. They want to be socially accepted. They want to feel a sense of personal worth . . . .

3. The task of the leader is to create a warm congenial atmosphere in which individuals feel free to bring out any attitudes and feelings they may have . . . .

4. The leader tries to get across to others that he accepts them as individual human beings.

Such a leadership philosophy is oriented towards accomplishing goals through the successful interaction with people. Rather than being goal oriented the leader is oriented towards people who in turn accomplish the mission.

Thus there will be a need for some reeducation of the leader . . . in such things as (1) giving orders, (2) handling grievances, (3) leading groups, (4) handling disciplinary problems, and (5) making decisions.[18]

Impact of the Organization on the Individual

Much has been written concerning the impact of the organization on the individual. While most behavioral science studies consider the impact of the organization on the individual, the following findings are considered in their particular subset of this subject to be the most appropriate.

The impact of the organization on the individual tends to be unfavorable when there is a conflict in the goals of both the individual and the organization. Conversely, the impact of the individual on the organization also tends to be unfavorable in such a situation. One major problem appears to be how to achieve both the individual's goals and the organization's goals simultaneously. Bennis[19] considers that attempting to reach these two seemingly incompatible goals is an essential task for management. In viewing effective leadership, he further conceptualized that effective leadership depends primarily on mediating between the individual and the organization in such a way that both can obtain maximum satisfaction. This particular opinion, shared by Herzberg, Likert, Argyris, McGregor, and many others, emphasizes the creating of conditions so that the subordinate is motivated by accomplishing challenging work in which he can assume responsibility rather than a course of action where working conditions are improved, salaries are raised, or jobs restructured. Allied to these concepts is the relationship of the leader's authority and the individual's freedom of operation. While various situations may require different relationships of authority and freedom, Bennis considers that "democracy is inevitable" in that optimum long-term goals can be achieved by a genuine delegation of authority to the individual.

An effective evaluation of the impact of the organization on the individual was accomplished by Rensis Likert in his overall evaluation of various systems

---

[18] *Ibid.,* p. 113.
[19] Warren G. Bennis, "Revisionist Theory of Leadership," *Harvard Business Review* (January–February 1961): 26–35.

of organization. In exploring organizational variations, he defined and labeled a continuum consisting of four "systems of organization" which are as follows:

1. Exploitative authoritative
2. Benevolent authoritative
3. Consultative
4. Participative group

In evaluating the above four systems of organization, Likert considered the following, which he labeled as operating characteristics:

1. Character of motivational forces
2. Character of communications process
3. Character of interaction–influence process
4. Character of decisionmaking process
5. Character of goal–setting
6. Character of control process
7. Performance characteristics

His research findings indicated that management systems similar to System 4 (the participative group):

> ... are more productive and have lower costs and more favorable attitudes .... Those firms or plants where System 4 is used show high productivity, low scrap loss, low costs, favorable attitudes, and excellent labor relations. The converse tends to be the case for companies or departments whose management system is well toward System 1. (Exploitative Authoritative) Corresponding relationships are also found with regard to any shifts in the management system. Shifts toward System 4 are accompanied by long-range improvement in productivity, labor relations, costs, and earnings. The long-range consequences of shifts toward System 1 are unfavorable. A science-based management, such as System 4, is appreciably more complex than other systems. It requires greater learning and appreciably greater skill to use it well, but it yields impressively better results, which are evident whenever accurate performance measurements are obtained.[20]

At present, Likert and his Institute for Social Research at the University of Michigan are working with several companies attempting to develop a System 4 type organization. These companies are exploring ways of using the principles and procedures of System 4 "... in mobilizing fully the noneconomic motives in coordination with effective use of economic needs."[21] Their primary goal is to maximize the benefits of a favorable impact of the organization on the individual employee.

Carroll Shartle[22] visualized the impact of the leader (or organization) on an individual in terms of how the leader performed certain acts. In an Ohio State University leadership study, he used a continuum of leadership performance to

[20] Rensis Likert, *The Human Organization* (New York: McGraw-Hill, 1967), p. 46.
[21] *Ibid.*, p. 191.
[22] Carroll L. Shartle, *Executive Performance and Leadership* (Englewood Cliffs, N.J.: Prentice-Hall, 1956).

112

record certain acts. In measuring, for example, the communication between the leader and subordinates, one continuum used by Shartle was: "He calls the Group Together to Discuss the Work." Five frequencies located along this continuum were: Always, Often, Occasionally, Seldom, and Never. In addition, leadership performance can be measured relative to a standard. Shartle suggests the following:

> The use of leader behavior description scales represents one method for evaluating supervisory and executive behavior. If, for example, an executive has an immediate staff of twelve people, six can describe his actual leader behavior and the remainder can describe the ideal leader behavior of a person in his position. Scores can then be compared.[23]

Another Ohio State University study by Fleishman, Harris, and Burtt determined how leadership was influenced by a specific training program for foremen and also by the leadership later provided by the foreman's own boss. The results of their study indicated that:

> The powerful influence of "leadership climate" may be our most important finding. Leadership behavior is not a thing apart but is imbedded in a social setting. Besides, the foreman is actually being "trained" every day by the rewards and example provided by his own boss. We are apt to lose sight of the fact that this every day kind of learning is more potent than a "one shot" training course.[24]

In considering the impact of the organization on the individual, the leadership climate in each particular situation is a major factor.

An important dimension in considering the impact of the organization on the individual is the personal identification that the individual may have with the organization and with his own particular role in the organization. Jennings, in his book *The Executive in Crisis*, substantiates this by stating:

> Those [executives] who arrive at the top seem to have made this strong identification with the administrative role .... He learns to identify with these ideas by means of seeing how others assume the administrative role. He may distantly identify with superiors and goal-achieving activities, but he is essentially using these identifications to show himself how to achieve personal identification with the authority and goals of his own administrative role.[25]

In further considering the impact of the organization on the individual, Jennings concludes that anxiety can be caused in part by a feeling of potential danger because of wanted or unwanted movement upward. He established the following four categories to depict specific situations:

1. Mobility upward is wanted and is impending.
2. Mobility upward is wanted and is not impending.

---

[23] *Ibid.*, p. 123.

[24] Edwin A. Fleishman, Edwin F. Harris, and Harold E. Burtt, *Leadership and Supervision in Industry* (Columbus, Ohio: Ohio State Univ., 1955), p. 423.

[25] Eugene Emerson Jennings, *The Executive in Crisis* (East Lansing, Mich.: Michigan State Univ., 1965), p. 171.

3. Mobility is not wanted and is impending.
4. Mobility is not wanted and is not impending.

With respect to the first category, a mild anxiety may develop because the individual fears an unknown future. "He may want the promotion but may fear it, and the ambivalence may generate formidable anxiety."[26] In the second category, the individual may perceive that he is not doing well and that his potential for promotion is mediocre at best. The anxiety in this case is the thought of remaining attached to the present job level. In the third category, anxiety, according to Jennings, is probably caused by the individual desiring to remain at the present level, but receiving cues that he is wanted in a higher and more responsible level. With respect to the fourth category, many individuals, according to Jennings, do not seem anxious when mobility is not wanted and is not impending. However, there may be other factors, such as an ambitious wife, that may cause other problems for this individual who apparently does not seem anxious. It appears that for more effective operations, the potential for anxiety in each of the four above cases should be understood by the leader's superior, and that promotion policies should be designed to minimize these anxieties.

Several writers have labeled various leadership styles. Jennings in his book *The Executive: Autocrat, Bureaucrat, and Democrat*,[27] categorized various major leadership styles as autocratic, bureaucratic and democratic. The current trend, however, seems to be to develop flexible categories.

> I would like to further develop the concept of a leadership continuum that has been produced by the works of Tannenbaum and Schmidt who point out that forces in the leader, forces in the group members, and forces in the situation apparently combine to make it necessary for a leader to respond at any given moment with a style of leadership appropriate to that situation.[28]

While Lippitt indicates that there are at least four relatively well-defined leadership styles—autocratic, benevolently autocratic, laissez-faire, and democratic—he concurs with others such as Rensis Likert concerning the dangers of stereotype classifications. Lippitt's opinion is as follows:

> In a very real sense I feel that it is not appropriate to classify leaders by stereotypes .... In similar fashion I feel that classifying organizations as authoritative or participative may do a disservice to the reality of situational needs and demands.[29]

A general implication from much of the literature reviewed is that large organizations such as Army are self-generators of employee dissatisfaction. Further, that large organizations by the very nature of their size require conformity and thus restrict the individual. A study conducted by Lyman W. Porter did not support these notions. "Contrary to general belief, large companies

---

[26] *Ibid.*, p. 181.

[27] E. E. Jennings, *The Executive: Autocrat, Bureaucrat, Democrat* (New York: Harper & Row, 1962).

[28] Lippitt, *Organizational Renewal* (New York: Meredith Corp., 1969), p. 87.

[29] *Ibid.*

114

produce more favorable management attitudes, greater challenges, and less conforming behavior than do smaller companies."[30] Porter concludes that large organizations can generate:

> ... At least as favorable management attitudes as small companies, in terms of job challenges and the kind of behavior seen as necessary for job success .... If we are to be concerned with the effects of organizations on individuals, we should direct our attention to the internal structure of organizations rather than to their sheer external size. Our findings indicate that big companies need not be apologetic either for their bigness or for their effects on their managers.[31]

The attempt by organizations to " 'install a generator' in the employee has been demonstrated to be a total failure."[32] According to Frederick Herzberg, employees will not necessarily be motivated by improved working conditions, shuffling of tasks, or even a raise in salary. Herzberg states that:

> The absence of such "hygiene" factors as good supervisor-employee relations and liberal fringe benefits can make a worker unhappy, but their presence will not make him want to work harder. Essentially meaningless changes in the tasks that workers are assigned to do have not accomplished the desired objective either. The only way to motivate the employee is to give him challenging work in which he can assume responsibility.[33]

Katz and Kahn[34] view the concept of role as the major means for the conceptual interfacing of the individual and the organization.

> Each person in an organization is linked to some set of other members by virtue of the functional requirements of the system which are heavily implemented through the expectations those members have of him; he is the focal person for that set. An organization can be viewed as consisting of a number of such sets, one for each person in the organization.[35]

Within an organization, some individuals adapt to roles that they would not assume outside of the organization.

> They may wear uniforms or costumes which they would not otherwise wear. They are likely to adopt certain styles and formalities in interpersonal relations which are not elsewhere in evidence. Above all, their behavior in organizations shows a selectivity, a restrictiveness, and a persistence which is not to be observed in the same persons when outside the organization.[36]

[30] Lyman W. Porter, "Where is the Organization Man?" *Harvard Business Review* (November–December 1963): 53.

[31] *Ibid.*, p. 61.

[32] Frederick Herzberg, "One More Time: How Do You Motivate Employees?," *Harvard Business Review* (January–February 1968): 53.

[33] *Ibid.*

[34] Daniel Katz and Robert L. Kahn, *The Social Psychology of Organizations* (New York: John Wiley and Sons, 1966).

[35] *Ibid.*, p. 197.

[36] *Ibid.*, p. 199.

An extensive study by Joan Woodward[37] concerning organizational theory and practice focused on the effects of change. After she presented a theoretical framework and a case study, she described a followup investigation pertaining to the impact of change within a large organization. It is interesting to note that role changes compatible with the interests of individuals met little resistance while role changes that threatened or appeared to threaten the maintenance of individual interests faced considerable resistance. Training and indoctrination of leaders should, according to Woodward, include the development of a sensitivity of the leader towards the needs of subordinates. This sensitivity would aid in the implementation of change.

In an analysis of (1) organizational innovativeness, and (2) interpersonal competence, Chris Argyris[38] arrived at the following observations that have relevance to this book. "Modern organizations may not survive unless they are able to innovate. It is equally clear that the costs of innovation are growing rapidly while the useful life span for any new idea is decreasing."[39]

Pertaining to interpersonal competence, he noted that:

> Problems may be "solved" so permanently, that people do not speak to each other again . . . . If individuals with relatively low interpersonal competence are aware of relevant problems, they should not be able to solve them; or if they are able to solve them, they should do so at a cost to the problem-solving processes involved.[40]

In attempting to describe the characteristics of the organization beyond the traditional one of today, Argyris[41] emphasizes that:

> The pyramidal structure has not been overthrown . . . . Management in the organization of the future will give much more thought to its basic values and planning as to how they may be implemented . . . . How does it intend to adapt to, and become integrated with the environment? What influences should it attempt to change the environment?[42]

Values pertaining to effective organizational operations will be expanded to incorporate the necessary system capable of adjusting to the environment.

> The "old" values regarding influence will still be maintained to be used for the appropriate conditions. The "new" values regarding influence will be added to, not substituted for, the old . . . . The organization will require people who are not threatened by, but actually value, psychological success, self-esteem, self-responsibility, and internal commitment.[43]

[37] Joan Woodward, *Industrial Organization: Theory and Practice* (London: Oxford Univ. Press, 1965).

[38] Chris Argyris, *Organization and Innovation* (Homewood, Ill.: Richard D. Irwin and the Dorsey Press, 1965).

[39] *Ibid.*, pp. 1–2.

[40] *Ibid.*, p. 4.

[41] Argyris, *Integrating the Individual and the Organization* (New York: John Wiley and Sons, 1964).

[42] *Ibid.*, pp. 272–273.

[43] *Ibid.*, pp. 273–274.

Thousands of studies pertaining to military psychology were scanned in the preparation of this section of this chapter. Pertinent studies were then reviewed. The majority lacked scientific thoroughness and tended to describe how to accomplish a particular training and development task. Several studies in military psychology, however, were particularly excellent and relevant. The following two studies are representative of several others:

1. *The American Soldier* study by Stouffer, Suchman, DeVinney, Star, and Williams published in 1949.
2. *The Professional Soldier* study by Janowitz published in 1960 and revised in 1971.

During World War II, the Research Branch of the Information and Education Division of the War Department accumulated a considerable amount of data pertaining to social psychology. A grant furnished by Carnegie Corporation of New York enabled Stouffer, et al.[44] to prepare four volumes for the analysis and interpretation of this data. Finally published in 1949, the volumes consisted of the following:

I. *The American Soldier: Adjustment During Army Life.*
II. *The American Soldier: Combat and its Aftermath.*
III. *Experiments on Mass Communication.*
IV. *Measurement and Prediction.*

These studies consisted of a major recording and analysis of World War II attitudes and values of military personnel. Typical of this data is the portion concerning attitudes toward leadership and social control. It is interesting to note that many of the attitudes of enlisted personnel towards officers have changed little since World War II. The following pattern of attitudes sampled during World War II continues to be pertinent:

1. In any given survey, relatively new recruits tended to have more favorable attitudes toward officers than did men with longer service.
2. At later stages of the war, men tended to have less favorable attitudes toward officers than did men in the same rank and longevity groups in earlier surveys.
3. At a given time period, the smallest proportion of favorable attitudes tended to be found in the relatively inactive overseas theaters; the highest proportion of favorable attitudes tended to be found among combat troops; the proportion favorable among troops in the United States who had not gone overseas tended to be intermediate between these two groups.
4. The better educated enlisted men, rank and longevity held constant, tended to be less favorable in attitudes toward officers than less educated men. [45]

In the late 1950's Morris Janowitz conducted a major study to provide a social and political portrait of the American professional soldier. In his book,

[44]Samuel A. Stouffer, *et al.,* "The American Soldier: Adjustment During Army Life," *Studies in Social Psychology in World War II,* vol. 1 (Princeton: Princeton Univ., 1949).
[45]*Ibid.,* p. 364.

The Professional Soldier,[46] he describes "the professional life, organizational setting, and leadership of the American military as they have evolved during the first half of this century."[47] In providing an analysis of professionals in violence, he used five major predictions as a point of departure. These predictions and a brief explanation are as follows:

1. *Changing Organizational Authority.* There has been a change in the basis of authority and discipline in the military establishment, a shift from authoritarian domination to greater reliance on manipulation, persuasion, and a group consensus . . . .

2. *Narrowing Skill Differential Between Military and Civilian Elites.* The new tasks of the military require that the professional officer develop more and more of the skills and orientations common to civilian administrators and civilian leaders . . . . The concentration of personnel with "purely" military occupational specialties has fallen from 93.2% in the Civil War to 28.8% in the post-Korean Army . . . .

3. *Shift in Officer Recruitment.* The military elite has been undergoing a basic social transformation since the turn of the century. These elites have been shifting their recruitment from a narrow, relatively high, social status base to a broader base, more representative of the population as a whole . . . .

4. *Significance of Career Patterns.* Prescribed careers performed with high competence lead to entrance into the professional elite, the highest point in the military hierarchy at which technical and routinized functions are performed. By contrast, entrance into the smaller group—the elite nucleus—where innovating perspectives, discretionary responsibility, and political skills are required, is assigned to persons with unconventional and adaptive careers . . . .

5. *Trends in Political Indoctrination.* The growth of the military establishment into a vast managerial enterprise with increased political responsibilities has produced a strain on traditional military self-images and concepts of honor . . . . Current indoctrination in the armed forces is designed to eliminate the civilian concept of the "military mind." The "military mind" has been charged with traditionalism and with a lack of inventiveness. The new doctrine stresses inventive and continuous innovation. The "military mind" has been charged with an inclination toward ultra-nationalism and ethnocentrism. Military professionals are being taught to de-emphasize ethnocentric thinking, since ethnocentrism is counter to national and military policy. The "military mind" has been charged with being disciplinarian. The new doctrine seeks to deal with human factors in combat and large-scale organizations in a manner conforming to contemporary thought on human relations. In short, the new indoctrination seems to be designed to supply the military professional with opinions which he feels obliged to form as a result of his new role, and to which he was expected to be indifferent in the past.[48]

The significance of Janowitz's contribution is that it fairly accurately reflects the development of a career Army officer's set of beliefs during the Korean War period. A logical extension of his analysis could have predicted, to some extent, today's social and political behavior of the same officers. Janowitz accomplished

[46]Morris Janowitz, *The Professional Soldier* (New York: Free Press, revised 1971).
[47]*Ibid.*, p. vii.
[48]*Ibid.*, pp. 7–13.

a fairly accurate forecast when in 1960 he stated that:

> Much of this indoctrination is designed to develop a critical capacity and a critical orientation. Will the growth of critical capacities be destructive of professional loyalties, or will it be productive of new solutions? Will the present increased effort to politicize the military profession produce negative attitudes? In the United States any such hostility is hardly likely to lead to open disaffection; it is more apt to cause quiet resentment and bitterness.[49]

JAIM RESEARCH RELATED TO THIS STUDY

As an extension of the three subjects elaborated previously in this section ((1) The Learning Process; (2) Impact of the Organization on the Individual; and (3) Military Studies Relative to this Study, the review of related research will conclude by narrowing its scope towards specific JAIM research related to this study. While all of the major uses of the JAIM instrument will not be elaborated in this review, Appendix A describes the test instrument and the bibliography lists all major references of JAIM research.

The majority of the following research was conducted concurrent with this study. It is apparent to me that most of the predictions and forecasts are rather conservative and fail to attack beyond a range that can be adequately defended. An objective of the study described in this chapter will be to extend beyond the security afforded by previous JAIM research.

Two major features of the JAIM that facilitated its application to this study were its capability to discriminate between occupational groups and its capability to be administered equally well via mail. The following related studies also reveal how the JAIM can, with a reasonable degree of reliability, discriminate between various roles of individuals, pertaining to their associated self-reported behavioral style scales.

In 1965, a study was conducted pertaining to the goals of inservice training for juvenile court judges.[50] "The key findings of the JAIM inquiry have been the identification of common orientations and the description of possible points of conflict between the professions participating in the work of the juvenile court system."[51] The professions examined were patrolmen, youth officers, lawyers, social workers and judges. A monograph pertaining to this study[52] suggests that a mutual awareness and sensitivity towards the self-reported beliefs of the various groups involved would aid in their communication and general interface in working towards their common objective. It concluded that the improvement of inservice training for the juvenile court judge along these lines would aid the court in meeting the needs of both children and society.

A doctoral dissertation[53] by Shirley McCune in 1966 provided a significant

---

[49] *Ibid.*, p. 13.

[50] Regis H. Walther and Shirley D. McCune, *Socialization and Work Styles of the Juvenile Court* (Washington, D.C.: George Washington Univ., 1965).

[51] *Ibid.*, p. 70.

[52] *Ibid.*

[53] Shirley D. McCune, "An Exploratory Study of the Measured Behavioral Styles of Students in Five Schools of Social Work," Doctoral Dissertation (Washington, D.C.: Catholic Univ., 1966).

application of the JAIM instrument, as well as a major extension of previous JAIM research. She examined the self-reported beliefs of students in five schools of social work. In addition, she compared the self-reported beliefs of social work students with law students, business administration students, and education school students. An investigation of the differences in the self-reported beliefs among the five schools of social work provided 13 significant differences. "This analysis would suggest that each social work school develops some aspects of a unique culture in that varying philosophies, geographical locations, students and community milieu are in operation."[54]

The three other groups of students consistently differentiated from social work students in nine of the 32 JAIM scales.

> Social work students can be differentiated from the three other professional groups studied by the values they place upon their work as it contributes to the society and gains the approval of others, as opposed to individual achievement. They tend to prefer an accommodating style when faced with aggressive behavior and desire to maintain the standards of the society. On the other hand, they do not select either directive or delegative leadership which makes use of external controls as a preferred style. In general, they may be described as society-or group-centered and evidence a dislike for forceful exertion of leadership.[55]

A study pertaining to personality variables and career decisions[56] completed in 1966 developed further the results of previous JAIM research. In prior studies, it was possible to differentiate between weak and superior performers within a profession and among superior performers in several different professions. This particular study investigated the possibility of an identical approach being used effectively to examine students entering a profession.

> It was found that the JAIM ... could be used to differentiate between law and social work students, among sub-specialties and schools and could also be used to measure change during an academic year. Finally, the JAIM was found to correlate significantly with school performance criteria such as school grades and field ratings.[57]

David Reimer[58] investigated the association between aspects of childhood experience and several variables, correlated with specific JAIM scales. Four of his predicted correlations significant at the .01 level are as follows:

> Acceptance was positively associated with Optimism; an optimistic outlook it seems would be most likely to result from the positive feelings of trust and security encouraged by parental acceptance. Standards correlated positively with Self

---

[54] *Ibid.*, p. 125.

[55] *Ibid.*, p. 131.

[56] Walther, *Personality Variables and Career Decisions: A Pilot Study of Law and Social Work Students* (Washington, D.C.: George Washington Univ., 1966).

[57] *Ibid.*, p. 16.

[58] David J. Reimer, "The Relationship Between Childhood Experience and Certain Variables Correlated with Occupational Choice and Performance," Master's Thesis (Washington, D.C.: George Washington Univ., 1967).

Confidence; this is interpreted as indicating that the superior achievement of individuals whose parents' standards for them are high results in greater self confidence. Domination was positively correlated with Directive Leadership and negatively correlated with Participative Leadership; this relationship is consistent with the principal of identification.[59]

A doctoral dissertation in 1969 by Robert C. Trojanowicz[60] reported a comparison of the self-reported beliefs of a group of policemen with a group of social workers.
The following results were obtained:

1. Twenty-five out of the thirty-two scales significantly differentiated social workers from policemen at the .01 level of confidence.
2. There was a differentiation of behavioral styles within the profession of social work depending on the work of the person in the organization . . . .
3. There was a differentiation of behavioral styles within the police profession depending on the rank of the person in the organization . . . .
4. There was a differentiation of behavioral styles within the social work profession depending on the area of specialization . . . .
5. There was a differentiation of behavioral styles within the police profession depending on the area of specialization.[61]

Edward M. Cross, in presenting a doctoral dissertation[62] in 1970, attempted to predict JAIM results on the basis of job analysis and then tested the accuracy of predictions by using worker analysis pertaining to occupational adjustment. He administered the JAIM questionnaire to a sample group of computer programmers to empirically test inferences developed by job analysis. Then a sample of programmers was used to cross-validate the results.

Two significant conclusions were reached. First, the set of constructs underlying the JAIM is useful for the inferential process of job analysis and provides a basis for improved research design addressing the relationships of individual differences in personality to work adjustment. Second, four traits measured by JAIM scales were associated with successful work adjustment in the computer programming occupation. (1) A high level of interest in mechanical activities (Mechanical Interests); (2) A high tendency to be motivated by results (Motivated by Results); (3) A low need for social interaction on the job (Social Interaction); (4) A low need for procedures and routines (Accept Routines).[63]

In the Navy, Commander William H. Robinson conducted an excellent study with the JAIM of the psychological dimensions of students attending

[59] Ibid., p. 41.
[60] Robert C. Trojanowicz, "A Comparison of the Behavioral Styles of Policemen and Social Workers," Doctoral Dissertation (East Lansing, Mich.: Michigan State Univ., 1969).
[61] Ibid., p. 2.
[62] Edward M. Cross, "The Behavioral Styles, Work Preferences and Values of an Occupational Group: Computer Programmers," Doctoral Dissertation (Washington, D.C.: George Washington Univ., 1970).
[63] Ibid.

the U.S. Naval War College during the 1969–70 academic year.[64] He found that individuals attending the Naval War College did not reflect the popular stereotype of the military mind.

> Critics of the military establishment have often cited the "military mind" as a disturbing element in international affairs. According to this criticism, long continued military service renders one's outlook aggressive, authoritarian, and basically antidemocratic. No research effort, however, has sought to examine the validity of this stereotype in the light of modern social science methodology. In this article the author uses a psychological testing vehicle to compare a group of military officers at the Naval War College with a group of civilian executives. He concludes that the popular stereotype of the military officer is not justified.[65]

The results of several independent studies using the JAIM instrument were compared to provide an extension of previous JAIM research.[66] A comparison of the self-reported beliefs of students from five professions (business, public administration, law, Army officer, and social work) furnished support for the following predictions:

> 1.   There are highly significant differences among students preparing for different professions.
> 2.   There are highly significant differences among students preferring different sub-specialties but these differences are less than the differences among professional student groups.
> 3.   There are highly significant differences between those who drop out of training and those who stay.
> 4.   There are highly significant differences between JAIM scores obtained at the beginning as compared with those obtained at the end of training.[67]

A followup study, currently in process, of West Point Cadets is being observed with interest. Five hundred West Point Cadets completed the JAIM at the beginning of their first year. JAIM scores will be related to school performance and peer group ratings. The JAIM will also be administered a second time to the same subjects to determine changes associated with training.

RESEARCH DESIGN

Earlier in this chapter, a review of related research was presented. The following section will describe the overall research design. Specific methodology will be considered and then a description of the theoretical framework of this study will serve to introduce the predictions. This section will conclude with the method for evaluating predictions.

[64] William H. Robinson, Jr., "An Element of International Affairs—The Military Mind," *Naval War College Review* 23, no. 3 (1970): 4–15.

[65] *Ibid.*, p. 4.

[66] Regis H. Walther, Shirley D. McCune, and Peter B. Petersen, *The Shaping of Professional Subcultures: A Study of Student Groups from Five Professions* (Washington, D.C.: George Washington Univ., 1968).

[67] *Ibid.*

To investigate the immediate effects of training and the stability of these effects, individuals were examined at the beginning of a six-month training program, again near the end of the training program, and then on a third occasion several years after departure from the training program. A copy of the identical test instrument was administered in each of these three situations. A total of 347 individuals were examined as both entering and graduating students. In addition, a total of 757 individuals were examined as both graduating students, and again years later after departing from Officer Candidate School. While this chapter will focus on the retesting of the same individuals, the results of hundreds of other individuals will also be reviewed. Table 8 is a summary of respondents who voluntarily provided their names and addresses for purposes of future examination.

Observations were made of the various aspects of student activities and many hours were spent in interviewing students and observing training. Entering students were usually administered the JAIM instrument during the end of the first week of training or the beginning of the second week of training. Graduating students were not usually sampled during their last week of training (the 23rd week) because of their concern with the impending events of graduation, leave, and their new assignment. The 20th week seemed most appropriate to examine typical graduating students.

Conditions of the testing facilities were reasonably equal during 1967 when questionnaires were administered to officer candidate students. A reasonably uniform verbal briefing was conducted prior to the administration of all questionnaires to students. Initially during the briefing, students were instructed not to complete blanks on the answer sheet pertaining to their name. They were further informed that their answers would, in no way, be used against them or even in their favor by the U.S. Army. The stated concept of an evaluation of a class average answer, rather than an evaluation of individual answers, seemed to help reduce most of the personal apprehension of students in completing the questionnaire. After the examination had started, students were then asked to provide their names and home addresses on a voluntary basis if they were interested in completing the questionnaire again several years after they departed from Officer Candidate School. Those persons reexamined approximately three years after graduation were mailed a copy of the identical questionnaire during the summer of 1970. Many of the individuals voluntarily reexamined approximately three years after departure from Officer Candidate School did not graduate and most of the individuals reexamined during 1970 were no longer members of the U.S. Army.

Figure 1 represents the response to this address survey which was initiated on May 3, 1970 and concerned 2,785 individuals. Each envelope sent contained a letter explaining the nature of the study, a preprinted post card for a reply, and a handwritten 12-word personal note. Each note was addressed with the individual's given name in handwritten form and contained an original signature.

TABLE 8

SUMMARY OF RESPONDENTS WHO VOLUNTARILY PROVIDED
THEIR NAMES AND HOME ADDRESSES

Category*	Number
Entering Students	1,613
Individuals not Qualifying for Other Categories	305
Graduating Students**	1,383
Individuals 3 Years after Departure from Officer Candidate School***	1,802

* 347 individuals were examined as both entering and graduating students. 210 of these individuals completed questionnaires when reexamined years after departure from Officer Candidate School.

** 757 of these graduating students were retested years after departure from Officer Candidate School.

*** All individuals in this category were previously examined while attending Officer Candidate School. Many failed to graduate. Most individuals are no longer members of the U.S. Army.

Seventy-seven percent, or 2,145 of the individuals who provided their names and addresses years earlier, were located and returned the enclosed post card. With the exception of one individual, they indicated a willingness to again complete the questionnaire. The percentage of individuals who did not reply to the address survey was 15.5 percent or 431 of the individuals who provided their names earlier. The number of individuals who did not answer the May 3, 1970 address survey was reduced from 913 men on August 3, 1970 to 431 men mainly because of the mailing of a second personal note, request, and preaddressed post card for a reply. Of the individuals who initially provided their names and home addresses, 33 or approximately 1.2 percent were deceased prior to the survey conducted during May 1970. Most of these men were killed in action in Vietnam. In addition, one man was reported as missing in action in Vietnam.

After individuals returned the post cards containing their current addresses, and were subsequently mailed questionnaires, the problem in data collection was then in receiving completed answer sheets. Uncompleted answer sheets received were returned immediately to the senders with a personal note requesting completion. There were 2,144 JAIM packets mailed to former officer candidate students starting on June 5 and daily thereafter as post cards were received. A letter of reminder requesting the return of completed answer sheets was dispatched on July 23 to 551 men, September 3 to 410 men, and September 14 to 51 men. Figure 2 presents an accounting of the response to the mailing of questionnaires. Approximately 84 percent or 1,802 individuals returned

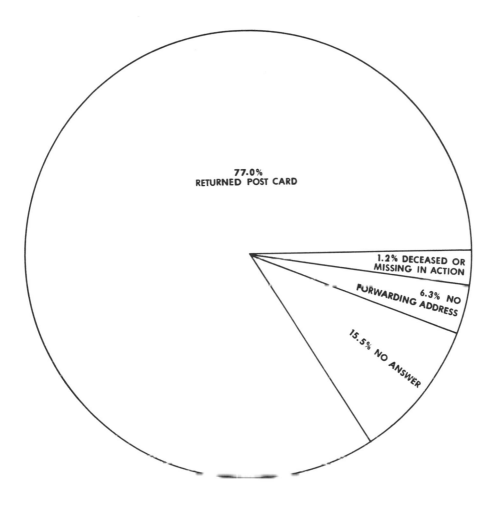

Figure 1 Response to Address Survey*

Category	Percent	Number
Returned Post Card	77.0	2,145**
No Forwarding Address	6.3	175
No Answer	15.5	431
Deceased or Missing in Action	1.2	34
TOTAL	100.0	2,785

* Of those capable of responding 83.3% returned post cards.
** Of this amount, one anonymous post card contained a negative response.

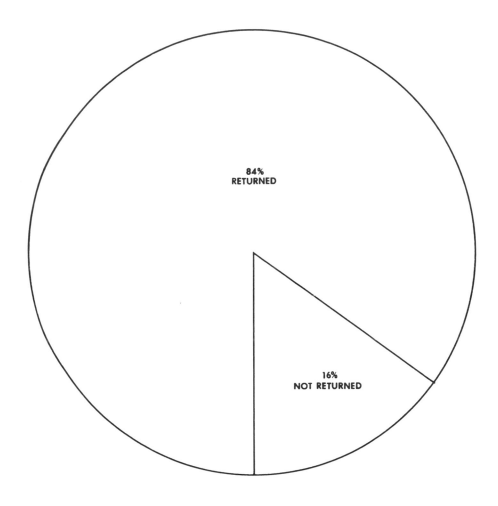

84%
RETURNED

16%
NOT RETURNED

Figure 2   Response From Mailing Questionnaires

Category	Percent	Number
Returned Completed Answer Sheets	84	1,802
Completed Answer Sheets Not Returned	16	342
TOTAL	100	2,144

completed questionnaires. The remainder, 342 persons, did not return completed questionnaires.

DESCRIPTION OF SAMPLE

The average age of a group of individuals tested as both entering and graduating students was 21.88 years, at the time of their entry to Officer Candidate School. Their age distribution is reflected on the first histogram in Table 9. The educational level of these individuals is also represented in Table 9. It is interesting to note that while various officer programs concentrate on the commissioning of college graduates, the Officer Candidate School program, in obtaining its input from the enlisted ranks, was faced with the problem that in 1969 only 10 percent of the newly drafted enlisted personnel were college men. "In 1969, of 283,000 men drafted only 28,500 were college men—10%, in a country where 40% of the college-age young do, in fact, go to some kind of college."[68] The majority of these individuals entered the Army as volunteers. While 60.5 percent volunteered, 39.2 percent were inducted and .3 percent entered active duty when their National Guard units were called to active duty. There were 34.4 percent who had previously participated in ROTC training but had not completed ROTC training. The remaining 65.6 percent indicated that they never participated in ROTC training. Individuals sampled at the time of entrance to Officer Candidate School were relatively new members of the U.S. Army. Their average length of service was 6.83 months. The distribution of their longevity is represented in the last histogram in Table 9. The distribution of the highest grade held by these men prior to reporting to Officer Candidate School was that 64.4 percent were privates, 32.6 percent were privates first class, 1.2 percent were corporals or specialists fourth class, and 1.8 percent were sergeants, specialists fifth class, or higher in grade. It should be noted that the individuals sampled were rather new Army members with an average longevity of 6.8 months and that their grades categorized them as junior enlisted personnel.

THEORETICAL FRAMEWORK

Entrance to Officer Candidate School is voluntary and on graduation each student is commissioned as a second lieutenant. Early in the training progarm, it becomes evident to the individual student that he must conform to behavioral standards as well as academic standards. Most entering candidates find themselves in an environment requiring a different role to which they are accustomed. To survive and graduate, the student is encouraged to adapt to the school's environment and to assume new roles. Entering students that later tend to graduate acquire new roles consistent with the reward and punishment standards of the school and their peers. During the six-month training program, many of these new roles probably become part of the individual's personality and self-conception.

[68] Ward Just, "Soldier," *Atlantic* (October 1970), p. 77.

TABLE 9

CHARACTERISTICS OF 347 MEN AT TIME OF ENTRANCE
TO OFFICER CANDIDATE SCHOOL

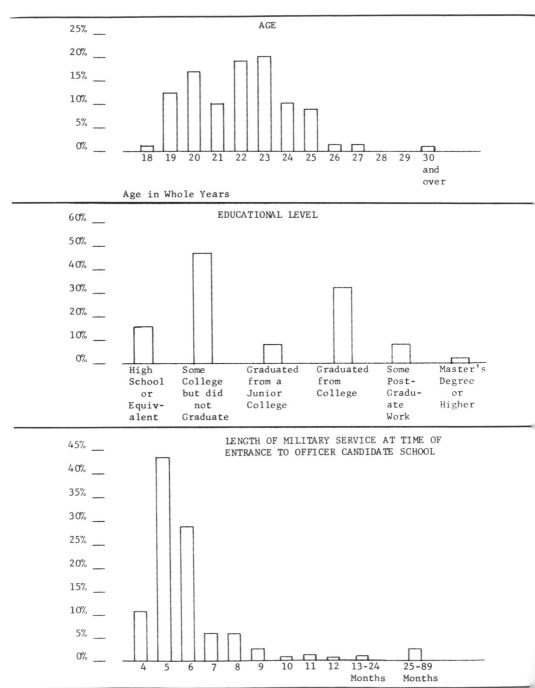

It is conceptualized that successful students, after becoming aware of the specific standards required by the school and their peers, probably adjust their roles to accommodate these standards. As the course progresses, it is further considered that the personal qualities of these individuals (other than aptitude, or knowledge) also adjust and become compatible with the individual's newly acquired roles. If being successful is measured in terms of conforming to the established standards of the program, it appears that those individuals who do not assume the correct roles will depart from school prior to graduation. The majority of persons who fail to graduate voluntarily depart from the school after it appears to them that further effort on their part in working towards graduation is fruitless. Some individuals who do not meet the prescribed standards are "turned back" to more junior classes and many of them eventually graduate. It appears that almost all entering students, if they desire to apply themselves, can graduate; however, approximately a third of the entering students normally fail to graduate. It appears that these individuals, as a group, do not adapt or are not particularly interested in adapting to the required new roles.

> The hopeful candidate is now subjected to a nearly catastrophic experience, which breaks down to a large extent his previous personality organization. His previous valuations fail him, and in order to find a basis for self-respect, he must adopt new standards or escape from the field. His high motivation to become an officer usually rules out the latter alternative. At the same time, new, appropriate attitudes are built up and established. The catastrophic experience provides a kind of purgatory, a definite demarcation from the candidate's enlisted incarnation that puts a barrier between the new officer and his enlisted memories. It has some of the characteristics of a conversion experience, or the ordeal of a medieval knight. The effect of this ordeal on the officer candidate is not only to attack his previous personality, but to exert a positive influence in the desired direction.[69]

While graduates of Officer Candidate School acquire roles commensurate with those needed as a junior officer, it appears that these roles are not necessarily appropriate for more sophisticated assignments. It is further conceptualized that the roles acquired during the individual's Officer Candidate School experience will diminish in importance as a further socialization process occurs pertaining to the individual and higher level assignments.

> Only in the most primitive of organizational forms, however, is the influence of the organization over the member manifest solely in terms of uniformity of behavior. As organizations become more complex, the division of labor and the specialization of tasks prescribe very different patterns of behavior for different roles. The need for reliability of role performance, however, becomes no less; on the contrary, it increases with the complexity and sophistication of the organization.[70]

[69] Stouffer, et al., "The American Soldier: Adjustment During Army Life," *Studies in Social Psychology in World War II* (Princeton: Princeton Univ., 1949), 1: 389.
[70] Katz and Kahn, *The Social Psychology of Organizations* (New York: John Wiley and Sons, 1966), p. 200.

The theoretical framework of this study first concentrated on the acquisition of new roles by those individuals who successfully completed training. These roles reflect adjustment by the student to the established standards of the total school environment including the standards of peers. Self-reported beliefs commensurate with these roles are conceptualized as changing to a lesser extent during the training program. It was further conceptualized that behavior acquired during the individual's Officer Candidate School experience will diminish in importance to the individual as a further socialization process occurs relative to the individual's interaction with increasingly higher level assignments. As new roles are assumed to cope with these new situations, the effects of training at Officer Candidate School will tend to diminish. Commensurate with these changes in roles, associated self-reported beliefs will also change.

The following assumptions are applicable to both predictions used in this study:

1. The standards and techniques used by the Officer Candidate School authorities in evaluating students remained constant during the sampling period.

2. The system of rewards and punishments for students remained constant during the sampling period.

3. The Job Analysis and Interest Measurement instrument is reliable and valid.

Introduction to First Prediction

In selecting the specific self-reported beliefs that would be most likely influenced by training, the results of an earlier study that I conducted were considered (Chapter 3). Of the 32 scales previously examined, 15 of these scales were significant at the .01 level. In addition, there seemed to be a logical reason for these statistical results in terms of expectations of change that would be reasonably expected to occur during Officer Candidate School training. These 15 scales are incorporated in the first prediction and are presented in Table 10.

First Prediction

The self-reported beliefs of a group of individuals participating in Officer Candidate School training changes significantly during training. Compared with when they were entering students, the same group of 347 individuals measured again as graduating students tends to significantly change its self-reported beliefs as presented in Table 10. A confidence level of .05 will be used as a test of significance relative to each scale presented in Table 10.

TABLE 10

RESULTS OF TRAINING*

Scales	Predicted Increase or Decrease**
Degree of Self-Confidence	+
Prefers Supervisory Activities	+
Prefers Activity Frequent Change	+
Values Approval from Others	−
Degree of Perseverance	+
Influences by Persuasive Leadership	+
Influences by Being Self-Assertive	+
Move Toward Aggressor	−
Move Against Aggressor	+
Prefers Independence	+
Prefers Directive Leadership Style	+
Prefers Participative Leadership Style	
Prefers Delegative Leadership Style	+
Motivates by Knowledge of Results	+
Believes in External Controls	+

---

* Predicted significant change in the average self-reported beliefs of group of 347 entering students compared with when they become graduating students. A confidence level of .05 will be used as a test of significance relative to each scale presented. For this prediction to be confirmed, 3 or more scales must be significant at the .05 level of confidence pertaining to the predicted increase or decrease.

** Plus (+) indicates average score for 347 individuals as graduating students is higher. Minus (−) indicates average score for 347 individuals as graduating students is lower.

Introduction to Second Prediction

In considering the stability of the graduating students' self-reported beliefs, it was conceptualized that those scales that changed the most during training would probably be the least stable. The 15 scales selected for the first prediction as being the most likely to change during training were now considered in terms of their lack of stability following graduation. Research findings and views developed by Mosel, Katz and Kahn, Herzberg, Argyris, and Miller, presented earlier in this chapter were considered in conjunction with empirical observations in order to develop a further evaluation of specific scales that would tend to be least stable. Those selected represent 11 of the 15 considered in the first prediction and one additional scale that appeared to be applicable. These 12 scales are incorporated in the second prediction and are reflected in Table 11.

Second Prediction

The effects of training at Officer Candidate School tend to diminish following graduation. Therefore, there will be a significant difference in the self-reported

TABLE 11
STABILITY OF TRAINING*

Scales	Predicted Increase or Decrease**
Degree of Self-Confidence	—
Prefers Supervisory Activities	—
Values Approval from Others	+
Influences by Persuasive Leadership	—
Influences by Being Self-Assertive	—
Move Toward Aggressor	+
Move Against Aggressor	—
Prefers Directive Leadership Style	—
Prefers Participative Leadership Style	+
Motivates by Knowledge of Results	—
Believes in External Controls	—
Prefers Group Participation	+

* Predicted significant difference in self-reported beliefs between a group of 757 individuals examined as graduating students and the same group of individuals examined again years after graduation. A confidence level of .05 will be used as a test of significance relative to each scale presented. For this prediction to be confirmed, 3 or more scales must be significant at the .05 level of confidence pertaining to the predicted increase or decrease.

** Plus (+) indicates average score for group of 757 individuals three years after graduation is higher. Minus (—) indicates average score for group of 757 individuals three years after graduation is lower.

beliefs between a group of 757 graduating students and the same group of individuals examined again years after graduation. A confidence level of .05 will be used as a test of significance pertaining to each scale presented in Table 11.

METHODS OF EVALUATING PREDICTIONS

Two statistical analysis techniques will be used in the evaluation of predictions. The t-test will be used for comparisons between groups pertaining to specific scales, and a binomial probability distribution will be used to test the predictions in whole. While a t-ratio can be determined in terms of a one-tailed or a two-tailed test, the more conservative two-tailed test will be applied in this study even though the direction of a difference in averages had been predicted in every case. The critical value of t used in this analysis will be t < 1.97 pertaining to significance at the .05 level. Both predictions consist of a series of other predictions related to increases or decreases in selected scales. The first prediction consists of 15 predicted increases or decreases in certain scales, while the second prediction consists of 12 predicted increases or decreases in selected scales.

In an analysis where a relatively large number of scales are evaluated, there is a possibility that at least one apparently significant relationship caused by chance alone will appear. For example, an analysis with an .05 level of significance and 15 scales will result, on the average, in .75 relationships occurring entirely due to chance. The probability of these relationships occurring can be estimated by computing the average and the standard deviation of the binomial distribution and approximating the binomial probabilities through use of the normal curve.[71] This approach is relatively conservative in that it does not provide for the result of a predicted outcome which is significant at high levels such as the .001 level of confidence. With respect to the first prediction, two relationships out of fifteen can be expected to be significant at the .05 level five percent of the time and therefore, three correct predictions out of fifteen concerning predicted intensity and direction will be necessary to confirm the first prediction. The same decision rule can be used for the second prediction since reducing the number of scales from 15 to 12 does not change the number of significant relationships which could occur due to chance.

CONTROL

If individuals experience a significant change in certain of their self-reported beliefs while attending Officer Candidate School, there is a possibility that exposure to the influences of the Army's environment, rather than attending Officer Candidate School, is, in part, responsible for this change. A control group to provide for this possibility could consist of comparable individuals serving in the Army but not attending Officer Candidate School during the same period of time. Unfortunately, such a control group was not used. However, data is available that can be examined to determine to a reasonable extent the effect of exposure to the Army's environment rather than from attending Officer Candidate School. Inasmuch as individuals enter Officer Candidate School with varying amounts of prior service, a comparison of self-reported beliefs at the time of entry to Officer Candidate School in terms of the length of prior service should reveal those differences that can be attributed to exposure to the Army's environment.

A comparison of a group of men having four months prior service at the time of entry to Officer Candidate School with a group of men having five to nine months prior service at the time of entry reveals no significant differences in self-reported beliefs in terms of t-test results and no relevant differences in terms of a comparison of standard scores. Therefore, within the overall framework of using subjects as their own control, it can be concluded that exposure to the influences of the Army's environment rather than attending Officer Candidate School will not be responsible for any significant changes experienced by the test group while they attend Officer Candidate School.

[71] Allen L. Edwards, *Statistical Methods for the Behavioral Sciences* (New York: Holt, Rinehart and Winston, 1964), pp. 221–224.

FINDINGS AND ANALYSIS

This section will evaluate both predictions. Each of the 15 scales relating to the first prediction, which concerns the effect of training, will be evaluated as well as the entire first prediction. Then the second prediction concerning the stability of training will be tested, first relative to its 12 scales, and then for the significance of the prediction as a whole. Following the findings of the second prediction, an analysis will be offered. The section will conclude with an elaboration of results pertaining to 210 individuals tested on three occasions and other relevant findings.

EFFECT OF TRAINING

First Prediction

Compared with when they were entering students, the same 347 individuals examined again as graduating students significantly changed 14 out of 15 previously selected beliefs in the directions predicted. This prediction is affirmed.

Table 12 presents the results of the first prediction.

ANALYSIS

There was a significant difference in 14 scales obtained from the identical 347 Officer Candidate School students before and after training. When compared with themselves later as graduating students, these men scored significantly higher as entering students on the following scales (listed in order of significance):

Values Approval from Others
Prefers Participative Leadership Style
Move Toward Aggressor

When measured again approximately six months later, near the completion of their training, these individuals scored significantly higher on the following scales (listed in order of significance):

Influences by Persuasive Leadership
Believes in External Controls
Influences by Being Self-Assertive
Move Against Aggressor
Degree of Self-Confidence
Prefers Supervisory Activities
Degree of Perseverance
Prefers Directive Leadership Style
Motivates by Knowledge of Results
Prefers Activity Frequent Change
Prefers Independence

TABLE 12

DIFFERENCES IN SELECTED SELF-REPORTED BELIEFS OF OFFICER
CANDIDATE SCHOOL STUDENTS BETWEEN
TIME OF ENTRANCE AND GRADUATION

Scales	Predicted Increase or Decrease	t-test Results*	Level of Confidence	Prediction Confirmed
Degree of Self-Confidence	+	+ 6.58	.001	Yes
Prefers Supervisory Activities	+	+ 6.43	.001	Yes
Prefers Activity Frequent Change	+	+ 3.70	.001	Yes
Values Approval from Others	—	−11.17	.001	Yes
Degree of Perseverance	+	+ 5.37	.001	Yes
Influences by Persuasive Leadership	+	+ 8.54	.001	Yes
Influences by Being Self-Assertive	+	+ 7.66	.001	Yes
Move Toward Aggressor	—	−5.38	.001	Yes
Move Against Aggressor	+	+ 7.01	.001	Yes
Prefers Independence	+	+ 2.41	.05	Yes
Prefers Directive Leadership Style	+	+ 5.33	.001	Yes
Prefers Participative Leadership Style	—	−6.19	.001	Yes
Prefers Delegative Leadership Style	+	+ 1.24	n/a	No
Motivates by Knowledge of Results	+	+ 3.90	.001	Yes
Believes in External Controls	+	+ 8.43	.001	Yes

* Plus (+) indicates average score for 347 individuals as graduating students is higher. Minus (—) indicates average score for 347 individuals as graduating students is lower.

It can be concluded that, as a group, these men changed their self-reported beliefs during the time they participated in Officer Candidate School training. It appears from these results that this shaping process emphasizes an insistence on immediate task performance with the results obtained through persuading, directing, or supervising other people.

These findings tend to substantiate the following observations made of Officer Candidate School graduating students:

1. They placed a high value in being a leader. In their leader subordinate relations they preferred a directive style of leadership. In addition, they considered that specific instructions should be given to subordinates and that most subordinates require external controls.

2. In relations with their peers they placed little value in the approval of others. This was particularly applicable when receiving the approval from others conflicted with the accomplishment of their mission. In reacting to a belligerent individual they preferred to counterattack rather than appease him. In their actions with their peers they tended to be very competitive.

3. They tended to be self-confident and independent. They preferred frequent changes in their activities and also placed a high value on perseverance.

While the nature of the developed change may be that desired for young combat officers, the use of these characteristics for effective personal interaction at higher levels of responsibilities seems to be doubtful.

STABILITY OF TRAINING

The second prediction specifically addresses the subject of the stability of the effects of Officer Candidate School training. It was conceptualized that beliefs acquired during an individual's Officer Candidate School experience will tend to revert to the individual's initial beliefs when he returns to the work situation after his departure from training.

Second Prediction

There will be a significant difference in 12 selected JAIM scales between scores obtained at the time of graduation from Officer Candidate School and

TABLE 13

DIFFERENCES IN SELECTED SELF-REPORTED BELIEFS OF 757 MEN
BETWEEN TIME OF GRADUATION AND RETESTING
THREE YEARS LATER

Scales	Predicted Increase or Decrease*	t-test Results	Level of Confidence	Prediction Confirmed
Degree of Self-Confidence	—	+4.78	n/a	No
Prefers Supervisory Activities	—	+11.10	n/a	No
Values Approval from Others	+	—2.59	n/a	No
Influences by Persuasive Leadership	—	—0.99	n/a	No
Influences by Being Self-Assertive	—	—2.43	.05	Yes
Move Toward Aggressor	+	—0.73	n/a	No
Move Against Aggressor	—	—1.70	n/a	No
Prefers Directive Leadership Style	—	—11.94	.001	Yes
Prefers Participative Leadership Style	+	+5.69	.001	Yes
Motivates by Knowledge of Results	—	—1.49	n/a	No
Believes in External Controls	—	—10.33	.001	Yes
Prefers Group Participation	+	+.95	n/a	No

*Plus (+) indicates average score for group of 757 individuals approximately three years after graduation is higher. Minus (—) indicates average score for group of 757 individuals three years after graduation is lower.

136

those obtained approximately three years later, and the direction will be opposite from the change occurring during training. Table 13 presents the results of the test of the second prediction. This prediction could possibly be confirmed in that four of the twelve scales showed significant differences in the predicted direction. The decision rule required that three or more scales show significant differences. It should be noted, however, that three other scales showed highly significant differences in a direction opposite from what was presented. In view of this inconsistency, the second prediction is not confirmed.

ANALYSIS

While the findings of Katz and Kahn, Mosel, Fleishman and Shartle tend to indicate that the work environment and leader exert a major influence on the attitudes of the individual, I incorrectly believed that this influence was a relatively uncomplex phenomenon. It was inferred in the second prediction that beliefs acquired in training would, over time, simply revert towards their configuration prior to training. This was an incorrect inference. Results pertaining to the second prediction suggest that this prediction was not adequately formulated. A better formulation would have been that individuals tend to revert to previous beliefs when negative reinforcement is present in the postgraduation period. Also that beliefs tend to continue to change in the same direction as in training when positive reinforcement is present during the postgraduation period, and that beliefs tend to remain the same as acquired in training when neither a positive nor negative reinforcement is present in the postgraduation period. However, such a revised formulation should consider the possibility that a slight positive influence might tend only to maintain the level of a belief acquired by training. Also to be considered is the possibility that an absence of positive or negative influence might tend to permit a reversion of the belief to a configuration held prior to training.

When the same group of 757 individuals were tested approximately three years after graduation, their self-reported beliefs pertaining to the scale "Prefers Participative Leadership Style" increased significantly (as predicted), and there was a significant decrease (as predicted) in the scores associated with the following scales (listed in order of their significance):

Prefers Directive Leadership Style
Believes in External Controls
Influences by Being Self-Assertive

It appears that these individuals experienced problems in applying directive leadership procedures that had been perhaps acceptable to fellow Officer Candidate School students, but not acceptable to enlisted personnel having a different outlook toward the U.S. Army. As negative reinforcement influences were experienced by these young officers, the intensity of the beliefs that previously increased during training was now subsequently decreased.

An additional mechanism involved in the determination of the officer personality

is the passing-on of aggression .... The existence of his thwarted aggressive ten-
dencies makes him more likely to assume an autocratic role in accordance with
traditional Army structure .... He puts a high value on official "GI" ways of
doing things, and rationalizes that what was good for him must be good for those
under his command.[72]

The need for adequate operational control of subordinates is stressed during
training, and thus the individual student seems to acquire a belief that people
require external controls. Interestingly, approximately three years after graduation the same individuals reflect a significant decrease in their views that
people require external controls. It is speculated that negative reinforcement
influences played a major part in this change. While the graduating student
tends to be competitive and seeks to pursue his own goals when they are in
competition with the goals of others, the same group of men, approximately
three years later, tend to decrease their self-assertiveness. The marked decrease
in the scales "Prefers Directive Leadership Style," "Believes in External
Controls," and "Influences by Being Self-Assertive" is matched by a significant
increase in the scale "Prefers Participative Leadership Style." It is speculated
that positive reinforcing influences pertaining to participative leadership were
mainly responsible for this change.

RESULTS PERTAINING TO 210 INDIVIDUALS TESTED ON THREE OCCASIONS

Up to this point in this chapter, a total of 347 individuals were examined as
both entering and graduating students. In addition, 757 individuals were
examined both as graduating students and again several years after departing
from Officer Candidate School. Persons reexamined approximately three
years after graduation were mailed a copy of the identical questionnaire used
during Officer Candidate School. Effects could be measured because the same
individuals were examined either before and after training, or after training
and three years later.

It seemed worthwhile to analyze the results of only those individuals who
had been examined on three occasions. A review of the respondents indicated
that 210 individuals were tested on three occasions: (a) as entering students,
(b) as graduating students, and (c) again approximately three years after
graduation. The original research predictions formulated prior to an analysis of
the data connected with this chapter will be examined in this analysis. No
attempt will be made to predict and confirm results inasmuch as the original
predictions were not stated in terms of these 210 individuals.

RESULTS PERTAINING TO THE EFFECT OF TRAINING

Compared with when they were entering students, the same 210 individuals
examined again as graduating students significantly changed 14 out of 15

[72] Stouffer, *et al., op. cit.,* p. 390.

TABLE 14

DIFFERENCE IN SEVERAL BELIEFS OF A GROUP OF 210
MEN BETWEEN TIME OF ENTRANCE AND GRADUATION

Scales	t-test Results[a]	Standard Scores[b]	
		Time of Entrance	Time of Graduation
Degree of Self-Confidence	+6.00***	−7	35
Prefers Supervisory Activities	+5.84***	16	51
Prefers Activity Frequent Change	+2.02*	56	77
Values Approval from Others	−9.16***	−32	−80
Degree of Perseverance	+3.81***	12	39
Influences by Persuasive Leadership	+6.38***	25	65
Influences by Being Self-Assertive	+5.11***	89	120
Move Toward Aggressor	−3.40***	−37	−56
Move Against Aggressor	+4.78***	36	73
Prefers Independence	+2.08*	−8	3
Prefers Directive Leadership Style	+3.49***	112	147
Prefers Participative Leadership Style	−4.33***	−56	−91
Prefers Delegative Leadership Style	+1.91	−44	−38
Motivates by Knowledge of Results	+3.15**	−23	0
Believes in External Controls	+6.35***	103	148

[a] Plus (+) indicates higher average score for 210 individuals as graduating students. Minus (−) indicates lower average score for 210 individuals as graduating students.

* $p < .05$
** $p < .01$
*** $p < .001$

[b] Average of norm group has been equated to zero and the standard deviation to 100.

self-reported beliefs. (See Table 14.) Specific results of training correlated in terms of observations and results from the test instrument are as follows:

1. Repeated emphasis during training on being self-confident resulted in a substantial increase in the self-confidence of graduating students. This increase in self-confidence is also attributed to their successful completion of this difficult course.

2. Supervisory activities as occupational preferences increased in importance during training for these individuals as they prepared for their future role as platoon leaders.

3. Their strong preference at the beginning of training for work that provides a lot of excitement and a great deal of variety increased considerably during training.

4. In the process of arriving at a decision during training, mission

accomplishment received considerable priority over pleasing others. During training, their value of the approval of others decreased from an initially low value to a significantly lower value. This lack of concern for the approval of others, while appropriate for the training situation, might not be appropriate in later assignments.

5. There was substantial attrition of students, both voluntary and involuntary, during this rigorous training program. Perseverance, therefore, is definitely an asset to the individual who desires to graduate. It is interesting to note that the importance given to perseverance increased from a high value at the time of starting the program to a significantly higher value at the time of graduation.

6. Empirical observations support the test results in that these individuals significantly increased the importance they placed on persuasive leadership. During training, these individuals demonstrated that they have no difficulty in expressing their opinions before a large group. In addition, a prerequisite for graduation is effective performance in various leadership positions during training.

7. As entering students, these men tended to do well under conditions of competition and stress. During the training program, their self-assertiveness significantly increased. The competitive nature of the course is probably reflected in this increase. While an individual who is highly self-assertive may do well as a junior officer, his potential for further success may depend on his ability to limit his self-assertiveness.

8. Entering students placed a low value in behaving diplomatically when someone acts toward them in a belligerent or aggressive manner. This low value became substantially lower during training.

9. When given the choice of appeasing, or counterattacking a belligerent individual, these men prefer to counterattack. Their high value for this preference significantly increased during training.

10. While there was a significant increase in independence during training, it is noted that these individuals scored relatively low as entering students. This can be attributed partially to the constraints placed on entering students.

11. At the start of training, students tended to place a low value on a leadership style that would delegate decisionmaking authority to individual subordinates. At the end of training, there was little change in this view.

12. Both before and after training, these men placed considerable importance on directive leadership. It should also be noted that their impression of the importance of directive leadership increased significantly during training. While this degree of directive leadership may be effective at the small unit level, it appears that it probably will not be effective for higher level assignments.

13. During training, participative leadership was not considered as an effective leadership style for platoon leaders in combat. It follows then that the low value held by individuals when they entered the program would change to a considerably lower value during training.

14. When they entered training, students tended to disagree with the view that people are motivated best by the knowledge of their results. Instead, they strongly considered that a leader obtains the best results through rewards and punishments. At the conclusion of training, these students placed a significantly higher value in the view that individuals are best motivated by the knowledge of their results.

15. Their strong preference for a leader who tells them specifically what to do increased substantially during training. This preference emphasized a strong regard for discipline and a view that most people require external controls.

RESULTS PERTAINING TO THE STABILITY OF TRAINING

It was conceptualized earlier that beliefs acquired during an individual's Officer Candidate School experience will tend to revert to the individual's initial beliefs when he returns to the work situation after his departure from training. Earlier in this chapter, this prediction was not confirmed. Results pertaining to the stability of training for 210 individuals are presented in Table 15.

The reverse learning effect of the scale "Prefers Directive Leadership Style" as it decreases in value years later to a position lower than when measured prior to training is worthy of consideration. The resulting boomerang effect pertaining to the scale "Prefers Directive Leadership Style" is as follows:

Graduating Students*	Men 3 Years After Graduation*	Men 3 Years After Graduation*
vs	vs.	vs.
Entering Students	Graduating Students	Entering Students
3.49	−5.91	−2.98

*A positive t-value indicates this group higher and a negative t-value indicates this group lower.

It can be speculated that the negative reinforcing influences experienced by these 210 young officers during the period 1967–70 were so strong that their feelings toward directive leadership not only reverted back to their original score, but decreased to a point considerably lower than they held prior to Officer Candidate School training.

Results pertaining to the four scales that formed the basis of the four predictions years earlier (as reported in Chapter 3) are illustrated in Charts 1–4. These results are indicated in terms of the identical group of 210 men tested on three occasions. Hopefully, these results will "put to rest" the subject of change during training and the stability of this change.

TABLE 15

Difference in Several Beliefs of a Group of 210 Men between Time of Graduation and Retesting Approximately Three Years Later

Scales	t-test Results[a]	Standard Scores[b]	
		Time of Graduation	3 Years After Graduation
Degree of Self-Confidence	+2.13	35	42
Prefers Supervisory Activities	+3.41	51	75
Values Approval from Others	+ .40	—80	—80
Influences by Persuasive Leadership	—1.58	65	51
Influences by Being Self-Assertive	—2.13*	120	107
Move Toward Aggressor	+0.14	—56	—61
Move Against Aggressor	—1.09	73	66
Prefers Directive Leadership Style	—5.91***	147	88
Prefers Participative Leadership Style	+2.93**	—91	—62
Motivates by Knowledge of Results	—0.13	0	—7
Believes in External Controls	—6.72***	148	103
Prefers Group Participation	—1.79	—17	—25

[a] Plus (+) indicates higher average score for group of 210 individuals approximately three years after graduation. Minus (—) indicates lower average score for group of 210 individuals approximately three years after graduation.

*p. <.05
**p. <.01
***p. <.001

[b] Average of norm group has been equated to zero and the standard deviation of 100.

Other Relevant Issues

The results of this research may shed some light on other relevant issues. Although no predictions were formulated with respect to the following issues, an analysis has been made of the data obtained in connection with this study to determine possible answers to the following:

1. Will scores obtained by using the test instrument at the time of entry into the training program discriminate between those who will eventually graduate and those who will voluntarily depart from the program prior to graduation?

2. Will scores obtained by using the test instrument at the time of entry into the training program discriminate between those who will remain in the Army years later and those who will depart from the Army years later?

3. Will scores obtained by using the test instrument at the time of entry into the training program discriminate between those who will both graduate and remain in the Army years later and those who will not graduate and depart from the Army years later?

CHART I

COMPARISON OF THE IDENTICAL GROUP OF 210 MEN ON THREE OCCASIONS PERTAINING TO THE EXTENT TO WHICH THEY EXERT LEADERSHIP IN INTERPERSONAL SITUATIONS *·

| TIME OF ENTRANCE TO OCS¹ | TIME OF GRADUATION FROM OCS | 3 YEARS AFTER GRADUATION FROM OCS |

* Size of figure pertains to standard scores for the JAIM scale "Influences by Persuasive Leadership." This scale measures the degree to which the individual exerts leadership in interpersonal situations. Persons scoring high report that they have no difficulty giving a speech or reciting before a large group; that they often take the leadership in groups; and that they like best in a job the opportunity to get results through persuasion or negotiation.

CHART 2

COMPARISON OF THE IDENTICAL GROUP OF 210 MEN ON THREE OCCASIONS PERTAINING TO THE EXTENT TO WHICH THEY VALUE THE APPROVAL OF OTHERS*

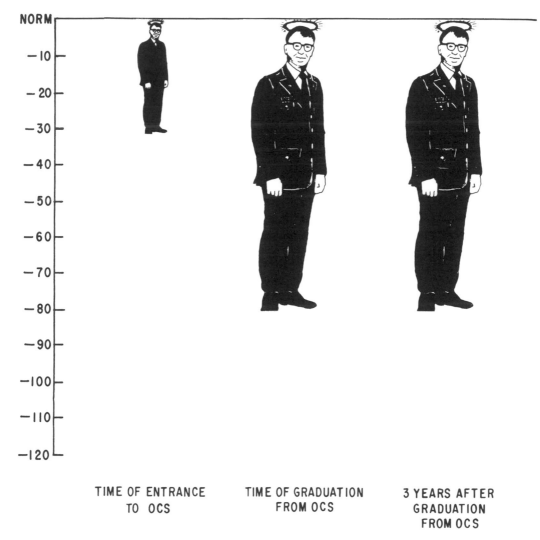

TIME OF ENTRANCE TO OCS

TIME OF GRADUATION FROM OCS

3 YEARS AFTER GRADUATION FROM OCS

* Size of figure pertains to standard scores for the JAIM scale "Values Approval from Others." This scale measures the degree to which the individual values himself by obtaining the approval of others. Persons scoring high consider it most important to have congenial peers; to be well liked; and like to please others through their work; and like to be considered gracious, attractive, and pleasant.

CHART 3

COMPARISON OF THE IDENTICAL GROUP OF 210 MEN ON THREE OCCASIONS PERTAINING TO THE EXTENT TO WHICH THEY INFLUENCE OTHERS BY BEING SELF-ASSERTIVE *

TIME OF ENTRANCE TO OCS	TIME OF GRADUATION FROM OCS	3 YEARS AFTER GRADUATION FROM OCS

* Size of figure pertains to standard scores for the JAIM scale "Influences by Being Self-Assertive." This scale measures the degree to which the individual tends to pursue his own goals when they are in competition with the goals of others. Persons scoring high say that it is important to avoid being diverted from doing what is right in order to please someone; that they do better under competition or stress; and that they are proficient in athletic games.

145

CHART 4

COMPARISON OF THE IDENTICAL GROUP OF 210 MEN ON THREE OCCASIONS PERTAINING TO THE EXTENT THEY PREFER SUPER-VISORY ACTIVITIES *

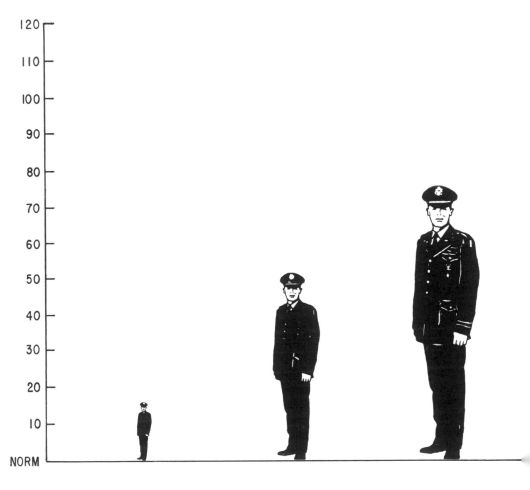

TIME OF ENTRANCE TO OCS'

TIME OF GRADUATION FROM OCS

3 YEARS AFTER GRADUATION FROM OCS

* Size of figure pertains to standard scores for JAIM scale "Prefers Supervisory Activities." This scale measures the degree to which the individual likes to plan and supervise the work of other people. Persons scoring high on this scale find that they get along best when they know what they want and work for it; they are generally striving to reach some goal they have established for themselves and like to supervise others in the carrying out of difficult assignments.

146

TABLE 16

SELF-REPORTED BELIEFS DIFFERENTIATED BY SELECTION AND TRAINING

Scales	Comparison of Entry Scores: 833 Graduates vs 328 Quitters[a]	Comparison of 347 Men Before and After Successful Completion of Training[a]
Extent of Optimism	5.73***	−1.61
Degree of Self-Confidence	8.34***	6.58***
Belief in Moral Absolutes	2.60**	−2.42*
Belief in Slow Change	−0.53	2.84**
Prefers Problem Analysis	0.30	2.53*
Prefers Social Interaction	4.23***	−2.63**
Prefers Mechanical Activities	−1.40	0.85
Prefers Supervisory Activities	6.13***	6.43***
Prefers Activity Frequent Change	4.05***	3.70***
Values Status Attainment	4.07***	1.13
Values Social Service	−2.51*	−1.95
Values Approval from Others	−2.36*	−11.17***
Values Intellectual Achievement	1.03	2.89**
Values Role Conformity	1.22	1.68
Degree of Perseverance	3.94***	5.37***
Extent of Orderliness	3.97***	4.57***
Prefers to Plan Ahead	2.51*	0.0
Influences by Persuasive Leadership	5.67***	8.54***
Influences by Being Self-Assertive	3.66***	7.66***
Move Toward Aggressor	0.09	−5.38***
Move Away from Aggressor	3.07**	4.19***
Move Against Aggressor	2.92**	7.01***
Prefers Routine	−0.06	−2.49*
Identifies with Authority	2.14*	−3.85***
Prefers Independence	0.22	2.41*
Prefers Directive Leadership Style	3.32***	5.33***
Prefers Participative Leadership Style	−0.82	−6.19***
Prefers Delegative Leadership Style	−2.23*	1.24
Motivates by Knowledge of Results	1.12	3.90***
Believes in External Controls	1.28	8.43***
Prefers Being Systematic Methodical	−0.37	−4.78***
Prefers Group Participation	2.42*	−1.30

[a] A positive t-value indicates graduating students are higher in this particular scale while a negative t-value indicates that graduating students are lower as pertains to this particular scale.

* < .05 with t = 1.97
** < .01 with t = 2.58
*** < .001 with t = 3.30

TABLE 17

DIFFERENTIATION BY SELECTION

Group of 833 Entering Students who later graduate are higher on these scales		Group of 328 Entering Students who later voluntarily depart training are higher on these scales	
Scales	t-test Results	Scales	t-test Results
Degree of Self-Confidence	8.34	Move Away from Aggressor	—3.07
Prefers Supervisory Activities	6.43	Values Social Service	—2.51
Extent of Optimism	5.73	Values Approval from Others	—2.36
Influences by Persuasive Leadership	5.67	Prefers Delegative Leadership Style	—2.23
Values Intellectual Achievement	5.19		
Prefers Social Interaction	4.23		
Values Status Attainment	4.07		
Prefers Activity Frequent Change	4.05		
Extent of Orderliness	3.97		
Degree of Perseverance	3.94		
Influences by Being Self-Assertive	3.66		

With respect to the first additional issue considered relevant, it was found that scales which measured change during training also differentiated at the time of entry between those who would eventually graduate and those who would later voluntarily depart from Officer Candidate School prior to graduation. This seemed to indicate that the effects of selection and training were, to a substantial degree, similar. This relationship is presented in Table 16. It is interesting to find that the intensity and direction of change in many scales is rather similar. While Table 16 shows a comparison of those differences that may be attributed to selection with those differences that may be attributed to

148

TABLE 18

Group of 347 Students Higher on These Scales at Time of Graduation		Identical Group of 347 Students Higher on These Scales at Time of Entry	
Scales	t-test Results	Scales	t-test Results
Influences by Persuasive Leadership	8.54	Values Approval from Others	−11.17
Believes in External Controls	8.43	Prefers Participative Leadership Style	−6.19
Influences by Being Self-Assertive	7.66	Move Toward Aggressor	−5.38
Move Against Aggressor	7.01	Prefers Being Systematic, Methodical	−4.78
Degree of Self-Confidence	6.58	Move Away from Aggressor	−4.19
Prefers Supervisory Activities	6.43	Identifies with Authority	−3.85
Degree of Perseverance	5.37	Prefers Social Interaction	−2.63
Prefers Directive Leadership Style	5.33		
Extent of Orderliness	4.57		
Motivates by Knowledge of Results	3.90		
Prefers Activity Frequent Change	3.70		

training, Tables 17 and 18 attempt to simplify this complex relationship. Table 17 concerns differences attributed to selection. Entering students are categorized into two groups in Table 17; those who later graduate, and those who later voluntarily depart from training prior to completing the course. A comparison of the scores of entering students relative to these two categories indicates that there is a significant difference in their self-reported answers pertaining to the JAIM scales. This significant difference is quite similar to the differences attributed to training in Table 18. In Table 18, a comparison is

TABLE 19

Group of 184 men who years later remain in Army are higher in these scales at time of entry into training		Group of 599 men who years later departed from the Army are higher in these scales at time of entry into training	
Scales	t-test Results	Scales	t-test Results
Prefers Supervisory Activities	3.88	Values Intellectual Achievement	−2.27
Belief in Moral Absolutes	2.90	Values Approval from Others	−2.13
Extent of Orderliness	2.66		
		Prefers Problem Analysis	−2.07
Prefers Activity Frequent Change	2.46	Move Away from Aggressor	−1.96
Influences by Persuasive Leadership	2.44		
Degree of Perseverance	2.43		
Values Role Conformity	2.19		
Prefers Mechanical Activities	2.18		
Believes in External Controls	2.17		

made of the scores obtained from the same individuals before and after training. The similarity of results shown in both Tables 17 and 18 indicates that the configuration of scales attributed to training is similar to the configuration of scales attributed to selection.

With regard to the second issue considered relevant, it was found that JAIM scores obtained at the time of entry did discriminate significantly between those individuals who would remain in the Army years later and those who would depart from the Army years later. (See Table 19.)

With respect to the third issue considered relevant, information obtained years later pertaining to graduation and retention was used to group the entering scores of individuals so that a comparison could be made between those who graduated and remained in the Army with those who did not graduate

TABLE 20

Comparison of Those who Graduate and Remain
in Army with Those who do not
Graduate and Depart Army

Group of 175 men who graduated and remained in Army are higher in these scales at time of entry into training		Group of 174 men who did not graduate and who departed Army are higher in these scales at time of entry into training	
Scales	t-test Results	Scales	t-test Results
Prefers Supervisory Activities	6.09	Move Away from Aggressor	−2.88
Degree of Self-Confidence	3.95	Prefers Problem Analysis	−2.17
Influences by Persuasive Leadership	3.73	Values Approval from Others	−1.96
Influences by Being Self-Assertive	3.47		
Extent of Orderliness	3.44		
Prefers Directive Leadership Style	3.44		
Prefers Activity Frequent Change	3.41		
Extent of Optimism	3.39		
Belief in Moral Absolutes	3.33		
Prefers Social Interaction	3.07		

and subsequently departed from the Army. Results are shown in Table 20. These scores obtained at the time of entry into training clearly show that there is a significant difference between these two groups and that the JAIM instrument can discriminate between these two groups.

The above study pertained to Engineer Officer Candidate School located at Fort Belvoir, Virginia, and it was assumed that Engineer Officer Candidate School was representative of others in operation at that time. During September 1968, the results of the study at Engineer Officer Candidate School were cross-validated by a replication at Infantry Officer Candidate School located at Fort Benning, Georgia. The questionnaire, used earlier, was administered to 170 entering students and 101 graduating students. It was predicted that the significant differences found at Engineer Officer Candidate School between entering and graduating students would be found also at Infantry Officer Candidate School. Out of 19 predictions, 11 were confirmed at the .05 level or better. Although not statistically significant, seven out of the remaining eight predictions were in the predicted direction. There was a remarkably similar difference in self-reported beliefs between groups of entering and graduating students at both Engineer Officer Candidate School and Infantry Officer Candidate School. In addition, graduating students from both schools had similar standard scores on selected JAIM scales (see following chart). It was concluded from these results that the two schools had a very similar effect on their students.

During 1970, there was a reevaluation of the Officer Candidate School training process by testing a group of 42 men as both entering students and as graduating students at Engineer Officer Candidate School. There was a significant difference in the average self-reported beliefs of these 42 men between the time they entered Officer Candidate School and the time they departed. These findings substantiate earlier studies that indicated that Officer Candidate School tends to change the self-reported beliefs of the individual in terms of basic beliefs, activity preferences, personal values, and behavioral styles. These changes can be predicted. Changes in self-reported beliefs during Officer Candidate School training in 1970 were similar to those changes during Officer

STANDARD SCORES*

Scales	199 Graduating Students From Engineer Officer Candidate School (1966)	101 Graduating Students From Infantry Officer Candidate School (1968)
Prefers Social Interaction	−8	4
Prefers Supervisory Activities	46	50
Values Approval from Others	−102	−84
Influences by Being Self-Assertive	125	120
Move Toward Aggressor	−79	−84
Move Away from Aggressor	−34	−53
Move Against Aggressor	67	85
Prefers Directive Leadership Style	145	129
Prefers Participative Leadership Style	−100	−100
Prefers Delegative Leadership Style	−21	−23
Believes in External Controls	148	122

*The standard scores are based on a norm group selected from over 50 occupational groups with the mean of the norm group set at zero and the standard deviation at 100.

152

Candidate School training conducted during 1966, 1967, and 1968. It is interesting to note that changes during training were of a lesser intensity during 1970 because entering students during 1970, compared to entering students during 1967, had more of the desired characteristics to begin with. It should be noted also that graduating students during 1970 had less of the desired characteristics than did the graduating students sampled during 1967. It appears that changes in American society may have altered the desired characteristics of graduates as perceived by both the school authorities and by the individuals themselves.

CONCLUSIONS AND RECOMMENDATIONS FOR FURTHER RESEARCH

During the study described in Chapter 3, a comparison was conducted of selected self-reported beliefs between a group of 561 entering students and a group of 319 graduating students attending the Engineer Officer Candidate School. The set of selected self-reported beliefs of each of these two groups was significantly different; however, the effect of training could not be measured because the same individuals were not tested as both entering and graduating students. In the normal course of events, most of the individuals who failed to graduate actually resigned from the program rather than wait to be selected for relief by the school authorities. There was a possibility that this self-selection departure process would further prevent an accurate analysis between entering and graduating students. If individuals with certain beliefs were encouraged to remain while others with certain beliefs were selected to fail, it could be possible that instead of developing junior officers, the school was selecting men to become junior officers. A more likely possibility to account for the difference between groups of entering and graduating students was a combination of training and selection.

In contrast to this earlier study, the purpose of the study described in this chapter was to investigate the effect of U.S. Army Engineer Officer Candidate training and the stability of this training when measured again years after departure from Officer Candidate School. The JAIM inventory was administered at the beginning of a six-month training program, again near the end of the training program, and then on a third occasion several years after departure from the training program. A total of 347 individuals were examined as both entering and graduating students. In addition, a total of 757 individuals were examined both as graduating students and again years later after departing from Officer Candidate School.

The following assumptions were used in this study:

1. The standards and techniques used by the school authorities in evaluating students remained constant during the sampling period.
2. The system of rewards and punishments for students remained constant during the sampling period.

3. The JAIM instrument is reliable and valid.

CONCLUSIONS

1. The self-reported beliefs of a group of individuals participating in Officer Candidate School training changes during training. As graduating students, individuals tend to reflect changes in the previously predicted scales. They score higher on the following scales:

Influences by Persuasive Leadership
Believes in External Controls
Influences by Being Self-Assertive
Move Against Aggressor
Degree of Self-Confidence
Prefers Supervisory Activities
Degree of Perseverance
Prefers Directive Leadership Style
Motivates by Knowledge of Results
Prefers Activity Frequent Change
Prefers Independence

They score lower on the following scales:

Values Approval from Others
Prefers Participative Leadership Style
Move Toward Aggressor

It can be concluded that, as a group, these men changed their self-reported beliefs during the time of training. This change was considered as tending to reflect adjustment by the student to the established standards of the school environment including the standards of peers.

2. In some cases, there was a significant difference between scores obtained at the time of graduation from Officer Candidate School and those obtained approximately three years later. This prediction pertaining to the lack of stability of Officer Candidate School training was not confirmed because of the erratic results of the predictions as a whole. It should be noted that several of these self-reported beliefs continued to change significantly in the same direction as during training. This suggests that those beliefs that receive positive reinforcement following graduation tend to increase, and that those beliefs that receive negative reinforcement following graduation tend to decrease in intensity. In addition, those scales that receive neither positive nor negative reinforcement tend to remain approximately the same.

It is speculated that a slight positive influence might only tend to maintain the level of the belief acquired by training. Also, that an absence of positive or negative influence might tend to permit a reversal of a belief to that configuration held prior to training.

3. Although no predictions were formulated, an analysis of the data in connection with this study indicated that scores obtained by using the test

instrument at the time of entry into the training program effectively discriminate the following:

a. Between a group of men who will eventually graduate and a group of men who will voluntarily depart from the program prior to graduation.

b. Between a group of men who will remain in the Army approximately three years later and a group of men who will depart from the Army approximately three years later.

c. Between a group of men who will both graduate and remain in the Army approximately three years later and a group of men who will not graduate and who will depart from the Army approximately three years later.

RECOMMENDATIONS FOR FURTHER RESEARCH

1. Differences in JAIM scores associated with selection, training, and retention were considered in this study. The extent of the graduate's performance as an officer was not considered. It would be worthwhile to compare students' JAIM scores with the officer efficiency indexes[73] the same individuals receive later as officers. This may provide an insight in predicting future performance.

All officers in the sample who were on active duty during 1970 were in the grade of captain at that time. A further evaluation of the relationship of performance and JAIM scores previously sampled would be to isolate those individuals in the sample who receive an early promotion[74] from captain to major. Then study the prior JAIM scores of these individuals for common characteristics. While it was possible to somewhat isolate the effects of training and selection and to predict to a lesser extent the stability of acquired self-reported beliefs, it will be more difficult to isolate the characteristics associated with what is required for "excellent" performance.

2. I also recommend that these individuals continue to be tested as they mature further and reach various levels of their civilian or military careers.

CLOSING REMARKS

This study investigated the effect of training at a particular Officer Candidate School. Certain questions concerning the immediate effects of training and the stability of these effects three years later were answered. It is clearly recognized that this study had several limitations. In completing the JAIM questionnaire, the perception of the individual was involved. This limited the evaluation to an

---

[73] Officer efficiency index: A composite of an individual's officer efficiency report results during a prescribed period. No longer officially used to determine promotions or assignments. Occasionally used in official U.S. Army personnel research studies.

[74] Normally 5 percent of those individuals selected for promotion to the grade of major consist of captains considered by the promotion board as outstanding but who are too junior pertaining to longevity to meet conventional promotion criteria. In their case, part of the longevity requirement is waived and they are promoted prior to their peers.

average of how hundreds of individuals perceived conditions rather than precise reality. A further limitation was that the factors that influenced these men to change during and after training were not isolated in detail. While much has been written about training, very little has been written concerning the effect of Officer Candidate School training and the stability of this training. I hope that this study will, in some small measure, help fill the void and provide information beneficial to both the Officer Candidate School authorities, and to individuals who are conducting similar research.

Chapter 5

EFFECTS OF COMBAT ON THE BELIEFS OF INFANTRYMEN

The effects of combat on individuals returning to civilian life are viewed by Levy[1] as a psychological disorientation that is detrimental to society. He reported a common tendency in a group of 60 randomly selected former combat marines to carry into civilian life the "unbridled violence" that served them well in combat. In contrast, Moskos[2] considers that American enlisted men return to their civilian roles with qualities that are beneficial to society. Moskos found that compared with when they entered the Army, these men return to civilian life more mature and better suited to contribute to society. A third finding was indicated by Stouffer, *et al.* concerning the WW II veteran. "Personal readjustment problems of varying degrees of intensity are disclosed by the veterans in this study. But the 'typical' veteran pictured in some quarters as a bitter, hardened individual does not emerge from this survey."[3]

It is evident that there is a wide divergence of findings concerning the overall effects of combat. What then are the effects of combat on the beliefs of enlisted infantrymen? The purpose of this chapter is to describe an investigation of the differences in certain self-reported beliefs when the same group of enlisted infantrymen are evaluated while in Vietnam, and then again after they return to the United States.

People differ in the way they respond to various situations that they experience in their lives. The nature of this response affects their effectiveness and the satisfaction they receive from the results of their performance in different situations. American enlisted infantrymen in combat in Vietnam found themselves in a setting requiring them to assume different roles from those to which they have been accustomed. It is believed that during the period these individuals were stationed in Vietnam, many of their new roles probably became

---

[1] Charles Levy, "The Violent Veterans," *Time* (March 13, 1972), pp. 45–46.

[2] Charles C. Moskos, Jr., *The American Enlisted Man* (New York: Russell Sage Foundation, 1970).

[3] Samuel A. Stouffer, *et al.,* "The American Soldier: Combat and its Aftermath," *Studies in Social Psychology in World War II,* Vol. 2 (Princeton: Princeton Univ., 1949), p. 631.

part of their personality and self-conception. It is also considered that upon returning to the United States, these individuals further changed their personality and self-conception.

THEORETICAL FRAMEWORK

An analysis of differences in self-reported beliefs should consider the influences that caused these differences. In this study, the influences of combat are seen in terms of the following: (a) the environment, (b) the formal organization, and (c) the informal organization. The terms "formal organization" and "informal organization" are viewed within the framework described by Likert[4] pertaining to the characteristics of different management systems.

The effects of these influences are intensified by their interrelationships. Thus, stress experienced by the individual soldier is caused by a combination of the environment (i.e., tropical climate and the presence of Viet Cong), the formal organization (i.e., policies and procedures to follow), and the informal organization (i.e., responsibilities to comrades). During WW II, a report by a Special Commission of Civilian Psychiatrists[5] in describing stress as a major characteristic of combat discussed the following interrelationship of the above three types of influence.

> Adjustment to combat . . . means not only adjustment to killing, but also adjustment to danger, to frustration, to uncertainty, to noise and confusion, and particularly to the wavering faith in the efficiency or success of one's comrades and command.

INFLUENCES BY THE ENVIRONMENT

The discomforts of the Mekong Delta are often viewed by infantrymen in terms of heat, humidity, and muddy rice paddies. Heat rash, insects, and forms of immersion foot are prevalent. While these discomforts may be considered as important environmental factors, the major environmental factor for subjects in this study was surviving a potential life or death encounter with the Viet Cong. These encounters ranged from a face-to-face struggle to stepping on a landmine.

Unlike the sophisticated improvements in weapon systems, and command and control systems, today's infantrymen have many of the same human qualities of those individuals who fought in WW II. It seems ironic that the specific unit represented in this study was one of the many military organizations studied by Stouffer, *et al.*, during WW II. During WW II, it appeared to Stouffer, *et al.*, that stress was caused by a number of reasons. These reasons, not necessarily in order of their importance, are listed below.

1. Threats to life and limb and health.
2. Physical discomfort—from lack of shelter, excessive heat or cold, excessive

[4] Rensis Likert, *The Human Organization; Its Management and Value* (New York: McGraw-Hill, 1967).
[5] Report of Special Commission of Civilian Psychiatrists Covering Psychiatric Policy and Practice in the United States Army Medical Corps, European Theater, April 20–July 8, 1945, p. 12.

moisture or dryness, inadequacy of food or water or clothing; from insects and disease; from filth; from injuries or wounds; from long-continued fatigue and lack of sleep.

3.   Deprivation of sexual and concomitant social satisfactions.

4.   Isolation from accustomed sources of affectional assurance.

5.   Loss of comrades, and sight and sound of wounded and dying men.

6.   Restriction of personal movement—ranging from the restrictions of military law to the immobility of the soldier pinned down under enemy fire.

7.   Continual uncertainty and lack of adequate cognitive orientation.

8.   Conflicts of values:

      a.   between the requirements of duty and the individual's impulses toward safety and comfort;

      b.   between military duty and obligations to family and dependents at home, to whose well-being the soldier's survival is important;

      c.   between informal group codes, as of loyalty to comrades, and the formal requirements of the military situation which may sometimes not permit mutual aid;

      d.   between previously accepted moral codes and combat imperatives.

9.   Being treated as a means rather than an end in itself; seemingly arbitrary and impersonal demands of coercive authority; sense of not counting as an individual.

10.   Lack of "privacy"; the incessant demands and petty irritations of close living within the group.

11.   Long periods of enforced boredom, mingled with anxiety, between actions.

12.   Lack of terminal individual goals; poverty and uncertainty of individual rewards.[6]

While most of the above reasons for stress pertain to environmental influences, it is acknowledged that several of these reasons can be attributed mostly, or in part, to influences from the formal and informal organization.

Influences by the Formal Organization

The formal organization in this study is the 3rd Battalion, 60th Infantry (3/60), 2nd Brigade, 9th Infantry Division. The following represents a successful combat operation in terms of the goals and *modus operandi* of this organization. Approximately 75 percent of the men in the study participated in this particular battle. It is typical of many other battles in which, at one time or another, all of the subjects participated. An account of this tactical operation is also cited in order to describe the elements of surprise, firepower, and violence of action with which these individuals were often associated.

On February 14, 1969, three companies of the 3/60 fought against an estimated main force Viet Cong company in the Mekong Delta. Immediately prior to the battle, the 3/60 conducted airmobile operations in the Mo Cay District of Kien Hoa Province. At approximately 2:00 p.m., an Air Force forward air controller, operating in the adjacent district of Giong Trom, observed several armed Viet Cong crossing a stream in a sparsely populated area. This indicated the possibility of a larger force in the same vicinity. For-

[6] Stouffer, *et al., op. cit.,* p. 77.

tunately, the commander of the 3/60, his artillery liaison officer from the 3/34th Artillery, and the helicopter company commander (162d Assault Helicopter Company) were airborne in the same helicopter in the vicinity of the observation made by the forward air controller. Company D, airborne in helicopters near Mo Cay, was diverted to the vicinity of the observed enemy. While the infantry was en route, the forward air controller coordinated an air strike by Air Force F-100 fighter jets in the area where the Viet Cong had been observed. During the later phases of the 10–15 minute air strike, the artillery liaison officer fired and adjusted an artillery preparation on two areas considered by the commander of the 3/60 as potential landing sites. The air strike and artillery fires drove several squads of the armed enemy from their camouflaged positions and out into open areas.

The commander of Company D received a fragmentary order via radio while airborne. Subsequently, while still airborne, he briefed his platoon leaders by radio. The landing zone selected by the battalion commander was marked with a smoke grenade by the lead helicopter gun ship. Members of Company D arrived by helicopter and were able to observe the activated smoke grenade. This helped them to make a rapid aerial reconnaissance of their objective area. The use of helicopters enabled the battalion commander to specifically indicate the landing zone, direction to the objective, and distance to the objective. Preparatory fires by the helicopter gun ships of the supporting airmobile company started simultaneously with the completion of the air strike and artillery preparation. Company D, upon landing, moved rapidly from its landing zone towards the enemy. Helicopters from the airmobile company then promptly landed Company A in a position on the opposite side of the stream from Company D. Next, Company C was airlifted from the flight deck of the barracks ship APL-30, which lay at anchor in the Ben Tre River some three miles distant. Company C completed the cordon by landing south of the enemy force. The helicopters were then used to reinforce Companies A and D with the remaining portions of their respective units. As the cordon contracted, fire teams from Troop D, 3d Squadron, 5th Air Cavalry located in helicopters flying at an altitude of 5–25 yards, engaged enemy troops who were firing from bunkers along the stream.

During the operation, air strikes conducted by members of the Air Force 306th and 510th Tactical Fighter Squadrons continued to impact on enemy positions within the cordoned area. Medical evacuation helicopters evacuated wounded U.S. personnel from landing zones 500–800 yards to the rear of infantry contacts. Helicopters from the cavalry provided suppressing fires during the airmobile medical evacuation. On the return trip to the supply base, helicopters that previously delivered a resupply of ammunition to the infantry, evacuated Viet Cong wounded, Viet Cong prisoners, and recovered the bodies of two American soldiers who had been killed in the battle. A helicopter smoke ship, organic to the 162d Assault Helicopter Company, provided a smoke screen in an attempt to conceal from the enemy the helicopter landings and takeoffs.

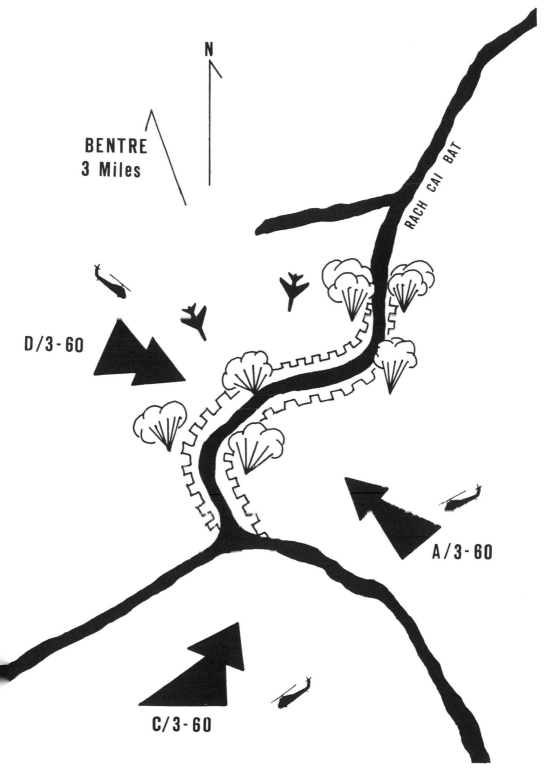

N

BENTRE
3 Miles

RACH CAI BAT

D/3-60

A/3-60

C/3-60

In many respects, the procedures that were followed by infantrymen during WW II have changed drastically. The formal organization is no longer an infantry battalion moving together on foot towards the high ground. Today's advances in technology have aided the infantryman in the accomplishment of his mission; however, there are some disadvantages. Communications within the formal organization which rely more heavily on radio seem to lack the effectiveness gained by a face-to-face discussion. In many cases, movement by helicopter requires the infantryman to rapidly orient himself with regards to the enemy and the terrain immediately prior to a skirmish. Fragmentary orders require a stronger reliance on the standing operating procedures of the formal organization. In many respects, infantrymen are more closely tied to the policies and procedures of the formal organization. However, at times the relative isolation of small groups may strengthen the infantrymen's reliance on the informal organization.

Influences by the Informal Organization

Informal organizations, in regard to the study reported in this chapter, may consist of portions of a rifle squad or portions of a rifle platoon. In some cases, they consist of an entire 11-man rifle squad or an entire 45-man rifle platoon. In exceptionally well-performing squads and platoons, the informal and formal organizations are often one and the same. In such instances,[7] all social forces are available to support efforts needed to achieve the organization's goals.

An analysis of the data concerning this study indicated that when a group of 80 enlisted infantrymen from the 3rd Battalion, 60th Infantry were in combat they tended to be more sensitive to the needs of their friends. Perhaps the daily stress of combat and adverse environmental conditions encouraged a feeling of comradery that was welcome in Vietnam, but no longer needed after these men returned to the United States. This feeling of comradeship, and perhaps the possibility of death in combat, may be responsible, at least in part, for this sensitivity. It seems ironic that it takes the horrors of war to cause individuals to become more sensitive in their interactions with their friends. It is certainly most unfortunate that these desirable qualities did not tend to carry over substantially after these men returned to the United States.

In discussing the influence of the informal organization, it is interesting to consider an account of a young sergeant who was a highly valued member of an informal organization. Sergeant Blye's performance is representative of other extraordinary acts by many of the subjects in this study during the same general period of time.

On the afternoon of May 7, 1969, Sergeant Blye distinguished himself while on a reconnaissance operation in Kien Hoa Province south of Ben Tre. When his platoon was hit by heavy small arms and automatic weapons fire, Sergeant Blye immediately deployed his men and began to direct their return fire.

[7] Likert, *op. cit.*

162

Specialist 4th Class David Donaldson (Elwood, Pennsylvania), radio-telephone operator, Company D, 3rd Battalion, 60th Infantry, 9th Infantry Division takes a break during an operation near Mo Cay. Photo by Allen T. Rockoff, 221st Signal Company, U.S. Army.

Noticing that a machine gun was jammed in one of his key positions, Sergeant Blye, completely ignoring his own safety, raced approximately 30 yards across open terrain under very heavy enemy fire to the gun position. Exposing himself to the enemy fire, he worked fervently to repair the jammed weapon. After finally restoring the weapon to working order, Sergeant Blye stood up in the face of the intense enemy fire and brought a devastating volume of fire on the enemy, routing them from their positions and allowing his wounded comrades to be aided.

The individual cited in the above combat operation is a 21-year-old black, born and raised in Myrtle Beach, South Carolina. He attended Myrtle Beach High School where he won the Golden Hammer award as the best industrial arts student. He was drafted into the Army in August 1967 and received basic training at Fort Gordon, Georgia, and advanced individual training at Fort Ord, California. Later he was assigned to the Jungle Warfare School in Panama where he became an instructor. In July 1968, he volunteered for duty in Vietnam. While in Vietnam, he earned two Silver Stars for heroism, two Bronze Stars for achievement and service, four Air Medals for meritorious actions in connection with air assaults, and a Purple Heart.

In an earlier battle, Sergeant Blye's officer platoon leader was wounded and was subsequently evacuated. In the absence of an officer, Sergeant Blye took command of the platoon. Members of the platoon viewed him as a dependable friend as well as a competent leader. His platoon was one of the best in the battalion. Sergeant Blye's success as a leader can be attributed, in part, to the support he received from the platoon members. He was fortunate in being the leader of a platoon where the formal and informal organizations were identical.

METHOD

OBSERVATIONS OF INFANTRYMEN IN VIETNAM

The group of individuals in this study were observed in Vietnam for approximately 200 days. As commander of the battalion during this period, I had many opportunities to observe the behavior and characteristics of these men who were members of the rifle companies in this particular battalion. In considering the many observations made, the following five appear to be the most significant:

1. The infantrymen represented in this study tended to place a high value on what their peers thought of them. In combat, the importance to them of acceptance by their peers was often reflected in their lack of self-assertiveness in situations when they were encouraged by their superiors or by the nature of events to compete with their peers.

2. While involved in combat operations, the men represented in this study appeared to have a strong identification with their immediate superiors.

The officer who commanded the personal respect and loyalty of his men could mobilize the full support of a willing followership; he therefore had at his disposal the resources of both the formal coercive system and the system of informal group controls. If, however, the officer had alienated his men and had to rely primarily on coercion, the informal sanctions of the group might cease to bear primarily on the combat mission. [8]

3. The unselfish nature of the infantrymen observed was apparent, particularly in their genuine concern for their friends. The dependence on one another for safety in combat may have been a factor in this comradeship. In addition, individuals seemed to place an extraordinary value in tasks involving interactions with their associates and especially in participating in social activities involving their friends.

4. A common complaint by these infantrymen was the frequency of changes in their combat operations. Typical complaints were "hurry up and wait" and "not another change in today's plans!" Sometimes these complaints were justifiable, while at other times a change in the situation required a change in plans.

5. While in Vietnam, the infantrymen represented in this study seemed to dislike being considered ambitious. In many cases, competent and highly productive individuals avoided receiving the traditional military rewards that pertain to high status and prestige. Perhaps this was due to their desire to be one of the "boys" rather than to be considered a "hero" or "showoff" by their companions. Also, motivation to some degree may have been missing due to the type of war in which they were engaged.

The observations described above were considered when the predictions for this study were formulated.

PREDICTIONS

Several predictions will be presented in the form of the differences in self reported beliefs found when the same group of individuals are evaluated in both a combat setting in Vietnam and again after they return to the United States. These differences will be attributed to the removal of the influences of combat. The purpose for posing these predictions is to further examine the observations of the group of 80 enlisted infantrymen listed earlier in this chapter. The differences predicted below are not intended to include all of the differences pertaining to this situation. However, they are selected as being representative of many obvious differences that became apparent during empirical observations.

Compared with when they were stationed as infantrymen in Vietnam, the same group of 80 individuals, after they return to the United States, will tend to significantly change several of their self-reported beliefs.

1. *Differences Attributed to Influences by the Formal Organization* Influences by the formal organization are important in combat, therefore,

[8] Stouffer, *et al., op. cit.,* p. 118.

the following changes in Job Analysis and Interest Measurement (JAIM) scales are predicted:

a. Scores for the scale "Identifies with Authority" will be significantly lower after these men return to the United States. This scale measures the degree to which the individual identifies with his superior and tries to please him.

b. Scores for the scale "Prefers Activity Frequent Change" will be significantly higher after these men return to the United States. This scale measures the degree to which the individual likes to be actively engaged in work providing a lot of excitement and a great deal of variety.

2. *Differences Attributed to Influences by the Informal Organization* Influences by the informal organization are important in combat; therefore, the following changes in JAIM scales are predicted:

a. Scores for the scale "Values Approval from Others" will be significantly lower after these men return to the United States. This scale measures the degree to which the individual values himself by obtaining the approval from others.

b. Scores for the scale "Prefers Social Interaction" will be significantly lower after these men return to the United States. This scale measures the degree to which the individual likes work involving interactions with people.

c. Scores for the scale "Influences by being Self-Assertive" will be significantly higher after these men return to the United States. This scale measures the degree to which the individual tends to pursue his own goals when they are in competition with the goals of others.

d. Scores for the scale "Prefers Group Participation" will be significantly lower after these men return to the United States. This scale measures the degree to which the individual identifies himself with a highly valued group.

e. Scores for the scale "Values Status Attainment" will be significantly higher after these men return to the United States. This scale measures the degree to which the individual values himself by his achievement of the status symbols established by his culture.

PROCEDURE

While stationed in Vietnam during 1969, 321 enlisted infantrymen assigned to the rifle companies of an infantry battalion completed the JAIM questionnaire. During 1970, after they returned to the United States, many of these individuals were contacted and indicated a willingness to complete the same questionnaire again via mail. At the conclusion of the study, 80 questionnaires completed in the United States were suitable for analysis.

Concurrent with testing infantrymen in a combat setting, 121 enlisted men assigned to a relatively safe rear area in Vietnam also completed this questionnaire during 1969. In 1970, after they returned to the United States, many of these men were contacted again. At the conclusion of the study, 53 questionnaires completed via mail in the United States for this group were suitable for analysis. The group of individuals who were assigned to a relatively safe rear area will be used as a control group. Both the test group and control group were retested in the United States in connection with the study described in Chapter 4.

RESULTS

Table 21 indicates the results. Compared with when they were stationed as infantrymen in Vietnam, the same group of individuals after they returned to the United States significantly changed several of their self-reported beliefs.[9] Of the seven predictions stated earlier, five are confirmed and two are not confirmed inasmuch as five out of seven scales are significant at least at the .05 confidence level pertaining to the predicted increase or decrease. Both the group of 80 enlisted infantrymen and the control group had significant changes in their response to the JAIM questionnaire when it was administered on the second occasion. While differences were generally similar for both the group of 80 enlisted infantrymen and the control group, the intensity of the changes were noticeably stronger in the case of the group of 80 enlisted infantrymen. In analyzing the changes that are applicable for both the group of 80 enlisted infantrymen and the control group, it is considered that Americans stationed in Vietnam are confronted with influences that require them to assume different roles from those to which they had been accustomed. It is conceptualized that, to some degree, many of these new roles probably became part of their personality and also that these new roles are responsible, at least in part, for changes in their self-reported beliefs. It was further conceptualized that on returning to the United States, individuals in both groups further changed their self-reported beliefs. Specifically, the results of the predictions pertaining to the group of 80 enlisted infantrymen are interpreted as follows:

1. *Differences Attributed to Influences by the Formal Organization*
    a.   In many instances, the survival in combat of the individuals in the group of 80 enlisted infantrymen depended on the competence of their immediate superior. It was predicted that individuals would identify less with authority after they returned to the United States. Results indicated that individuals retested in the United States had a decrease in the value they placed in the scale "Identifies with Authority." This decrease, however, was not statistically significant and the prediction was not confirmed.
    b.   During 1969, the nature of tactical operations in Vietnam required

[9] Zero is the norm for Table 21 (pertaining only to the standard scores). This was determined by setting zero in place of the average scores representing over 50 occupational groups in the United States. Theoretically, no particular occupational group exactly fits the norm. The purpose of this norm is to establish a "bench mark" so that the scores different groups of people receive will have relative meaning. It should be recognized that major differences in response may be essential for top performance in different environments. Therefore, the reader should not make a general assumption that "lowest" indicates "worst."

TABLE 21

DIFFERENCE IN SEVERAL SELF-REPORTED BELIEFS FOR A GROUP OF 80
MEN BETWEEN TIME OF TESTING IN VIETNAM AS A MEMBER OF AN
INFANTRY BATTALION AND RETESTING IN THE UNITED STATES
APPROXIMATELY ONE YEAR LATER

Scales	Test Group						Control Group[a]	
	Predicted Increase or Decrease[b]	t-test Results[c]	Prediction Confirmed	Standard Scores[d]		t-test Results	Standard Scores	
				Vietnam	US		Vietnam	US
Identifies with Authority	—	−1.59	No	−12	−31	− .04	− 6	− 7
Prefers Activity Frequent Change	+	+2.45**	Yes	−29	− 4	−0.42	− 7	−12
Values Approval from Others	—	−2.72***	Yes	16	−14	−1.81*	− 6	−26
Prefers Social Interaction	—	−3.62***	Yes	− 3	−46	−1.44	− 6	−24
Influences by Being Self-Assertive	+	+ .69	No	38	45	.95	51	62
Prefers Group Participation	—	−1.83*	Yes	0	−23	−2.19*	24	− 8
Values Status Attainment	+	+2.04*	Yes	−23	− 1	−0.97	− 6	−16

[a] Control group consisted of 53 individuals assigned to a relatively safe rear area in Vietnam during the same time period members of the test group were assigned to the rifle companies of an infantry battalion engaged in combat in Vietnam. Both the test group and the control group were retested in the United States approximately one year later via mail.

[b] Plus (+) indicates a higher average score for the group of individuals when retested. Minus (−) indicates a lower average score for the group of individuals when retested.

[c] Computed on the basis of a one-tailed distribution.

*p < .05
**p < .01
***p < .001

[d] Average of norm group has been equated to zero and the standard deviation to 100.

frequent changes in daily operational plans. Many of the soldiers expressed a dislike for these constant changes. Persons scoring low on this scale indicated that they like to finish one task before starting another. After returning to the relatively conventional influences of the United States, there was a significant increase in the value placed in the scale "Prefers Activity Frequent Change." The prediction concerning this scale was confirmed. (See Chart 5.)

2. *Differences Attributed to Influences by the Informal Organization*

a. The infantrymen, while stationed in Vietnam, tended to have a high degree of concern for the approval of their actions by their friends. Persons scoring high on the scale "Values Approval from Others" considered it important to obtain the approval of their peers. In addition, they believed that it is most important to have congenial coworkers, to be well-liked, and to please others through their work. As predicted, there was a significant decrease in the scale "Values Approval from Others" after the individuals returned from Vietnam. It is speculated that the exceptionally high concern for what their friends thought of them during combat accounts for this difference as well as the need for teamwork and mutual support in time of stress. (See Chart 6.)

b. The group of 80 enlisted infantrymen placed an unusually high value on their interactions with their peers. It is understandable that this value would decrease after these individuals returned from Vietnam. Results indicated that there was, in fact, a significant decrease in the scale "Prefers Social Interaction" between the time of testing in Vietnam and retesting approximately one year later. The prediction pertaining to "Prefers Social Interaction" was confirmed. (See Chart 7.)

c. It was predicted that when individuals return from Vietnam, their increased independence would lead them to place a higher value on being self-assertive. Persons scoring high indicated that it is important to avoid being diverted from doing what is right in order to please someone; that they do better under competition or stress; and that they are proficient in athletic games. In Vietnam, it seemed that a high value was placed on teamwork while conversely a low value was placed on competition among individuals. The results indicated that, compared with their answers in Vietnam, individuals having returned to the United States placed a slightly higher value on the scale "Influences by Being Self-Assertive;" however, this increase was not found to be statistically significant and the prediction was not confirmed. (See Chart 8.)

d. The nature of events in Vietnam encouraged individuals to identify with a group of peers. Persons scoring high indicated that they like best to work as a member of a group and do not like to work apart from other people. As predicted, there was a decrease in the value given to the scale "Prefers Group Participation" after these individuals returned from Vietnam. (See Chart 9.)

e. Individuals in the test group observed in Vietnam did not appear to place any particular value in the attainment of status. Persons scoring high on this scale indicated that they prefer to be considered ambitious and successful; like to have a job which is recognized to be important or desirable; and think that the ideal job is one which shows they were a success and had achieved high status and prestige. It was predicted that there would be a

CHART 5

SOLDIERS RETURNING FROM VIETNAM:
EXTENT OF THEIR PREFERENCE FOR FREQUENT CHANGES IN THEIR ACTIVITIES

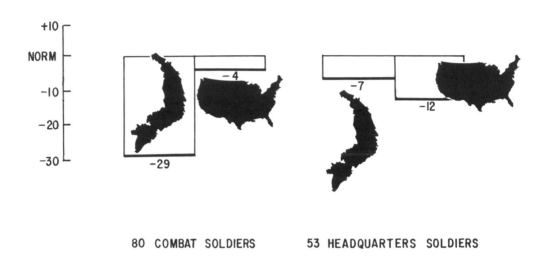

80 COMBAT SOLDIERS   53 HEADQUARTERS SOLDIERS

CHART 6

SOLDIERS RETURNING FROM VIETNAM:
EXTENT OF THEIR VALUE FOR THE APPROVAL FROM OTHERS

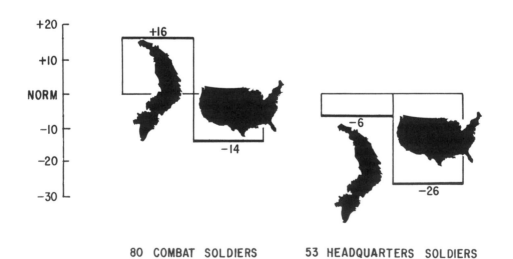

80 COMBAT SOLDIERS   53 HEADQUARTERS SOLDIERS

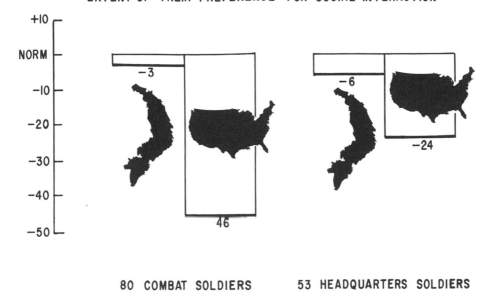

CHART 7

SOLDIERS RETURNING FROM VIETNAM:
EXTENT OF THEIR PREFERENCE FOR SOCIAL INTERACTION

80 COMBAT SOLDIERS   53 HEADQUARTERS SOLDIERS

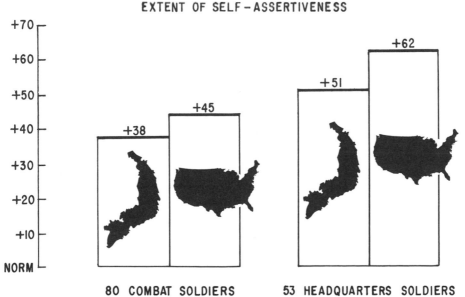

CHART 8

SOLDIERS RETURNING FROM VIETNAM:
EXTENT OF SELF-ASSERTIVENESS

80 COMBAT SOLDIERS   53 HEADQUARTERS SOLDIERS

CHART 9

SOLDIERS RETURNING FROM VIETNAM:
EXTENT OF THEIR PREFERENCE FOR GROUP PARTICIPATION

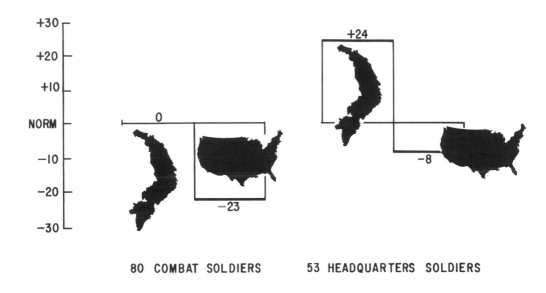

80 COMBAT SOLDIERS   53 HEADQUARTERS SOLDIERS

CHART 10

SOLDIERS RETURNING FROM VIETNAM:
EXTENT OF THEIR PREFERENCE FOR STATUS

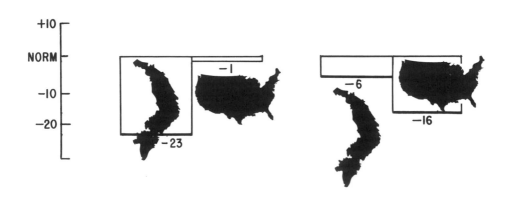

80 COMBAT SOLDIERS   53 HEADQUARTERS SOLDIERS

significant increase in the self-reported evaluation of the scale "Values Status Attainment" when individuals returned to the United States. This prediction was confirmed.

In contrast, the control group, while observed in Vietnam, seemed to place a relatively higher value on status. It is interesting to note that the standard scores for both groups in the United States moved in the opposite direction from those scores in Vietnam. (See Chart 10.)

SUMMARY OF FINDINGS

Compared with after they returned to the United States, the same group of individuals, when they were stationed as infantrymen in Vietnam, placed a significantly higher value on the approval from others, on social interaction, and on group participation. Conversely, a lower value was placed on the attainment of status. While both the group of 80 enlisted infantrymen and the control group changed to some degree after they returned to the United States, the group of 80 enlisted infantrymen experienced a greater degree of change. This is attributed to the removal of these men from combat. The nature of these changes clearly indicates, as pertains to this particular study, that the effects of combat on the beliefs of infantrymen are not detrimental to society.

Chapter 6

RETENTION OF YOUNG LEADERS

An important consideration in most organizations is the retention of young leaders. The U.S. Army is particularly interested in retaining officers after they complete their first term of service. The purpose of this chapter is to indicate how to improve the retention of junior officers in the Army. To accomplish this, an examination will be conducted of the differences in self-reported beliefs between a group of 358 individuals who remained in the Army and a group of 919 individuals who departed. In addition, an analysis will be made of the reasons why one group departed and of the major goals in life for both groups combined. It is acknowledged that numerous studies concerning retention have been conducted and that efforts along this line will be continued. It is hoped, however, that the study reported in this chapter will provide an insight pertaining to retention that has not been previously fully developed.

It is recognized that this analysis must consider the impact of the Army's current problems on those individuals examined. These problems are abundantly reflected in contemporary news reports. A typical contemporary analysis by Johnson and Wilson featured in a leading newspaper is as follows:

> Today's American Army is fighting its most threatening battle, a struggle for survival as an institution. It faces what top commanders agree is the most complicated crisis in its history . . . . The elements of the chaotic conditions that affect the contemporary United States Army wherever it is stationed, in Germany, or Vietnam, or at home (are): crime, drugs, racial conflict, rebellion against officers, boredom, and attitudes that always have been anathema to armies.[1]

Senior officials within Headquarters, Department of the Army, recognize that serious problems do exist. The following statement by Lieutenant General William E. DePuy indicates that the critical nature of the situation is well understood. "Last year was bad for the Army, one of the worst since before World War II."[2] Action is being taken in an attempt to correct the many

---

[1] Haynes Johnson and George C. Wilson, "Army in Anguish," *Washington Post* (September 12, 1971), p. 1.

[2] George P. Hunt, "Our Four–Star Military Mess," *Life*, June 18, 1971, pp. 50–68.

problems facing the Army today. Specific objectives stated by General William C. Westmoreland are as follows:

> We must revitalize, rebuild, and rejuvenate the United States Army . . . . We will do this by breaking out of the Vietnam strait-jacket; by bringing our professionalism to its highest level ever; by making service life more appealing; and by improving our public support . . . .[3]

SIMILAR STUDIES

Although the study reported in this chapter is concerned with officers who graduated from Officer Candidate School, a review of the results of similar studies may be helpful.

The following study pertains to graduates of the United States Military Academy. In April 1970, the Deputy Chief of Staff for Personnel, U.S. Army, directed that a study be conducted pertaining to the problems of retaining in the Army members of the United States Military Academy Class of 1966. As of June 1970, 23 percent of the Class of 1966 had resigned. In the past 12 years, the average rate of resignations four years after graduation was 15½ percent. A detailed study indicated the following:

> 1. When USMA graduates perceive themselves to have a "black mark" on their record which might slow their career progression in relation to that of their contemporaries, they may very well resign so as to "save face." It would be too painful to remain on active duty for the first major selection round and see all one's classmates' names on the list, but not one's own . . . .
> 2. In line with this finding, the losses from the Class of 1966 represent considerable self-selection out.
> 3. Given a chance to select from 70 reasons those which were instrumental in causing their resignations, above average performers evidenced a sharply different reply pattern from that given by average and below average performers:
>> a. Above-average performers are highly ambitious men . . . . They consider themselves under-utilized by the Army. They want to go where their abilities can be fully recognized. They feel that this place is in the civilian sector.
>> b. Average performers accomplish all assigned duties in a satisfactory manner. But deep down they are not driven by ambition. They are ego-centered, middle-class, and suburban. Work is a means to an end. The end is family life, a house and garden, and vacations. Thus, they object to family separations . . . .
>> c. Below average performers are bitter. They are highly critical of Army activities which relate to performance . . . . They blame the system for their personal "failure" . . . .
> 4. The principal dissatisfiers . . . common to the three groups . . . relate to excessive family separations and the prospects of another tour in Vietnam.
> 5. Pay and fringe benefits rate relatively low in the list of dissatisfiers.[4]

---

[3] William C. Westmoreland, General, U.S.A., Speech delivered at Fort Benning, Georgia, September 24, 1971.

[4] Robert Leider, *Why They Leave: Resignations from the USMA Class of* 1966, A U.S. Dept. of the Army Study, (July 6, 1970), pp. 1–3–1 to 1–3–3.

The President's Commission on an All-Volunteer Armed Force recommended the following to President Nixon on February 20, 1970:

> We unanimously believe that the nation's interests will be better served by an all-volunteer force, supported by an effective stand-by draft, than by a mixed force of volunteers and conscripts; that steps should be taken promptly to move in this direction; and that the first indispensable step is to remove the present inequity in the pay of men serving their first term in the armed forces.[5]

It is interesting to note that an improved pay scale for men serving their first term was considered as the first step towards enhancing an All-Volunteer Armed Force. In contrast to an emphasis on monetary rewards considered paramount by the President's Commission on an All-Volunteer Armed Force, William L. Hauser observed that:

> Junior officers are willing to forego the higher pay and settled conveniences of civilian life if the Army offers them psychic rewards in the form of professional achievement. What they often see, however, is a lack of professionalism among senior field grade officers nearing the end of foreshortened careers.[6]

A reenlistment attitude survey prepared in March 1970 by Behavior Systems, Inc. of Philadelphia, Pennsylvania, provided relevant information concerning the current attitudes of soldiers. The objective of one analytical approach was to sort the results of individual questionnaires into groups having common attitudes toward life in the Army. Four major groups of individuals with common attitudes toward Army life appeared to attract persons with the following characteristics:

> 1. The group which has an orientation to security consists of older, married men with a better than average education and a somewhat higher level of reenlistment.
> 2. The group which has an orientation to travel has younger, single men with a moderately better level of education and reenlistment.
> 3. The group which has an orientation to patriotism is composed of young, single draftees primarily Caucasian with a significantly better education.
> 4. The group which has an orientation to status has older, married blacks who enlisted in the Army in the first place and who have reenlisted. This group has significantly better than average public school education.[7]

The results of the Behavior Systems, Inc. survey were further analyzed by the advertising firm of N. W. Ayer and Son, Inc. Philadelphia, Pennsylvania. Advertising guidelines were prepared for Headquarters, Department of the Army, and other ideas obtained from the study were presented as subjects needing further investigation. Two such subjects were as follows:

[5] William H. Meckling, Executive Director, *The President's Commission on an All-Volunteer Armed Force* (Washington, D.C.: U.S. Government, February 1970), p. iii.

[6] William L. Hauser, "Professionalism and the Junior Officer Drain," *Army,* (September 1970): 16–22.

[7] U.S. Department of the Army, "Reenlistment Study: An Attitudinal Survey," a summary of data prepared by Behavior Systems, Inc., March 1970, p. 30.

1. All men, even reenlistees, have a low opinion of Army life and careers. Dramatic programs are needed to improve this situation and build enthusiasm, pride, professionalism. A disturbing aspect of this is that attitudes toward an All-Volunteer Army were no different (i.e., no more positive) among career oriented men than noncareer men.

2. Indications are that counselors seldom address themselves to the personal objections or problems surrounding reenlistment, but are likely to go by the book in pointing out benefits .... A program should be developed to get counselors more involved in men's personal considerations.[8]

Major J. C. Miller, as a member of the U.S. Air Force, conducted an excellent officer motivation study in 1966. It is titled *A Study in Officer Motivation (New View)*. This study investigated the problem of retention and effective use of young Air Force officers. It evaluated officer motivation by determining the factors which these officers considered important in their decision to remain in the Air Force for a life's career. Miller's conclusions fell into three broad categories: (1) the young Air Force officer, (2) the importance of attitudes to these individuals and the Air Force, and (3) what determined the attitudes of these young officers.

With regard to the young Air Force officer, Miller concluded the following:

1. .... He is well educated with a high potential for growth. His greater education has made him more consciously aware of his psychological growth needs. He looks beyond just monetary and material benefits for satisfaction in job and career. Appeals to his lower order or avoidance needs only, are ineffective in satisfying his growth needs.

2. Young officers will endure hardships in their current jobs if they perceive an opportunity for progressing into higher level jobs in the future or for changing career fields.

3. The Air Force is not selectively retaining the better officer but is losing as many officers of high ability as of low ability.

4. The concepts of career and profession, as disseminated in recruiting and motivation literature, must be revised to conform to the perceptions of the young officers at whom such communications are directed ....[9]

Miller reported the following pertaining to the importance of attitudes to these individuals and the Air Force:

1. The attitudes of young officers are important and have a significant impact on the Air Force in terms of productivity, personal adjustment, and career intent. Satisfaction in job and career lead to increasing productivity, better personal adjustment, and favorable career intent. Conversely, dissatisfaction in job and career causes decreased productivity, deters personal adjustment, and produces unfavorable career intentions.

2. Different factors lead to attitudes of job and career satisfaction and dissatisfac-

[8] U.S. Department of the Army, "Advertising Guidelines From Reenlistment Research," a study prepared by N. W. Ayer & Son, Inc., March 1970, p. 7.

[9] J. C. Miller, *A Study in Officer Motivation (New View)* (Washington, D.C.: U.S. Air Force Studies and Analysis, November 1966), 2: 140.

tion in the Air Force.[10]

In relating the determinants of the attitudes of these young officers, Miller integrated his recommendations with these determinants.

1. To improve the retention and productivity of junior officers, the Air Force must provide them with the major factors which lead to job and career satisfaction and minimize or eliminate the major factors leading to job and career dissatisfaction . . . .

2. Career intentions of junior officers are related to the motivational content of their jobs. Air Force jobs vary widely in motivational content . . . .

3. Concurrent attention to both motivators and dissatisfiers is essential if the Air Force is to utilize more fully the potential of its junior officers.

4. Competent, motivated and sincere officers are needed to attract, supervise and counsel the new officers . . . . Classes in motivation using the New View approach . . . may also help in the supervisory area.

5. . . . . Specific conditions within each command which result in negative attitudes must be further determined in depth if effective corrective measures are to be applied.[11]

THEORETICAL FRAMEWORK

After considering the results of similar studies, the following theoretical framework pertains to a comparison of 358 men who decided to remain in the Army with 919 men who decided to depart. All of these men graduated from Engineer Officer Candidate School during 1967. They possessed the qualities needed for entrance to Officer Candidate School and those qualities needed to graduate. After these men spent three years on active duty as an officer, they were asked to indicate, during 1970, whether or not they desired to remain in the Army or to return to civilian life. All of the men were surveyed several months after they entered into a new term of service or departed from the Army.

Empirical observations suggest that there is a significant difference in the beliefs between a group of junior officers who decided to remain in the Army and a comparable group who decided to depart. It appears that those individuals who remained have strong, favorable opinions towards the Army. Their current roles in the organization tend to be commensurate with those that are expected of successful junior officers. They appear to be forceful in their actions, dependable in accomplishing their roles within the organization, and readily exhibit an overall behavior that is favorable towards the organization. These individuals tend to be motivated by their recent achievements as platoon leaders and company commanders.

Those individuals that elected to depart from the Army are less enthusiastic about their former organization. They tend to be less forceful in their actions and seem to spend more time in reaching more innovative decisions. They are dependable in accomplishing the requirements of their new roles, but when appropriate, are less absolute in this dependability. These individuals seem to be motivated by the hopes of achieving future accomplishments.

[10] *Ibid.*, p. 141.
[11] *Ibid.*, pp. 141–147.

178

METHOD

BACKGROUND

During 1966, research was conducted pertaining to hundreds of students attending Engineer Officer Candidate School at Fort Belvoir, Virginia.[12] Research conducted from 1967 to 1970 in connection with a doctoral dissertation (as presented in Chapter 4) further developed the original study. While both studies were concerned with the effect of training, the later study also focused on several questions related to retention. Concurrent with completing the test instrument [13] during 1970, individuals completed a biographical data questionnaire which provided information concerning their major goals in life and, if applicable, their major reasons for departing from the Army.

TEST INSTRUMENT

The test instrument, as indicated earlier, is the Job Analysis and Interest Measurement (JAIM). This instrument is a rather comprehensive questionnaire that has been used since 1957 in studies of over 50 occupational groups. The 125 multiple-choice items within the instrument provide measures for 32 scales relating to certain self-reported beliefs. It is recognized that the instrument does not measure aptitudes, training, or knowledge. According to the author of the instrument:

> Research with the JAIM has shown that certain self-reported beliefs are associated with the occupation a person chooses, his satisfaction with the occupation, and the quality of his work performance.[14]

PREDICTION

After considering the results of similar studies, and after observing the individuals relative to this study, it was predicted that the 358 men who elected to remain in the Army would differ significantly in their self-reported beliefs from the 919 men who elected to depart as shown in Table 22.

RESULTS

DIFFERENCE IN CERTAIN SELF-REPORTED BELIEFS

The self-reported beliefs held by the two groups are significantly different in 18 out of 32 scales. This data is presented in Table 22. The prediction is confirmed. Zero is the norm for Table 22 (pertaining only to the standard scores).

[12] Peter B. Petersen, and Gordon L. Lippitt, "Comparison of Behavioral Styles Between Entering and Graduating Students in Officer Candidate School," *Journal of Applied Psychology* 52, no. 1, pt. 1, (February 1968): 66–70.

[13] The Job Analysis and Interest Measurement (JAIM) is described in Chapter 1 and in Appendix A. Appreciation is expressed to Professor Regis H. Walther, author of the test instrument, for his guidance in the analysis of data.

[14] Regis H. Walther, *The Psychological Dimensions of Work: A Research Approach Through Use of a Self-Report Inventory* (Washington, D.C.: George Washington Univ., 1972).

TABLE 22

COMPARISON OF CERTAIN SELF-REPORTED BELIEFS BETWEEN A GROUP
OF 358 MEN WHO REMAINED IN THE ARMY AND A GROUP
OF 919 MEN WHO DEPARTED

Scales	Standard Scores for Those Who Remain[a]	Standard Scores for Those Who Depart	t-test Results[b]
Extent of Optimism	−2	−6	.73
Degree of Self-Confidence	20	33	−2.24*
Belief in Moral Absolutes	20	−10	5.05**
Belief in Slow Change	19	−1	3.34***
Prefers Problem Analysis	18	41	−4.33***
Prefers Social Interaction	14	−14	5.02***
Prefers Mechanical Activities	87	85	0.21
Prefers Supervisory Activities	85	69	2.72**
Prefers Activity Frequent Change	58	42	2.67**
Values Status Attainment	29	47	−2.39*
Values Social Service	−66	−66	0.14
Values Approval from Others	−90	−76	−2.74**
Values Intellectual Achievement	−14	22	−5.76***
Values Role Conformity	67	28	5.98***
Degree of Perseverance	32	31	.04
Extent of Orderliness	46	35	1.90
Prefers to Plan Ahead	−12	−3	−1.37
Influences by Persuasive Leadership	52	38	2.42*
Influences by Being Self-Assertive	114	100	2.33*
Move Toward Aggressor	−64	−59	−0.85
Move Away from Aggressor	−60	−34	−4.60***
Move Against Aggressor	69	53	2.40*
Prefers Routine	−4	−9	0.90
Identifies with Authority	−29	−33	0.83
Prefers Independence	20	25	−0.86
Prefers Directive Leadership Style	88	67	2.98**
Prefers Participative Leadership Style	−63	−54	−1.40
Prefers Delegative Leadership Style	−20	−12	−1.43
Motivates by Knowledge of Results	−7	−7	0.02
Believes in External Controls	86	81	0.89
Prefers Being Systematic, Methodical	19	37	−3.01**
Prefers Group Participation	−9	−32	4.16***

[a] Average of norm group has been equated to zero and the standard deviation 100.

[b] A positive t-value indicates that those who remain in Army are higher in this particular self-reported belief while a negative t-value indicates that those who remain in Army are lower as pertains to this particular self-reported belief.

* p < .05
** p < .01
*** p < .001

180

This was determined by setting zero in place of the average scores representing over 50 occupational groups. Theoretically, no particular occupational group exactly fits the norm. The purpose of this norm is to establish a "bench mark" so that the scores different groups of people receive will have relative meaning. It should be recognized that major differences in response may be essential for top performance in different fields. Therefore, a general assumption that "lowest" indicates "worst" should not be made.

The self-reported beliefs of these two groups differ as follows:

1. *Degree of Self-Confidence* This scale measures the degree to which the individual believes that he can, by his own action, influence future events. The group who departed from the Army placed a significantly higher value in this scale. As a group, they reported that they often become enthusiastic over new things or new plans, and that their ideas are often considered unusual and imaginative.

2. *Belief in Moral Absolutes* This scale measures the degree to which the individual believes in moral absolutes. As a group, the men who remained in the Army placed a significantly higher value in moral absolutes. (See Chart 11.) They tended to place considerable emphasis in the belief that moral principles come from an outside power higher than man; and that it is most important to have faith in something. Conversely, those who departed from the Army tended to consider that moral principles are not absolute and unchanging but depend on circumstances.

3. *Belief in Slow Change* This scale measures the degree to which the individual believes that change should be slow. The group who remained in the Army scored exceptionally higher than the group who departed. Those who remained tended to agree that it is usually best to do things in a conventional way; and that when things are going smoothly, it is best not to make changes which will disrupt things.

4. *Influences by Persuasive Leadership* This scale measures the degree to which the individual exerts leadership in interpersonal situations. Those who remained in the Army placed a higher value in this scale. They indicated that they have no difficulty expressing their opinions before a large group; that they often take the leadership within a group; and that what they like best in a job is the opportunity to get results through persuasion or negotiation.

5. *Influences by Being Self-Assertive* The degree to which the individual tends to pursue his own goals when they are in competition with the goals of others is measured by this scale. The group that remained scored higher on this scale and indicated that it is important to avoid being diverted from doing what is right in order to please someone; that they do better under competition or stress; and that they are proficient in athletic games.

6. *Move Away from Aggressor* This scale measures the degree to which the individual withdraws when someone acts toward him in a belligerent or aggressive manner. The group of men who departed from the Army placed a significantly higher value in this scale. They tended to consider that when a

CHART II

COMPARISON OF 358 MEN WHO REMAINED IN ARMY WITH 919 MEN WHO DEPARTED: Extent of Their Belief in Moral Absolutes *

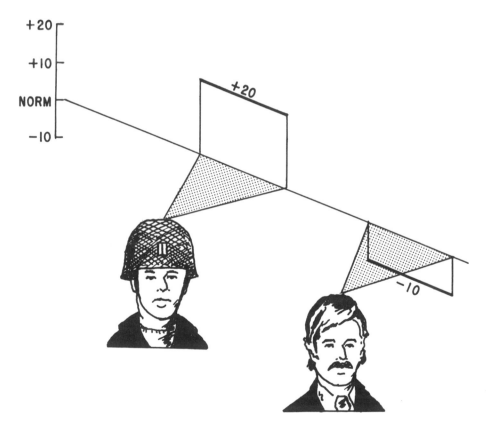

*Persons scoring high believe that moral principles come from an outside power higher than man; and that it is most important to have faith in something. Individuals scoring low believe that moral principles are not absolute and unchanging but depend upon circumstances.

person acts toward them in a dictatorial or domineering fashion, they keep away from him if they can.

7. *Move Against Aggressor* This scale measures the degree to which the individual counterattacks when someone acts toward him in a belligerent or aggressive manner. The group of men who remained in the Army placed a significantly higher value in this scale. They tended to consider that when someone crowds ahead of them in line, they do something about it; and if someone acts toward them in a dictatorial or domineering fashion they seek an occasion to have it out with him.

8. *Prefers Directive Leadership Style* This scale measures the degree to which the individual believes that a leader gets the best results by making decisions himself. The group of men who remained in the Army placed a higher value in directive leadership. They indicated rather strongly that an effective leader assigns each subordinate a specific job to do and sees that he does it the way it is supposed to be done.

9. *Prefers Being Systematic, Methodical* This scale measures the degree to which the individual uses systematic, methodical methods for processing information and reaching decisions. The group of men who departed from the Army scored significantly higher than the group of men who remained. Those who departed tended to believe that when they have a difficult decision to make and feel that they have enough facts that it is best to spend considerable time reviewing all possible interpretations of the facts before making a decision. In addition, they prefer the opportunity for careful consideration of all aspects of the problem and when they have an important problem to consider, they prefer to think it through alone.

10. *Prefers Problem Analysis* The degree to which the individual likes to analyze situations and develop ingenious solutions to problems is measured by this scale. Men who departed from the Army scored significantly higher on this scale. (See Chart 12.) This group of men prefers to be considered ingenious; likes to develop new ideas and approaches to problems and situations; and likes a job which permits them to be creative and original.

11. *Prefers Social Interaction* This scale measures the degree to which the individual likes work involving interactions with people. The group of men who remained scored exceptionally higher and related that they enjoy attending parties or social gatherings once a week or oftener; do not like to work apart from other people; and frequently entertain groups at home. (See Chart 13.)

12. *Prefers Supervisory Activities* The degree to which the individual likes to plan and supervise the work of other people is measured by this scale. Those who remained scored significantly higher than those who departed. The group of individuals who remained indicated that they get along best when they know what they want and work for it; that they are generally striving to reach some goal they have established for themselves and that they like to supervise others in carrying out difficult assignments.

13. *Prefers Activity Frequent Change* This scale measures the degree to which the individual likes to be actively engaged in work providing a lot of

CHART 12

COMPARISON OF 358 MEN WHO REMAINED IN ARMY WITH 919 MEN WHO
DEPARTED: Preference for Problem Analysis *

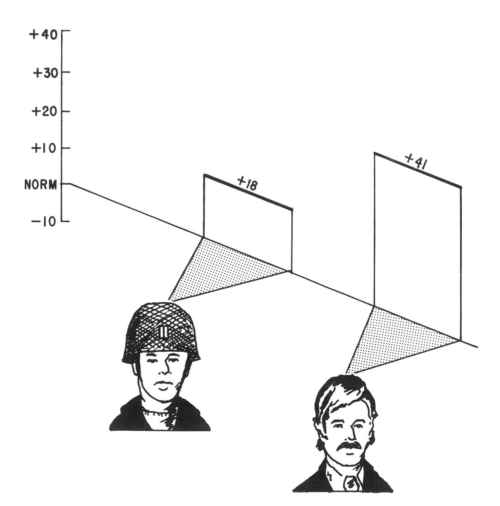

*This scale measures the degree to which the individual likes to analyze situations and
develop ingenious solutions to problems. Persons scoring high prefer to be considered
ingenious; like to develop new ideas and approaches to problems and situations; and like a
job which permits them to be creative and original.

CHART 13

COMPARISON OF 358 MEN WHO REMAINED IN ARMY WITH 919 MEN WHO DEPARTED: Preference for Social Interaction *

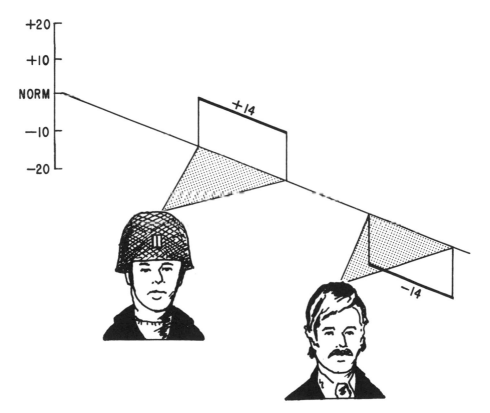

* This scale measures the degree to which the individual likes work involving interactions with people. Persons scoring high attend parties or social gatherings once a week or oftener; do not like to work apart from other people; and frequently entertain groups at home.

CHART 14

COMPARISON OF 358 MEN WHO REMAINED IN ARMY WITH 919 MEN WHO DEPARTED: Preference for Group Participation *

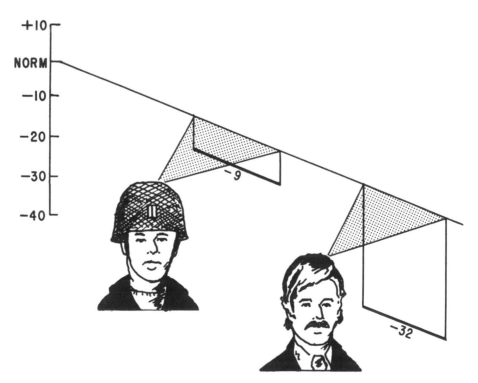

*This scale measures the degree to which the individual identifies himself with a highly valued group. Persons scoring high say they like best to work as a member of a group and do not like to work apart from other people.

excitement and a great deal of variety. The group of individuals who remained scored significantly higher on this scale. As a group, they indicated that they frequently enjoy taking part in a fight for good causes; sometimes enjoy dangerous situations; work best under a great deal of pressure and tight deadlines; and prefer a job in which there is a great deal of activity and opportunity to make frequent decisions. Conversely, the group of individuals who departed indicated that they tend to prefer finishing one task before they start another.

14. *Prefers Group Participation*   This scale measures the degree to which the individual likes to work as a member of a group. The group who remained scored significantly higher on this scale. (See Chart 14.) In addition, this group indicated that they have a strong preference for identifying themselves with a highly valued group.

15. *Values Status Attainment*   The degree to which the individual values himself by his achievement of the status symbols established by his culture is measured by this scale. The group of men who departed from the Army placed a significantly higher value in this scale. As a group, they prefer to be considered ambitious and successful; like to have a job which is recognized to be important or desirable; and think that the ideal job is one which shows they were a success and had achieved high status and prestige.

16. *Values Approval from Others*   This scale measures the degree to which the individual values himself by obtaining the approval of others. The group who departed from the Army placed a significantly higher value on this scale. As a group, they considered it most important to have congenial coworkers; to be well-liked; like to please others through their work; and like to be considered gracious, attractive, and pleasant.

17. *Values Intellectual Achievement*   The degree to which the individual values himself through his intellectual achievements is measured by this scale. Compared with those individuals who remained, those individuals who departed from the Army scored significantly higher concerning this scale. (See Chart 15.) The group of men who departed tend to like work which permits them to be creative and original; like to be considered ingenious, imaginative, intelligent, and brilliant; and believe that it is important to be intelligent and resourceful as opposed to having faith in something or being kind and considerate.

18. *Values Role Conformity*   This scale measures the degree to which the individual values himself according to how successfully he has conformed to the role requirements of society. The results were significantly higher for the group that remained in the Army. (See Chart 16.) In addition, they placed a high value in being considered reliable, dependable, trustworthy, and industrious.

REASON FOR DEPARTURE

The question in the biographical data questionnaire which asked, "What do you consider to be the *one major reason* why you departed?" was posed

187

CHART 15

COMPARISON OF 358 MEN WHO REMAINED IN ARMY WITH 919 MEN WHO DEPARTED: Extent of Their Value of Intellectual Achievement *

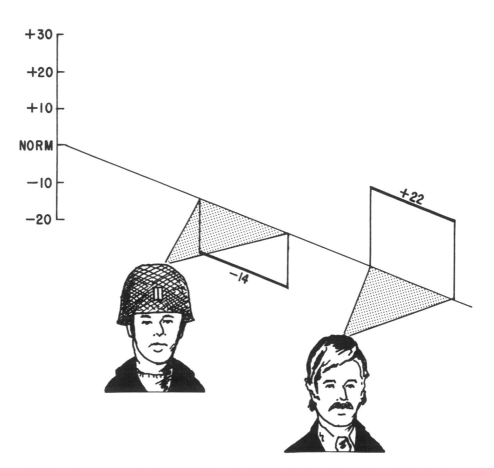

* This scale measures the degree to which the individual values himself through his intellectual achievements. Persons scoring high like work which permits them to be creative and original; like to be considered ingenious, imaginative, intelligent, and brilliant; and believe that it is important to be intelligent and resourceful as opposed to having faith in something, or being kind and considerate.

CHART 16

COMPARISON OF 358 MEN WHO REMAINED IN ARMY WITH 919 MEN WHO DEPARTED: Extent of Their Value for Role Conformity *

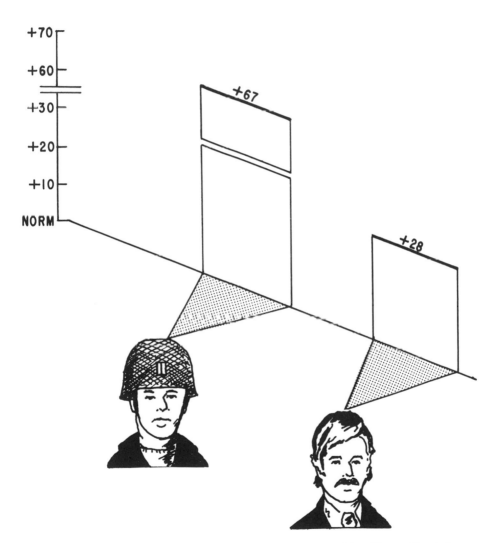

* This scale measures the degree to which the individual values himself according to how successfully he has conformed to the role requirements of society. Persons scoring high say that they prefer to be considered reliable, dependable, trustworthy, and industrious.

concurrent with other questions to the individuals who departed from the Army. The answers to this question are presented in Tables 23 and 24. Of the 919 individuals who departed from the Army, 299 elected to answer the question in narrative form.[15] A summary of these answers is presented in Table 24. An analysis of the findings reflected in Tables 23 and 24 indicates that the majority of those individuals who considered remaining changed their decision concerning an Army career and departed when their potential for a successful Army career seemed to diminish in their own opinion. This emphasizes the need for helping individuals achieve success in an Army career. By sincerely helping the young officer achieve success in his career, the Army will increase the current low rates of retention. Other reasons for departing indicated in Tables 23 and 24 also should be considered.

MAJOR GOAL IN LIFE

The majority of the 1,277 individuals sampled indicated that their major goal in life is to be successful in their career. While some of the goals tend to be abstract and idealistic, the majority are strongly linked with achieving success in a career. Table 25 reflects the answers to the question "What do you consider to be your major goal in life?" Of the 1,277 individuals who answered this question, 323 elected to answer in narrative form. Table 26 presents a summary of these answers.

DISCUSSION

IMPLICATIONS OF FINDINGS FOR IMPROVING RETENTION

There seems to be a common thread pertaining to retention that is found by examining: (a) the differences in self-reported beliefs between the group of men who remained in the Army and the group of men who departed, and (b) the reasons why the one group departed. The common thread is that the beliefs of these two significantly different groups were compatible with their career decisions. The group of men who remained in the Army is better qualified to cope with the current requirements of the organization. However, it should be considered that as these individuals change as they advance in grade, age, and responsibility for their own family, the requirements of the organization will also change. Also to be considered is the magnitude of change in the nature of interpersonal relations during the next decade. The question then becomes, which group is better suited during the 1970's and early 1980's for a life's career as an Army officer? Many of the individuals in the group that departed exhibited beliefs that would appear to be most appropriate for a career Army officer ten or fifteen years from now. Conversely, those who are in the group remaining in the Army seem to match quite closely the current requirements of the organization. The implication is that the organization, by changing some of

---

[15] I am grateful to Miss Carol McKenna for her assistance in sorting hundreds of narrative responses to questions asked in the biographical data questionnaire.

190

TABLE 23
MAJOR REASON FOR DEPARTING ARMY

24.7%: Not applicable (currently a member of U.S. Army).

25.0%: I did not intend to remain on active duty beyond that time required to fulfill my obligation.

17.5%: Disappointed with Army duty and my potential in the Army compared with civilian opportunities.

4.2%: The probability of repeated tours of duty in Vietnam.

5.2%: The desires of my wife and the welfare of our family.

23.4%: A reason that does not fit into any of the above categories. (These individuals elected to answer in narrative form. A summary of their narrative answers is presented in Table 24.)

TABLE 24
SUMMARY OF 299 NARRATIVE ANSWERS PERTAINING
TO MAJOR REASON FOR DEPARTING ARMY

In selecting a response to the question "What do you consider to be the one major reason why you departed?" 299 individuals considered that their major reason was not applicable to any of the first five categories presented in Table 23. They further elected to answer this question in narrative form. The following is a summary of these narrative answers:

REASONS RELATED TO EDUCATION

1.   12.9% indicated that they departed from the Army so that they could complete their education. Some individuals further indicated that additional education would prepare them for civilian careers that would offer better advancement opportunities than the Army.

2.   6.3% departed because they felt that their military potential was limited because they did not complete college. Many stated that their request for a civil schooling assignment was disapproved.

3.   5.0% indicated that they would consider rejoining the Army after completing college as a civilian.

REASONS CONCERNING PERSONNEL MANAGEMENT

4.   3.0% departed because they received an assignment with little bear-

TABLE 24 (Continued)

ing on personal interests or individual capabilities. A response by Robert B. is typical of several answers in this category. "Unable to pick my own type of assignment. Wanted to stay in Engineering but was told I must also have experience in command, staff, administration."

5. 2.4% departed because of what they considered to be unfair procedures concerning efficiency reports and promotions. The response of Daniel E. is typical. "I departed active duty because I felt that the Army was arbitrary to excess and therefore unfair in granting assignments; and the rating system, so important to one's success was totally unrealistic since it could in no way allow for personality conflicts which may develop and gives one person the "power of God" over another should he choose to use it in that way."

6. 2.4% indicated that constant relocation because of changing assignments was their major reason for departing the Army.

7. 1.1% stated that the major reason they departed was that an assignment they requested was disapproved.

REASONS RELATED TO LEADERSHIP

8. 8.2% indicated that their major reason for departing from the Army was the Army's lack of professionalism, wasteful procedures, "Mickey Mouse," and a lack of integrity.

9. 6.3% considered that their main reason for departing was that the Army stifled the individual and that they had no freedom. A response by Vernon A. is typical of the answers that are in this category. "The Army is a political body which restricts the individual and group from realizing their potential." The response of Richard K. is also typical of answers in this category. "Enjoyed responsibilities, job, working with people and career opportunity, however, did not enjoy 'army life'—i.e., living under orders from superiors 24 hours a day, regarding attendance at social activities and chain of command among wives (which is absolutely ridiculous)."

10. 7.0% indicated that their major reason for departure was because superiors had more concern for rank and title than their responsibilities. The response from Stephen L. is typical of the answers in this category. "I have had assignments from company level to engineer group headquarters and have found that the majority (75%) of the officers I dealt with did not honor the high ideals of the officer corps as was taught in OCS. I left active duty because I could not stand working with narrow-minded, self-centered, hypocritical officers who worried more about their own career than they did about their men's welfare or the job at hand."

11. 6.3% indicated that their major reason for departing from the Army

TABLE 24 (Continued)

was because of the incompetence of both officers and NCO's. Thomas H. furnished the following response which is typical of answers found in this category. "I left the military because I observed a substantial number of incompetents both officer and NCO serving in areas I served in."

12.   3.0% departed because of a personality conflict with their superior or because they received a low efficiency report.

13.   2.1% departed because of their sense of uselessness or because they could not fight the system. The response by Ivan L. is typical of the answers in this category. "I disliked the narrow-mindedness and the 'Army way is the only way' attitude."

14   0.6% departed because an Army career did not present a challenge.

CONFLICT OF GOALS

15.   3.0% departed because of their disagreement with the Vietnam War. The response by Jack P. is typical of the answers in this category. "My reason for departing from the service was that I disagreed totally with our Vietnam policy. Originally I thought that the answer to the Vietnam War would be found in a total military effort. The more I read on the subject, the more I became resolved to the idea that war is not the answer at all. I would not classify myself as a pacifist, but I am completely against the war in Vietnam. I want to serve my country, but I want to serve it in a peaceful way. I could not achieve this in the Army, therefore, when my obligation was fulfilled, I terminated my service."

16.   3.0% indicated that the Army ethic was in conflict with their personal code. For example: war vs. nonviolence.

LOW PAY

17.   1.1% departed because of low pay and limited advancement.

OTHER REASONS

18.   6.3% stated that their major reason for departing from the Army was that they thought that they would have more opportunities as a civilian.

19.   3.0% departed because of family responsibilities.

20.   2.1% departed from the Army because of the demands of their pre-Army careers (i.e., a family business).

21.   3.0% departed because of a medical disability.

22.   0.9% indicated that the major reason they departed from the Army

TABLE 24 (Continued)

was that they didn't want to get killed in Vietnam. A narrative response by Stephen D. tends to fall in this category. "I enjoyed the assignment to Vietnam because I had definite constructive and worthwhile goals. Only my chances of being killed kept me from extending my tour of duty."

23.   1.1% of those who departed indicated that their major reason for departing was that they would prefer to be a member of the U.S. Army Reserve.

24.   0.6% of those who departed stated that they are returning and in fact intended to eventually return when they initially departed.

25.   0.3% stated that they departed for no major reason.

26.   0.6% departed because they lacked career security and had a fear of a reduction in force.

27.   0.3% departed because the Army did not retain them.

28.   8.1% stated that they departed for a combination of several major reasons. A response by Ferdinand M. included a typical combination of reasons found in this category. "(a) A desire to complete university training through a civilian role. (b) Incompatibility of a military career with respect to a relationship with the type of women that generally interest me. (c) Incompatibility of my personal philosophy, moral standards, code if you will and that of the Army. (d) Widespread incompetency among the senior NCO and officer ranks (this is not intended to be a gross generalization bringing discredit to the service overall). (e) Repression."

TABLE 25

MAJOR GOAL IN LIFE FOR 1,277 MEN

5.6%:   The fulfillment of religious objectives.

3.1%:   To serve my country.

10.7%:   To be a good parent.

52.1%:   To be successful in my career.

3.2%:   To become very wealthy.

25.3%:   A reason that does not fit into any of the above categories. (These individuals elected to answer in narrative form. Their narrative answers are summarized in Table 26.)

2nd Lieutenant Edward Ridgley, Commanding Officer, Company C, 3rd Battalion, 47th Infantry, 9th Infantry Division calling in an air strike and artillery fire on Viet Cong who have his company "pinned down" following an ambush. This took place approximately a mile and a half west of the village of Ban Tra, on the banks of the Quan Tion River. (U.S. Army photo)

A company commander of a rifle company solves more leadership problems in several months of combat than many civilian executives are confronted with in a lifetime.

A major reason why many company grade officers, similar to Lieutenant Ridgley, depart from the Army is that they consider that their potential for a successful Army career is diminishing. It seems ironic that many of their self-perceived mistakes in performance or in the assignments they receive are not actually relevant. It appears that considerable progress could be made by dispelling many of their imagined career management problems.

TABLE 26

In selecting a response to the question "What do you consider to be your major goal in life" 323 individuals considered that their major goal was not included in any of the first five categories presented in Table 25. They further elected to answer this question in narrative form. The following is a summary of these narrative answers:

1.   18%:   *Family and Career Success*   The following are two typical answers.

George B.: "To be reasonably and realistically satisfied with a chosen profession, perform satisfactorily in that profession, and to have a stable and rewarding family life."

Larry E. indicated that his major goal was, "To become a good husband, father and a good provider; which would necessitate being successful at whatever career I decide."

2.   8%:   *Family, Marriage and Community*   Two   typical   answers are:

Ronald D.: "To be happy with a family, making enough money and having time to enjoy life."

Thomas C.: "To insure that my wife and myself live life to the fullest to include the rearing of children that will be an asset to the world."

3.   14%:   *Happiness and Contentment*   The following are two answers typical of this category.

Ronnie P.: "To be able to say, when I'm ready to die, that I have had a happy life."

Larry L.: "To find contentment through spiritual development and material wealth."

4.   14%:   *Social Contribution*

Ronald J. indicated that his major goal in life was "to make a meaningful contribution to society (particularly in the field of education)."

The goal of Boyce K. was "to contribute in a positive way to human happiness and joy in this world. I have chosen a career in medicine as a means to this end."

Kendrick T. stated his goal as "I want to feel that by my efforts I

TABLE 26 (Continued)

leave the world, or society, a better place (in my opinion) than it was and is."

5. 6%: *Live a Fulfilling Life*   The following are two typical answers.

Dale J.: "My goal is to be a creative, enlightened and tolerant person and I will attempt to live life to its fullest."

William W.: "To live a fulfilling life."

6. 4%: *Personal Satisfaction*

Francis B.: "My major goal combines those listed in (a) through (e) yet includes much more. That is, to be satisfied with myself as an individual who has accomplished all that is possible and probable for one human to do for himself and others. Total self-satisfaction."

Randel K. indicated that, "My major goal is to do the *best* I can in all situations; country, parent, and career. I must satisfy myself that I tried as hard as I could."

7. 4%: *Self-Realization*

Donald D.: "To be myself—which sounds like the normal thoughtless talk one hears around a college, but I have put thought into answering the question. I wish to work long hard hours until a goal is reached, then relax for a week or so until I'm ready to do it again. I wish to make enough money to live comfortably on, but the enjoyability of the work is more important than the salary."

8 3%: *Peace and Harmony*   The following two answers are typical of the answers in this category.

Gerald Y.: "To in the end look back over my life and be able to say that I have done my best not only for my country, but also my God. In short, to find peace in life."

Robert C. stated that his major goal was "Finding inner peace so that I might more effectively aid my brother. The 'beast' is in us all, the reason for being on earth probably nonexistent, and the time is short."

9. 2%: *In Search of a Goal*

An answer by Francis F. is typical. "At the moment I am interested in trying to understand life. The frustration of the Vietnam situation (in other words, a war with no real solution) was one of the latest experiences which has alienated me from the normal social process of

TABLE 26 (Continued)

career pursuit. I view my present attitudes as a temporary search."

10.   3%:   *Freedom and Independence*

James P. indicated the following: "I'm searching for a way of life that will have variety and freedom! I thought that the life style I'm looking for may be practical in another country outside the U.S.A.; so I decided to spend 2 or 3 years searching and sampling different ways of life. I've never been happy when I've worked, the routine has been depressing. The only time I've been 'happy' is when I've been travelling, looking and learning. I'm reluctant to surrender my freedom for the security and obvious economic benefits from regular employment."

11.   2%:   *Predetermined Purpose*   The following is a typical response.

"I feel that the living God, in whom I sincerely believe, has a definite plan for my life. My only goal is to fulfill that plan through a life of resourcefulness and hard work, using the talents given me."

12.   5%:   *Fulfillment of Personal Capacities*   These two responses are typical.

Philipp E.: "I intend to live, enjoy and be as productive in my profession as my talents will allow; to accept and deal with life as it is, not what I wish it would be."

Jean H. stated that his major goal in life was, "to use all my capabilities in the most effective manner in all situations. Also to continue the improvement of these capabilities as much as possible."

13.   2%:   *Pride in Accomplishment*

"My major goal in life is to be able to look back on my past and feel a sense of accomplishment, i.e., to feel that I had raised a family to the best of my ability, to feel that I have contributed something of value to at least one person and to feel that on passing I had done something to make this a better (city, county, state, country) to live in and the people in it, a better people."

14.   2%:   *Personal Interests*

An answer by Wolfgang M. was typical of this category. "Retire early and be able to pursue my own interests without having to worry about money."

15.   13%:   *Combination of Goals*

Clark V., like the others in this category, viewed his major goal in

TABLE 26 (Continued)

life as a combination of goals. "To serve the country that my children will live in. To improve this country through ecological balance, pollution control, resource recycling, and population control. To be a good parent and to attain for my family and myself a good education and income."

---

its current requirements now, will narrow the gap in differences between the group that departed and the group that remained. As a result, rates of retention will increase, and equally important, the organization will become more viable in the long run.

In an attempt to search for more detailed implications, this discussion will first focus on the self-reported beliefs that each group values highly, and on the results of a control group. Then this discussion will turn to an analysis of the specific reasons why the one group departed. The discussions will conclude by considering the major goals in life of both groups combined.

1. *Self-Reported Beliefs* People differ in the way they respond to various situations that occur in their lives. The nature of this response affects their effectiveness and the satisfaction they receive from the results of their performance in different situations. A sharp difference in self-reported beliefs is obvious in the following dichotomy.

  a. The group of 358 individuals who decided to remain in the Army placed a significantly higher value in the following:

    (1) To believe in moral absolutes.

    (2) To accomplish things in a conventional way, and when things are going smoothly, not to make changes which will cause a disruption.

    (3) To exert leadership in interpersonal situations and to get results through persuasion or negotiation.

    (4) To pursue their own goals when they are in competition with the goals of others.

    (5) To counterattack when someone acts towards them in a belligerent or aggressive manner.

    (6) To make decisions alone.

    (7) To interact with other people.

    (8) To plan and supervise the work of other people.

    (9) To be actively engaged in work providing a lot of excitement, and a great deal of variety.

    (10) To work as a member of a group and not apart from other people.

    (11) To conform to the role requirements of society.

  b. The group of 919 individuals who decided to depart from the Army placed a significantly higher value on the following:

    (1) To have self-confidence.

(2) To withdraw when someone acts toward them in a belligerent or aggressive manner.

(3) To use systematic methodical methods for processing information and reaching decisions.

(4) To analyze problems.

(5) To achieve the status symbols established by their culture.

(6) To obtain the approval of others.

(7) To attain intellectual achievement.

2. *Control* If there are significant differences between a group of individuals who remain in the Army and a group of individuals who depart from the Army, then it appears that these differences should also be apparent in a control group. Individuals tested in Vietnam (reported in Chapter 5) will be used as a control group. Their responses in Vietnam are segregated into two categories: (a) those who later remained in the Army, and (b) those who later departed from the Army. Differences as indicated in Table 27 are quite similar to those differences noted in Table 22. It can be concluded that these differences tend to be similar even though some of the biographical characteristics of the control group were unlike some of the biographical characteristics of the individuals who formerly attended Officer Candidate School. However, it should be noted that differences in self-reported beliefs, while tending to be similar in Tables 22 and 27, are not replicated in every case.

3. *Reasons for Departure* A major reason why many company grade officers depart from the Army is that they consider that their potential for a successful Army career is diminishing. It seems ironic that many of their self-perceived mistakes in performance or in the assignments they receive are not actually relevant. It appears that considerable progress could be made by dispelling many of their imagined career management problems. There is strong evidence to support the view that conditions that increase the actual and self-perceived potential of company grade officers will also tend to increase the retention of these individuals in the Army. Other major reasons why members of this group departed from the Army are as follows:

a. They did not intend to remain on active duty beyond that time required to fulfill their obligation.

b. They wanted to avoid repeated tours of duty in Vietnam.

c. They wanted to consider the desires of their wives and the welfare of their families.

d. They wanted to complete their education.

e. They were dissatisfied with current personnel management procedures.

f. They felt they had poor leadership.

g. They felt a conflict of their goals with the requirements of the organization.

4. *Major Goals in Life* While both groups were significantly different

TABLE 27

CONTROL: COMPARISON OF CERTAIN SELF-REPORTED BELIEFS BETWEEN
A GROUP OF 77 MEN WHO REMAINED IN THE ARMY
AND A GROUP OF 100 MEN WHO DEPARTED

Scales	t-test Results[a]
Extent of Optimism	1.77
Degree of Self-Confidence	4.54***
Belief in Moral Absolutes	1.25
Belief in Slow Change	1.43
Prefers Problem Analysis	1.14
Prefers Social Interaction	2.78**
Prefers Mechanical Activities	−0.94
Prefers Supervisory Activities	3.35***
Prefers Activity Frequent Change	2.12*
Values Status Attainment	−1.08
Values Social Service	.91
Values Approval from Others	−2.87**
Values Intellectual Achievement	1.04
Values Role Conformity	1.41
Degree of Perseverance	1.15
Extent of Orderliness	1.37
Prefers to Plan Ahead	1.72
Influences by Persuasive Leadership	3.45***
Influences by Being Self-Assertive	3.10**
Move Toward Aggressor	−3.01**
Move Away from Aggressor	2.22*
Move Against Aggressor	2.24*
Prefers Routine	1.28
Identifies with Authority	0.58
Prefers Independence	.63
Prefers Directive Leadership Style	4.18***
Prefers Participative Leadership Style	−1.99*
Prefers Delegative Leadership Style	−1.84
Motivates by Knowledge of Results	1.22
Believes in External Controls	2.03*
Prefers Systematic, Methodical	.04
Prefers Group Participation	1.05

[a] A positive t-value indicates that those who remain in Army are higher in this particular self-reported belief while a negative t-value indicates that those who remain in Army are lower as pertains to this particular self-reported belief.

    * p < .05
   ** p < .01
  *** p < .001

in many areas, it is noteworthy to find that their major goals in life were almost identical. A consolidation of goals for both groups reveals that the most often stated major goal in life is to be successful in their career. This tends to strengthen the above discussion concerning the importance of success in a career. Many other major goals in life that were stated tended to be idealistic and to reflect attitudes of their age group. Measures designed to increase retention should also consider these goals.

CLOSING REMARKS

While parts of this chapter tend to concentrate on isolating dissatisfaction, it is recognized that company grade officers expect to achieve more than the reduction of dissatisfaction. In many instances, they are reportedly seeking the satisfaction associated with the fulfillment of higher level needs such as accomplishing a job well or being in a position to apply their creative talents. The challenge of developing a leadership climate where lieutenants and captains can achieve satisfaction is applicable to those at field grade level, and can be extended to the general officer. The key in coping with many of the current problems in the Army may be found in leadership exercised at platoon and company level. It is here that the company grade officers can, in turn, create an environment where the individual soldier can develop many of his potentials and, hopefully, receive some satisfaction. Although considerable publicity has been given to extrinsic motivation, much needs to be accomplished in terms of intrinsic motivation where the individual is motivated not only because of external rewards but, also, because of the satisfaction that is derived by accomplishing the work itself.

Chapter 7

COMPARISON OF ARMY WAR COLLEGE STUDENTS WITH NORMS OF TEST INSTRUMENT AND OTHER GROUPS ASSOCIATED WITH THE ARMY

The U.S. Army War College is the Army's senior educational institution. The student body during the 1971–72 academic year consisted of 183 Army colonels and senior lieutenant colonels as well as 40 individuals having a comparable grade level from the Navy, Marine Corps, Air Force, Department of State, and other agencies of the Federal Government.

> The Senior Service College experience is designed to enhance the competence of selected officers with high general officer potential to assume key command and staff responsibilities at Department of the Army level and above.[1]

A considerable number of studies have been conducted to determine the characteristics of the American soldier. He has been scrutinized by sociologists, psychologists, nutritionists, anthropologists, and has been punched and prodded by investigators of almost every discipline imaginable to determine what makes him tick, and by so doing, to find ways and means to utilize his talents to the advantage of the Army and the soldier himself. However, there are very few studies that limit themselves exclusively to the beliefs of field grade Army officers.

In designing the research project described in this chapter, the principal motive was to prove that a study of the dimensions of 183 Army students attending the U.S. Army War College would provide an insight into the characteristics of individuals who will occupy the top leadership structure of the Army during the late 1970's and 1980's.

> During its 70-year history the Army War College has graduated some of the most illustrious military figures of the past century. Among the most distinguished alumni are Dwight D. Eisenhower, John J. Pershing, Omar N. Bradley, J. Lawton Collins,

[1] U.S. Department of the Army, *DA Circular No. 351–18: Senior Service College Selection System*, October 26, 1970.

George S. Patton and Alfred E. Gruenther.[2]

The following questions seemed relevant to such an undertaking:

1. What sort of a person is the Army officer who attends the U.S. Army War College?
2. How does he compare with other groups of Army personnel?
3. Do the findings contain any surprises?

Commander William H. Robinson[3] conducted a study of certain self-reported beliefs of students attending the U.S. Naval War College, Class of 1970. In comparing officers attending the Naval War College with a group of civilian executives, he concluded that the popular stereotype of the military officer, held by many critics of the military, is not justified. Instead of being venal, bumbling, and brutal, he was found to be optimistic, self-confident, and persuasive.

Early in the academic year 1972, a questionnaire similar to the one issued by Commander Robinson was administered to students attending the U.S. Army War College. Those tested completed the questionnaire on a voluntary basis with the understanding that the information obtained therefrom would be privileged. In view of this, responses have been averaged rather than identified with any individual.

METHOD

To answer these questions, the first action after the test was administered was to compare the test results obtained by the Army members of the U.S. Army War College class with the norms of the test. Then these individuals were compared with five other groups of personnel. Unlike the Naval War College study, this study was not concerned with the 40 individuals from other services and other governmental agencies. It was felt that the scores of the 183 Army students would be distorted by lumping them with the results obtained by the non-Army students attending the U.S. Army War College. These other individuals were considered as a group after the results of the Army students were analyzed.

THE TEST INSTRUMENT

The test used in this study was the Job Analysis and Interest Measurement (JAIM).[4] It is designed to measure self-reported beliefs.

RESULTS

The results obtained from the test administered to the U.S. Army War

[2] "U.S. Army War College," *U.S. Army War College Pamphlet,* January 1972.

[3] William H. Robinson, "An Element of International Affairs—The Military Mind," *Naval War College Review* (November 1970): 4–15.

[4] Appreciation is expressed to Professor Regis H. Walther, author of the JAIM, for his personal guidance concerning the analysis of data reported in this chapter.

College Class of 1972 indicate that Army members of the class differed significantly from the norms of the test, which are intended only as a point of reference. As an aid in analyzing the results of the many scales of the test, norms have been organized into four categories which pertain to an issue common to several scales. The first category "Basic Beliefs," for example, pertains to such scales as "Extent of Optimism" and "Degree of Self-Confidence." The results in terms of these four categories are listed below:

1. *Basic Beliefs* A person's basic beliefs often influence his response on the job. The nature of this response may considerably affect his performance and the satisfaction he receives from the result of his performance in different work situations.

While it is recognized that there are many basic beliefs, the following basic beliefs will be considered: (a) "Extent of Optimism," (b) "Degree of Self-Confidence," (c) "Belief in Moral Absolutes," and (d) "Belief in Slow Change."

Army members of the U.S. Army War College Class of 1972 scored significantly higher than the norms of the test instrument pertaining to the extent of their optimism, self-confidence, and belief in moral absolutes. In addition, they scored high in their belief that changes should be implemented slowly, rather than in a disruptive fashion.

The high degree of optimism and self-confidence evidenced by these Army students may be due in part to their good fortune in being selected to attend the U.S. Army War College. A less desirable assignment following graduation from the Army War College might reflect a lower score pertaining to these two scales. Army members of the U.S. Army War College Class of 1972 scored exceptionally high in their belief in moral absolutes. In this particular scale, persons who score high believe that moral principles come from an outside power higher than man, and that it is most important to have faith in something. Individuals who score low believe that moral principles are not absolute and unchanging but depend on circumstances. Their maturity and personal identification with the Department of the Army may be responsible for them placing a high value in the slow implementation of change.

2. *Activity Preferences* Individual preferences for various activities involve the anticipation of intrinsic satisfaction from the performance of certain tasks. U.S. Army War College students scored slightly higher than the norm in their preference for tasks that enable them to analyze problems and develop ingenious solutions. They also scored slightly higher than the norm pertaining to their preference for social activities involving interactions with people and they indicated an interest in working as a member of a group, rather than apart from others. They indicated strongly that they enjoyed mechanical activities and that they had an exceptionally strong preference for supervisory activities. They also expressed a strong preference for being actively engaged in work providing a lot of excitement and variety.

3. *Personal Values* Values are the criteria used by an individual when he judges his behavior.

Each of us has a set of standards or values about what is worthwhile and what is not, what we would like to be and what we would not. We use our standards to judge ourselves and our activities. These values are essential components of our self-concepts and are reflected in the meaning work has for us. Identical tasks performed in different contexts often differ dramatically in the degree to which they are valued. For example, to individuals who value helping others, clerical work in a hospital has quite a different meaning from clerical work in a real estate office. [5]

It is acknowledged that the values represented by the test are only a small portion of a person's total set of values. The following five values will be considered: "Values Status Attainment," "Values Social Service," "Values Approval from Others," "Values Intellectual Achievement," and "Values Role Conformity."

  a. *Values Status Attainment* This scale measures the extent to which the individual values himself by his achievement of the status symbols established by his culture. Scores for U.S. Army War College students were considerably higher than the norm. It should be noted that many of these individuals have already achieved many of the elements of status connected with their profession.

  b. *Values Social Service* The extent to which the individual values himself by contributing to social improvement is determined by this scale. It is to be expected that there would be a noticeable difference between Army students attending the U.S. Army War College and those individuals of a charitable nature, who are associated with a life's work of social service. Compared with the norm of the test instrument, Army students attending the U.S. Army War College placed a significantly lower value on the "Values Social Service" scale.

  c. *Values Approval from Others* This scale measures the degree to which the individual values the approval of others. The scores of Army students attending the U.S. Army War College pertaining to this scale differed by being significantly lower than the norm of the test instrument. In their process of arriving at a decision, it appears that mission accomplishment takes considerable priority over pleasing others.

  d. *Values Intellectual Achievement* The extent to which the individual values intellectual achievement is measured by this scale. Results indicated that a goal of intellectual achievement per se does not play a primary role within this group's set of values. However, it should be recognized that this group does exceptionally well in academic situations.

  e. *Values Role Conformity* This scale measures the degree to which the individual values conforming to the role requirements of society. Army students scored substantially higher on this scale. They preferred to be considered reliable, dependable, trustworthy, and industrious.

---

[5] Regis H. Walther, *The Psychological Dimensions of Work: A Research Approach Through Use of a Self-Report Inventory* (Washington, D.C.: George Washington Univ., 1972), p. 4.

4. *Behavioral Styles*

Individuals necessarily develop standard ways for dealing with recurring situations and reserve conscious information processing and decisionmaking for more significant occasions. This organization gives rise to characteristic types of performance or behavioral styles, conscious and unconscious, in various life situations.[6]

The following behavioral styles are considered pertinent to this study: (a) "Degree of Perseverance," (b) "Extent of Orderliness," (c) "Prefers to Plan Ahead," (d) "Influences by Persuasive Leadership," (e) "Influences by Being Self-Assertive," (f) "Move Toward Aggressor," (g) "Move Away from Aggressor," (h) "Move Against Aggressor," (i) "Prefers Routine," (j) "Identifies with Authority," (k) "Prefers Independence," (l) "Prefers Directive Leadership Style," (m) "Prefers Participative Leadership Style," (n) "Prefers Delegative Leadership Style," (o) "Motivates by Knowledge of Results," (p) "Believes in External Controls," (q) "Prefers Being Systematic, Methodical," and (r) "Prefers Group Participation."

a. *Degree of Perseverance* The degree to which the individual keeps at something, even when he is not particularly interested in it, is measured by this scale. Army members of the U.S. Army War College class scored significantly higher than the norm for this scale. Persons scoring high say that when working on a hobby, they concentrate for long periods of time and complete each project they start; that they do not tire easily and can work long and steadily; and that other people seldom find something after they have tried and given up. Individuals scoring low say that when they have something to do that doesn't interest them, they either do it after considerable pressure is put on them or they seldom get around to doing it.

b. *Extent of Orderliness* This scale measures the degree to which the individual has internal standards which he follows. Army students at the U.S. Army War College scored exceptionally high on this scale. They indicated that they like work which requires them to be extremely accurate and that they are usually very orderly.

c. *Prefers to Plan Ahead* This scale measures the degree to which the individual is a self-starter and directs his own activity toward goal achievement. Army students attending the U.S. Army War College did not score significantly different than the norm of the test instrument concerning the scale "Prefers to Plan Ahead." The actual result was a slight decrease from the norm. While many of these students are perceived by this observer as "self-starters," the nature of their work environment may have distorted several of their responses about directing their own activity towards goal achievement. Also, these individuals are aware that factors over which they have no control, i.e., federal budgets and world crises, can directly affect their future assignments and careers.

d. *Influences by Persuasive Leadership* and

e. *Influences by Being Self-Assertive* Some situations call for a

[6] *Ibid.*

207

considerable amount of persuasiveness. Other situations call for behavior which tends to be supportive and understanding of other people, and which contributes to the maintenance of harmonious relations. Still other situations require the individual to be assertive in the pursuit of his own goals when they are in competition with the goals of others. Finally, there are situations in which there is only a minor need for personally influencing the behavior of others. Scales that measure two major aspects of interpersonal influence are "Influences by Persuasive Leadership," and "Influences by Being Self-Assertive." Army members of the U.S. Army War College Class of 1972 scored exceptionally high on the scale "Influences by Persuasive Leadership." These students showed that they have little difficulty expressing their opinions before a large group and often assume leadership roles in group seminars. Direct observations of this group support the test results in that these individuals seem to enjoy the opportunity to get results through persuasion or negotiations. These students also scored exceptionally high on the "Influences by Being Self-Assertive" scale. The competitive nature of their profession is probably reflected in this score. Again, direct observation of these students by this researcher substantiates that they do well under conditions of competition and stress.

f, g, and h. *Reaction to Aggression* Job assignments differ in their requirements for dealing with aggressive behavior by others, and individuals differ in their preferred styles. Some people respond to aggressive behavior by attempting to win over or appease the aggressor, others respond by psychological or physical withdrawal, and still others respond by counterattacking. It is obviously desirable to be able to vary the strategy depending on the situation. It is assumed, however, that most individuals tend to rely on some strategy more than others. The test used measures three styles for dealing with an aggressor: "Move Toward Aggressor," "Move Away from Aggressor," and "Move Against Aggressor."

f.　*Move Toward Aggressor* The extent to which an individual attempts to behave diplomatically when someone acts toward him in a belligerent or aggressive manner is measured by this scale. Army students attending the U.S. Army War College differed from the norm by being significantly lower than the norm of the test instrument. It is evident that U.S. Army War College students would rather counterattack than win over a domineering person.

g.　*Move Away from Aggressor* This scale pertains to the extent to which the individual withdraws when someone acts toward him in a belligerent or aggressive manner. The scores of the War College students were exceptionally lower than the norm.

h.　*Move Against Aggressor* The extent to which the individual counterattacks when someone acts toward him in a belligerent or aggressive manner is measured by this scale. Army members of the Class of 1972 differed by scoring exceptionally higher than the norms concerning this scale. Observations of these individuals indicate that if someone acts toward them in a dictatorial or domineering fashion, they will confront the belligerent person and resolve the issue.

i. *Prefers Routine,*

j. *Identifies with Authority,* and

k. *Prefers Independence* These individuals do not prefer routines. Instead, their performance is at its best when they determine their own procedures. In an examination of the extent to which they identify with their superior and try to please him, these students scored much lower than the norm. Instead, their goals are in terms of excellent performance rather than in pleasing their superior. Their preference for independence was close to the norm.

l. *Prefers Directive Leadership Style,*

m. *Prefers Participative Leadership Style,*

n. *Prefers Delegative Leadership Style,*

o. *Motivates by Knowledge of Results,* and

p. *Believes in External Controls* Authority in an organization can be exercised in a number of ways. The leader can make all the decisions, or he can delegate a portion of them to individuals or to the group. Various styles of leadership are appropriate for different types of situations. This chapter focuses on the following three leadership styles: "Prefers Directive Leadership Style," "Prefers Participative Leadership Style," and "Prefers Delegative Leadership Style." It is recognized that there are other leadership styles that might be equally appropriate, but they are beyond the scope of this study.

Leaders differ in the types of controls they impose and the types of incentives they offer. Two relevant scales are: "Motivates by Knowledge of Results," and "Believes in External Controls."

Army members of the U.S. Army War College Class of 1972 preferred a directive leadership style, were tolerant of a delegative leadership style, and were strongly opposed to a participative leadership style. With respect to motivation, they considered that a leader gets the best results through rewards or punishment rather than through intrinsic motivation. In addition, they believed rather strongly that people require external controls.

q. *Prefers Being Systematic, Methodical* Decisions may require extensive analysis of the facts. These individuals do not usually prefer systematic, methodical methods for processing information and for reaching decisions. Their response was most appropriate considering their need for making rapid decisions.

r. *Prefers Group Participation* This scale measures the degree to which the individual identifies himself with a highly valued group. The scores of Army students attending the U.S. Army War College differed by being significantly higher than the norm for this scale of the test instrument. Persons scoring high say they like best to work as a member of a group and do not like to work apart from other people.

COMPARISON OF SIX GROUPS OF PERSONNEL

While it is interesting to compare these Army students with the norms of a test, it might be more meaningful to compare this group of individuals with five other groups of people associated with the Army. These intergroup comparisons will add meaning to the findings reported previously in this book. The Army members of the U.S. Army War College Class of 1972 will be compared with the following five other groups of personnel:

1. *Non-Army Members of the U.S. Army War College Class of* 1972 This group of 40 individuals has a degree of experience and grade level that is comparable to their 183 Army classmates reported previously in this chapter. These non-Army students consist of 10 Naval officers, 6 Marine officers, 16 Air Force officers, and 8 civilian employees of the Federal Government.

2. *Engineer Captains Tested During* 1970 These individuals completed the test in 1970 in connection with the study presented in Chapter 4. All members of this 358-man group had graduated from Engineer Officer Candidate School at Fort Belvoir, Virginia, during 1967.

3. *Infantrymen in Combat in Vietnam During* 1969 The 316 individuals tested in this group were members of rifle companies of an infantry battalion engaged in combat operations in the Mekong Delta. Responses pertaining to the self-reported beliefs of these combat infantrymen were similar to those reported in Chapter 5.

4. *Officer Candidate School Graduating Students Tested at Fort Belvoir During* 1970 These 148 men were examined during their last two weeks of Officer Candidate School training. They were all subsequently commissioned. These individuals were tested in connection with a replication of the study presented in Chapter 4.

5. *Former Officer Candidates During* 1967 *Who Did Not Graduate and Were Tested as Civilians During* 1970 These 182 men were tested in connection with the research project pertaining to the effect of training reported in Chapter 4.

RESULTS

Table 28 presents a summary of the results of this comparison. Zero is the norm for Table 28. This was determined by setting zero in place of the average scores of individuals representing over 50 occupations. Theoretically, no occupational group fits the norm. This is evidenced by the fact that there are usually very few zeros in tables like Table 28. As mentioned previously, the purpose of the norm is to establish a "bench mark" or "baseline" so that the scores of different occupations will have a relative meaning. For example, the reader's attention is invited to the first scale on Table 28 "Extent of Optimism." Both Army students and non-Army students in this study reported that they are optimistic. Inasmuch as their scores are positive (31 and 36 respectively), they placed a value higher than the norm on their extent of optimism. Conversely, the other four groups of individuals varied negatively from the norm (-2, -105, -21, and -30 respectively). The group with the strongest value for optimism is the one composed of non-Army members of the U.S. Army War College Class of 1972. Next would be their Army class-

210

TABLE 28

SCORES* FOR SIX GROUPS OF PERSONNEL WITH THE NORM BEING ZERO

	183 Army Members of the Army War College Class of 1972	40 Non-Army Members of the Army War College Class of 1972	358 Engineer Captains during 1970	316 Infantry-men in combat in Vietnam during 1969	148 OCS Graduating Students Belvoir 1970	182 Former Officer Candidates during 1967 did not Graduate, tested as civilians
Extent of Optimism	31	36	−2	−105	−21	−30
Degree of Self-Confidence	68	58	20	−120	23	−12
Belief in Moral Absolutes	71	62	20	17	−5	−16
Belief in Slow Change	39	17	19	11	−13	−5
Prefers Problem Analysis	9	22	18	−30	18	45
Prefers Social Interaction	13	27	14	−6	−1	−33
Prefers Mechanical Activities	43	10	87	86	46	100
Prefers Supervisory Activities	123	68	85	−22	48	3
Prefers Activity Frequent Change	51	72	58	−51	28	34
Values Status Attainment	51	79	79	−17	35	16
Values Social Service	−78	−56	−66	−19	−27	−44
Values Approval from Others	−84	−65	−90	18	−57	−58
Values Intellectual Achievement	−16	1	−14	−60	18	21
Values Role Conformity	39	7	67	24	8	29
Degree of Perseverance	29	−6	32	−8	39	30
Extent of Orderliness	57	10	46	2	37	28
Prefers to Plan Ahead	−15	−27	−12	−43	2	−10
Influences by Persuasive Leadership	88	61	52	−73	51	−6
Influences by Being Self-Assertive	100	90	114	19	99	84
Move Toward Aggressor	−62	−64	−64	−10	−48	−48

TABLE 28 (Continued)

Move Away from Aggressor	−53	−6	−60	11	−42	−22
Move Against Aggressor	69	22	69	13	63	38
Prefers Routine	−17	14	−4	61	−6	−5
Identifies with Authority	−24	−4	−29	−9	−14	−32
Prefers Independence	2	−5	20	−55	21	24
Prefers Directive Leadership Style	37	11	88	52	84	40
Prefers Participative Leadership Style	−24	2	−63	−55	−59	−26
Prefers Delegative Leadership Style	−6	−11	−20	14	−25	−20
Motivates by Knowledge of Results	−20	−5	−7	0	−25	5
Believes in External Controls	20	19	86	75	81	76
Prefers Being Systematic Methodical	−34	−39	19	38	16	38
Prefers Group Participation	17	5	−9	0	−24	−49

* Inasmuch as the groups of individuals vary in size, standard scores are used in this comparison. The standard scores for each group are determined by comparing the average response for each group pertaining to each scale with the norm. The norms of the test are equated to zero and the standard deviation of 100. Norms for the test instrument are based on a wide variety of occupational groups.

mates. Conversely, the group that placed the lowest value on optimism was the infantrymen in combat in Vietnam during 1969. Next to the lowest was the group of former officer candidates during 1967, who did not graduate, and were tested as civilians during 1970. Second from the lowest was the group of Officer Candidate School graduating students at Fort Belvoir during 1970. The group having the negative score closest to zero was the group of engineer captains tested during 1970. Stated differently, it can be concluded that the range of optimism from highest to lowest by group was reported as follows:

1. Non-Army members of the U.S. Army War College Class of 1972.
2. Army members of the U.S. Army War College Class of 1972.
3. Engineer captains tested during 1970.
4. Officer Candidate School graduating students, Fort Belvoir, 1970.
5. Former Officer Candidate School students during 1967, who did not graduate, and were tested as civilians during 1970.
6. Infantrymen in combat in Vietnam during 1969.

The reader should keep in mind when making an analysis of these scores that

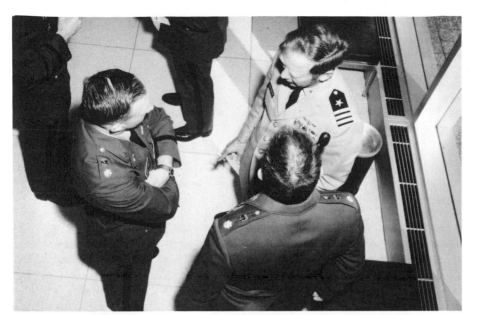

Top photo: An exchange of interservice views by three members of the U.S. Army War College Class of 1972. Bottom photo: Members of the class participating in one of their elective courses. There is a significant difference between the average scores of Army students attending the U.S. Army War College and the overall norms of the test instrument. These results are interpreted as being desirable for individuals in their capacity. It appears that the selection process for attendance at the U.S. Army War College is successful. Other differences are evident in a comparison of Army students attending the U.S. Army War College with several other groups of individuals associated with the Army.

213

The responses from six groups of individuals associated with the Army are quite different. Each group with its own set of characteristics is probably best suited for its own particular role. Above photographs depict typical representatives from each of the six groups described in this chapter.

while it may be understandable for students attending the U.S. Army War College to be optimistic, the same intensity of optimism may be quite dangerous for a group of soldiers confronting the reality of an armed enemy in combat. It should be recognized that major differences in response may be essential for top performance in different fields. Therefore, the reader should not make a general assumption that "lowest" indicates "worst."

It seems understandable that the scores of the Army students and the non-Army students attending the U.S. Army War College are somewhat similar. However, there are a few noticeable differences. (See Table 28.)

The range of differences between the six groups seems to emphasize that the beliefs of various groups associated with the same profession can be quite diverse. (See Table 28.) These findings tend to agree with the views of Stouffer, Janowitz, and Huntington that various groups of American soldiers are quite different in terms of their beliefs. The value of this data is that it reveals specific differences between the selected groups. These differences have direct implications for the formulation of personnel policies affecting these six groups. It appears that policies that have an impact on different groups within the same profession should consider these differences and be developed accordingly.

DISCUSSION

The following is an answer to the three questions posed earlier in this chapter:

1.   What sort of person is the Army officer who attends the U.S. Army War College? Answer:

a.   Compared with the norms of the test used in this study, Army officers attending the U.S. Army War College placed a significantly higher than average value in the following self-reported beliefs:

 (1) "Extent of Optimism"
 (2) "Degree of Self-Confidence"
 (3) "Belief in Moral Absolutes"
 (4) "Belief in Slow Change"
 (5) "Prefers Mechanical Activities"
 (6) "Prefers Supervisory Activities"
 (7) "Prefers Activity Frequent Change"
 (8) "Values Status Attainment"
 (9) "Values Role Conformity"
 (10) "Degree of Perseverance"
 (11) "Extent of Orderliness"
 (12) "Influences by Persuasive Leadership"
 (13) "Influences by Being Self-Assertive"
 (14) "Move Against Aggressor"
 (15) "Prefers Directive Leadership Style"
 (16) "Believes in External Controls"
 (17) "Prefers Group Participation"

b.   Compared with the norms of the test, Army officers attending the U.S. Army War College placed a significantly lower than average value in the following self-reported beliefs:

    (1)   "Values Social Service"
    (2)   "Values Approval from Others"
    (3)   "Values Intellectual Achievement"
    (4)   "Move Toward Aggressor"
    (5)   "Move Away from Aggressor"
    (6)   "Prefers Routine"
    (7)   "Identifies with Authority"
    (8)   "Prefers Participative Leadership Style"
    (9)   "Motivates by Knowledge of Results"
  (10)   "Prefers Being Systematic, Methodical"

c.   The following self-reported beliefs held by Army members of the U.S. Army War College Class of 1972 were at or near the average level compared with the norms of the test:

    (1)   "Prefers Problem Analysis"
    (2)   "Prefers Social Interaction"
    (3)   "Prefers to Plan Ahead"
    (4)   "Prefers Independence"
    (5)   "Prefers Delegative Leadership Style"

2.   How does he compare with five other groups of Army personnel? Answer:

The group of Army students attending the U.S. Army War College scored higher than all other groups pertaining to self-confidence, orderliness, a belief that changes should be executed slowly, and a belief in moral absolutes. They scored next to highest in optimism (their non-Army classmates scored highest). They were generally similar to other groups pertaining to perseverance, and in their negative value for their capability to plan ahead.

The Army members of the U.S. Army War College Class scored higher than all other groups concerning persuasive leadership. They scored next to highest in self-assertiveness (the group of engineer captains scored the highest).

When given the choice of appeasing, avoiding, or counterattacking a belligerent individual, Army members of the U.S. Army War College Class of 1972 would prefer to counterattack. Along with engineer captains, they received the highest score pertaining to a preference for counterattacking.

The group of Army students attending the U.S. Army War College scored lower than all other groups concerning a preference for routines. It is interesting to note that persons scoring low on a preference for routines indicate that they do not like to have a clear-cut written guideline or manual which tells them clearly what they are supposed to do. All of the groups scored generally the same in their negative value for an identification with authority. Rather than in pleasing their superiors, the goal of these groups tends to be in excellent performance. With regards to a preference for independence, Army members of the Class of 1972 scored closest to the norm. Other groups received a wide range of scores.

Army members of the Class of 1972 preferred a directive leadership style, were tolerant of a delegative leadership style, and were not in favor of a participative leadership style. Compared with other groups in this study, however, they placed the next to lowest value on directive leadership (their non-Army classmates placed the lowest). While their value for participative leadership was negative, it was the next to highest (highest value by their non-Army classmates). Their preference for delegative leadership (slightly negative) was the next to highest. The highest preference for delegative leadership was indicated by the group of infantrymen tested in Vietnam. Compared with other groups, Army members of the Class of 1972 scored next to lowest in the belief that a leader gets the best results through intrinsic motivation (Officer Candidate School graduating students scored the lowest). While they believed rather strongly that people require external controls, their score was next to lowest (lowest score was by their non-Army classmates).

Army members of the U.S. Army War College Class received the next to lowest score in a preference for being systematic, methodical (lowest score by their non-Army classmates).

Army students attending the U.S. Army War College scored higher than all other groups pertaining to their preference for supervisory activities and group participation. While they placed a high value in their preference for mechanical activities and problem analysis, their scores, compared with the other five groups, were next to lowest in each case. They placed a high value in social interaction; however, engineer captains placed a slightly higher value and non-Army members of the U.S. Army War College placed the highest value in social interaction. Their strong preference for activity frequent change was second from the highest (their non-Army classmates scored the highest and engineer captains scored next to highest).

Compared with other groups, Army members of the Class of 1972 received the highest score on the attainment of status and the lowest score in their preference for social service. They received the next to lowest score in their value of the approval from others and their relative value of the importance of intellectual achievement. All of the groups tended to place a high value in role conformity, while Army students attending the U.S. Army War College received a score generally the same as the other groups.

3. Do these findings contain any surprises? Answer:

In a search for surprising differences, it is interesting to find that these individuals are quite similar to civilian business executives and to Navy War College students. As a group, Army members of the U.S. Army War College Class of 1972 were found to be optimistic, self-confident, persuasive individuals who have a strong preference for being a leader. While they are aggressive and highly competitive in actions with their peers, they are strongly sensitive to the needs of their subordinates. In arriving at a decision, they tend to consider the facts rather than the relative popularity of various courses of action. In cases where the mission conflicts with the approval from others, they place little value in the approval from others. The responses of six groups of individuals associated with the Army are quite different. Each group with its own set of characteristics is probably best suited for its own particular role.

CHART 17

EXTENT OF SELF – ASSERTIVENESS *

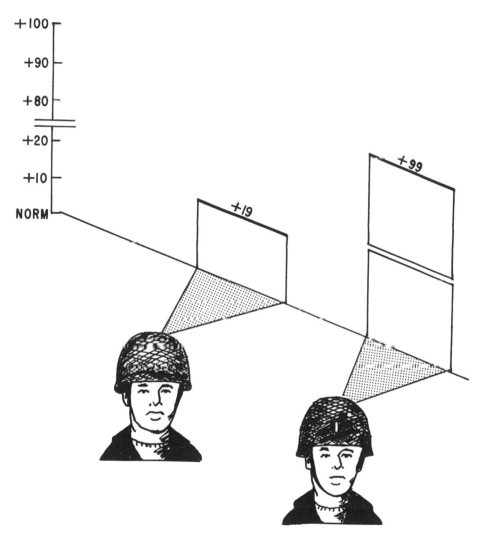

* Comparison is made of 316 infantrymen in combat in Vietnam during 1969 with 148 OCS graduating students at Fort Belvoir during 1970. The scale "Influences by Being Self-Assertive" measures the degree to which the individual tends to pursue his own goals when they are in competition with the goals of others.

CHART 18

EXTENT OF PREFERENCE FOR DIRECTIVE LEADERSHIP STYLE *

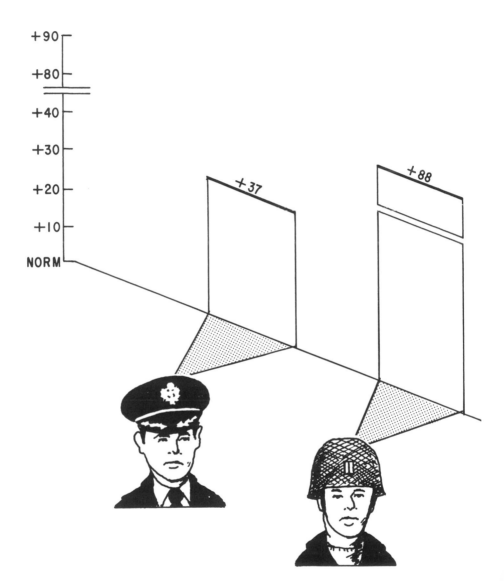

* Comparison is made of 183 Army members of the Army War College class of 1972 with 358 Engineer Captains during 1970. The scale "Prefers Directive Leadership Style" measures the degree to which the individual believes that a leader gets the best results by making decisions himself.

CHART 19

VALUE FOR THE ACHIEVEMENT OF STATUS *

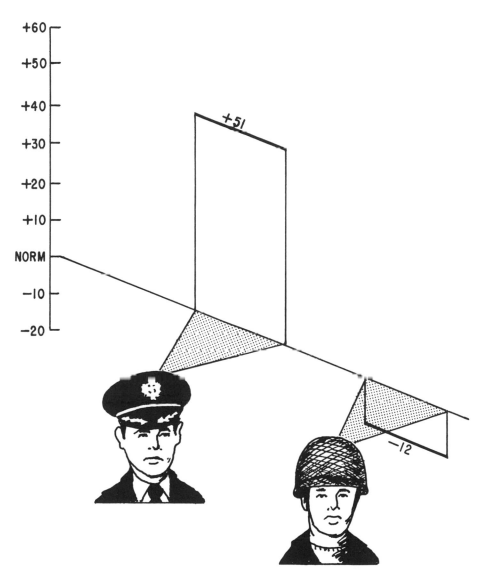

* Comparison is made of 183 Army members of the Army War College class of 1972 with 316 infantrymen in combat in Vietnam during 1969. The scale "Values Status Attainment" measures the degree to which the individual values himself by his achievement of the status symbols established by his culture.

CHART 20

VALUE FOR ROLE CONFORMITY *

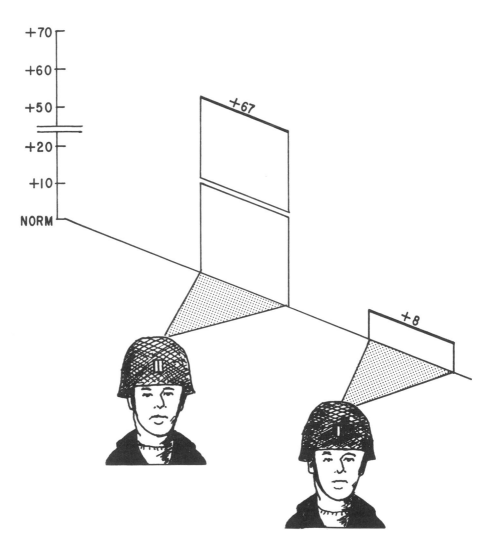

*Comparison is made of 358 Engineer Captains during 1970 with 148 OCS graduating students at Fort Belvoir during 1970. The scale "Values Role Conformity" measures the degree to which the individual values himself according to how successfully he has conformed to the role requirements of society.

CHART 21

COMPARISON OF SIX GROUPS: Extent of Optimism

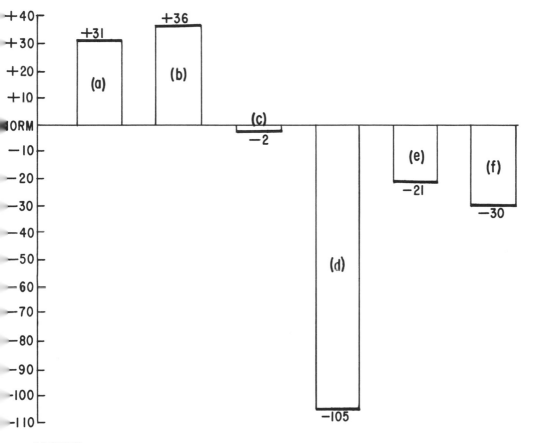

LEGEND:
  (a)   183 Army members of the Army War College Class of 1972.
  (b)   40 Non-Army members of the Army War College Class of 1972.
  (c)   358 Engineer captains during 1970.
  (d)   316 Infantrymen in combat in Vietnam during 1970.
  (e)   148 OCS graduating students at Fort Belvoir during 1970.
  (f)   182 Former officer candidates during 1967 who did not graduate and were tested as
            civilians during 1970.

CHART 22

COMPARISON OF SIX GROUPS: Extent of Belief in Moral Absolutes

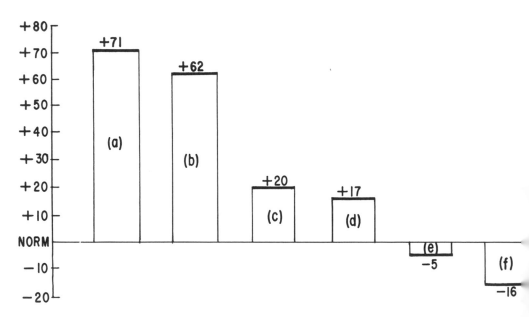

LEGEND:
- (a) 183 Army members of the Army War College Class of 1972.
- (b)   40 Non-Army members of the Army War College Class of 1972.
- (c) 358 Engineer captains during 1970.
- (d) 316 Infantrymen in combat in Vietnam during 1970.
- (e) 148 OCS graduating students at Fort Belvoir during 1970.
- (f) 182 Former officer candidates during 1967 who did not graduate and were tested as civilians during 1970.

CHART 23

COMPARISON OF SIX GROUPS: Preference for Supervisory Activities

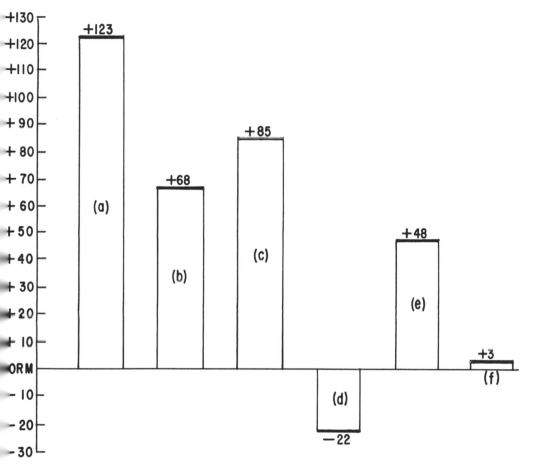

LEGEND:
- (a) 183 Army members of the Army War College Class of 1972.
- (b)   40 Non-Army members of the Army War College Class of 1972.
- (c) 358 Engineer captains during 1970.
- (d) 316 Infantrymen in combat in Vietnam during 1970.
- (e) 148 OCS graduating students at Fort Belvoir during 1970.
- (f) 182 Former officer candidates during 1967 who did not graduate and were tested as civilians during 1970.

CHART 24

COMPARISON OF SIX GROUPS: Extent of Value for the Approval From Others

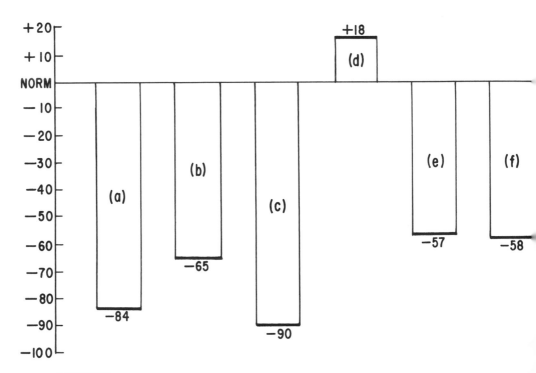

LEGEND:
- (a) 183 Army members of the Army War College Class of 1972.
- (b)   40 Non-Army members of the Army War College Class of 1972.
- (c) 358 Engineer captains during 1970.
- (d) 316 Infantrymen in combat in Vietnam during 1970.
- (e) 148 OCS graduating students at Fort Belvoir during 1970.
- (f) 182 Former officer candidates during 1967 who did not graduate and were tested as civilians during 1970.

Chapter 8

TURNING THE TIDE

The American soldier of the Vietnam War was described unfairly in much of the contemporary literature of that period. Deputy Secretary of Defense David Packard observed the following concerning the reporting of contemporary military events by critics of the military when he appeared before a Congressional subcommittee. "There are very few reports on the good things military people do; all they do, it seems is report on the mistakes."[1]

In addition to providing an argument in favor of the American soldier of the Vietnam War by furnishing an objective analysis of empirical evidence, the findings of this six-year research project will form the basis for the development of worthwhile conclusions and meaningful recommendations. A major problem in distilling an analysis presented in an academic setting to a form acceptable for general readership is that much of the scientific format and style needs to be reduced in order to improve the readability of the report. Conversely, those expecting a more academic approach will be disappointed in this summarized version. If this is the case, the reader is invited to examine the supporting research documents. Chapter 3, for example, is a condensed version of a master's thesis,[2] while Chapter 4 is a simplified version of a doctoral dissertation.[3]

A problem in connection with many research projects that are conducted in a military environment is that few individuals read the results, and even fewer individuals take appropriate action to implement the results. A classic case in point is the "Chapman Study"[4] of Korean War vintage. It seems that if Herschel Chapman's findings had been implemented properly they might have signaled

---

[1] U.S. Congress, House Committee on Appropriations, Subcommittee on Department of Defense, *Department of Defense Appropriations for* 1972, Hearings, 92nd. Cong., 1st sess., 1971.

[2] Peter B. Petersen, "A Comparison of Behavioral Styles Between Entering and Graduating Students in Officer Candidate School," Master's thesis (Washington, D.C.: George Washington Univ., February 1967).

[3] Petersen, "An Investigation of the Effect of Training," Doctoral Dissertation (Washington, D.C.: George Washington Univ., February 15, 1971).

[4] Herschel E. Chapman, *Officer Candidate School Evaluation and Training* (Fort Benning, Ga.: Infantry School, 1956).

a warning within the Officer Candidate School system in those days of rapid commissioning prior to the disaster of human judgment at My Lai. It is my opinion that the "Chapman Study" was unnoticed because it failed to receive widespread dissemination and because it failed to generate an audience of general readership. A major reason why an audience of general readership was not attracted was because the "Chapman Study" was couched in technical jargon. A summarized and simpler version of the "Chapman Study" is as follows:

During the Korean War, Herschel Chapman conducted a comparison of the combat leadership records of 139 Officer Candidate School graduates with their earlier records as officer candidates. He concluded that evaluations of students in Officer Candidate School provide significant predictions of their later success or failure as combat leaders. The correlation between combat preformance and certain Officer Candidate School ratings and scores were sufficiently positive to conclude that combat performance can be predicted in varying degrees by the results of Officer Candidate School peer ratings, tactical officer ratings, and company commander ratings.

More specifically, he determined the following:

1.   Combat performance can be predicted by the results of Officer Candidate School peer ratings, tactical officer ratings, and company commander ratings. These three ratings, which comprise the Officer Candidate School leadership rating, seem to indicate that leadership displayed in Officer Candidate School is an indication of the leadership that will be displayed in combat.
2.   Rifle qualification, physical fitness test scores, education and aptitude test scores do not predict combat performance. Also, there is no significant relationship between age and combat performance.
3.   Officer Candidate School academic rankings do not predict combat performance. The correlation of $-.80$ indicates, to a degree, that candidates ranking lower in academics tend to have a slight chance of better combat performance.
4.   Tactical officer and student ratings obtained midway through the course tend to indicate combat performance as good or better than similar ratings obtained near the end of the course.
5.   Officer Candidate School graduates assigned as combat platoon leaders during the Korean War tended to provide outstanding performances.

In learning a lesson from the causes of poor dissemination of the "Chapman Study," I have attempted to describe in clear terminology the findings of this research project, and provide clear conclusions that can be translated into meaningful recommendations. I make no apology for a simplistic approach that fails to "nit pick" the obvious. It is sincerely hoped that the implementation of these recommendations will help "turn the tide" in the current wave of problems facing the American soldier and the U.S. Army.

SUMMARY OF FINDINGS

1. CONTEMPORARY LITERATURE

In reviewing the contemporary literature pertaining to the American soldier of the Vietnam War, four major misperceptions by critics of the U.S. Army become evident. They are as follows:

a. *Training* Training tends to change the individual from a "normal well-adjusted" person into a robot or perhaps even into a manipulating leader complete with a Machiavellian *modus operandi.* Many of the extreme views in contemporary writing could be expressed in terms of a brainwashing system complete with the inoculation of a "Dr. Strangelove" vaccine.

b. *Effects of Combat* Soldiers returning from Vietnam are disoriented and tend to be a detriment to society.

c. *Retention* Those who make the Army a career are autocratic "hard-heads" incapable of employment in a free society.

d. *Comparison of Various Subgroups* There is a tendency in the current literature by critics of the Army to misjudge the characteristics of various subgroups within the Army. As a group, privates tend to be seen as oppressed pawns with a "Beetle Bailey" mentality. Junior officers as a group are often viewed as naive, and senior officers as a group tend to be perceived as manipulators of situations for their own career progression.

2. TRAINING

With respect to the misperception concerning training (see 1.a.), it is interesting to note the findings of this research pertaining to the immediate effects of training and to the stability of these effects. These findings indicate that the misperception of training held by some of the critics of the Army is false. There are, however, some significant changes in self-reported beliefs that occur during training. These changes are commensurate with the requirements for effective leadership at the junior officer level. They are beneficial to both the individual and to the organization.

Engineer Officer Candidate School Training Conducted During 1966 It appeared as no surprise to this former Officer Candidate School student that individuals change some of their self-reported beliefs while attending Officer Candidate School. In developing a master's thesis in 1966, it seemed worthwhile to measure how people change certain of their self-reported beliefs. A questionnaire[5] was administered to 561 entering students and 319 graduating students. The results indicated that entering students, compared with graduating students, placed a higher value in the approval from others. Graduating

[5] I am grateful to Professor Regis H. Walther, author of the Job Analysis and Interest Measurement (JAIM) used throughout this study, for his personal assistance in accomplishing much of the work described in this report.

students, as compared with entering students, tended to be more self-assertive, were more likely to be persuasive leaders, and were more prone to like supervisory activities.

Infantry Officer Candidate School Training Conducted During 1968   The study pertained to the Engineer Officer Candidate School located at Fort Belvoir, Virginia, and it was assumed that this Officer Candidate School was representative of others in operation at that time. During September 1968, the results of the study at Engineer Officer Candidate School were cross-validated by a replication at Infantry Officer Candidate School located at Fort Benning, Georgia. The questionnaire used earlier was administered to 170 entering students and 101 graduating students. It was predicted that the significant differences found at Engineer Officer Candidate School between entering and graduating students would also be found at Infantry Officer Candidate School. There was a remarkably similar difference between groups of entering and graduating students at both Engineer Officer Candidate School and Infantry Officer Candidate School. In addition, graduating students from both schools had similar standard scores on previously selected scales. It was concluded from these results that the two schools had a very similar effect on their students.

Further Research 1967-70   While the self-reported beliefs of entering and graduating students were significantly different, it was argued that the effect of training could not be measured because the same individuals were not tested as both entering and graduating students. In the normal course of events, most of the individuals who failed to graduate actually resigned from the program rather than wait to be selected for relief by the school authorities. There was a possibility that this self-selection departure process would further prevent an accurate analysis between entering and graduating students. If individuals with certain beliefs were selected to fail, it could be possible that instead of training men to become officers, the school was selecting men to become officers. It is more likely, however, that a combination of training and selection accounts for the difference between the two groups. In contrast to the earlier studies, further research developed in preparation of a doctoral dissertation[6] attempted to answer several previously unanswered questions.

Effect and Stability of Training: Engineer Officer Candidate School 1967-70   In 1967, 347 men were tested as both entering and graduating students. Scores on 14 out of 15 selected scales obtained at the time of graduation differed significantly from scores obtained at the time of their entrance to training.

Entrance to Officer Candidate School is voluntary and upon graduation each student is commissioned as a second lieutenant. Early in the training program it becomes evident to the student that he must conform to behavioral standards as well as academic standards. Most entering candidates find themselves in an

[6] The author is grateful for the financial support pertaining to the doctoral dissertation jointly furnished by the U.S. Army, George Washington University, and the U.S. Steel Corporation.

environment requiring a different role from that to which they are accustomed. To survive and graduate, the student is encouraged to adapt to the school's environment and to assume new roles consistent with the reward and punishment standards of the school and of his peers. During the six-month training program many of these new roles probably become part of the individual's personality and self-conception.

It is conceptualized that successful students, after becoming aware of the specific standards required by the school and their peers, will adjust their roles to accommodate these standards. As the course progresses, it is considered, also, that the beliefs of these individuals will adjust and become compatible with the individual's newly acquired roles. If being successful is measured in terms of conforming to the established standards of the program, it appears that the individuals who do not assume the correct roles will depart from school prior to graduation.

The majority of persons who fail to graduate voluntarily depart from the school after it appears to them that the difficult program is not worth the effort, or that further effort on their part in working towards graduation is fruitless. Some individuals who do not meet the prescribed standards are "turned back" to more junior classes and many of them eventually graduate. It is believed that almost all entering students, if they desire to apply themselves, can graduate; however, approximately a third of the entering students normally fail to graduate. It appears that these individuals as a group do not adapt or are not particularly interested in adapting to the required new roles.

It can be concluded that these men changed their self-reported beliefs during the time they participated in Officer Candidate School training. It appears from the results that the beliefs of these students were molded into a form required for them to perform their duties successfully as junior officers. The shaping process emphasizes an insistence on immediate task performance with results obtained through persuading, directing, or supervising other people. There is a considerable value placed in being self-assertive and in perseverance. The graduating student is action-oriented with a greater concern for the mission than for the welfare of his subordinates. However, this does not imply that he is not concerned with their welfare. It does imply that concern for subordinates is second only to the accomplishment of the mission. The graduating student has a set of beliefs that are probably the best suited to accomplish the short range goals of his profession, such as leading a platoon or commanding a company in combat. Subsequent duties, following about eight years of company grade assignments, will probably require another set of beliefs. Prior to that time, these men will receive additional training and become more experienced.

In considering the stability of the graduating student's self-reported beliefs, it was conceptualized that those self-reported beliefs that changed the most during training would probably be the least stable. When retested approximately three years after graduation from Officer Candidate School, significant changes in the reverse direction from that occurring during training were predicted for 12 scales. The results were that four scales were significant in the predicted direction, three in the opposite direction, and no significant difference was found for the remaining five scales. Thus the findings indicated that the stability of training was more complex than initially considered, probably a function of positive or negative reinforcement during the post-Officer Candidate School period.

Other Relevant Findings An analysis of the data in connection with this particular research project indicates that scores obtained by using the test instrument at the time of entry into the training program effectively discriminates:

1.   Between those who will tend to eventually graduate and those who will tend to voluntarily depart prior to graduation.
2.   Between those who will tend to remain in the Army years later and those who will tend to depart from the Army years later.
3.   Between those who will tend to both graduate and remain in the Army years later and those who will tend to both not graduate and depart from the Army years later.
4.   Between individuals at the time of entrance to Officer Candidate School and the same individuals approximately three years after departure.

Reevaluation of the Officer Candidate School Training Process During 1970 In 1970, 42 men were tested as both entering and graduating students. Scores on several of the JAIM scales obtained at the time of graduation differed significantly from scores obtained at the time of their entrance to training. These findings substantiate earlier studies that indicated that Officer Candidate School tends to change the self-reported beliefs of the individuals in terms of basic beliefs, activity preferences, personal values, and behavioral styles. These changes can be predicted. Changes in self-reported beliefs during Officer Candidate School training in 1970 were similar to those changes during Officer Candidate School training conducted during 1966, 1967, and 1968. It should be noted, however, that the changes were of a lesser intensity during 1970 because entering students at that time, compared to entering students during 1967, had more of the "desired" characteristics to begin with. It should also be noted that graduating students during 1970 had less of the "desired" characteristics than those sampled in 1967. Perhaps changes in American society may have altered the "desired" characteristics of graduates as perceived by both the school authorities and the individuals concerned.

3.   Effects of Combat

A major misperception by critics of the U.S. Army is that soldiers returning from Vietnam are disoriented and tend to be a detriment to society. The findings of this research project strongly indicate that this is not correct.

Compared with after they returned to the United States, the same group of individuals while they were stationed as infantrymen in Vietnam placed a significantly higher value on the approval from others, social interaction, and group participation, and conversely a lower value on the attainment of status. While both the group of 80 enlisted infantrymen and a control group changed to some degree after they returned to the United States, the group of 80 enlisted infantrymen experienced a greater degree of change which is attributed to the removal of the influences of combat. The nature of these changes clearly indicates that the effects of combat on the beliefs of infantrymen are not detrimental to society. An analysis of the data concerning this study indicates that when the members of the group of 80 enlisted infantrymen were in combat they tended to be more sensitive to the needs of their friends. Perhaps the daily stress of combat and the adverse environmental conditions of the Mekong Delta encouraged a feeling of comradery that was welcome in Vietnam, but no longer needed after these men returned to the United States. This feeling of comradeship, and perhaps the possibility of death in combat, may be responsible, at least in part, for this sensitivity. It seems ironic that it takes the horrors of war to cause individuals to become more sensitive in their interactions with their friends. It is certainly most unfortunate that these desirable qualities do not tend to carry over substantially after these men return to the United States.

4. RETENTION

Another misperception by critics of the U.S. Army is that individuals who make the Army a career are autocratic "hardheads" incapable of civilian employment in a free society. The findings of this research project clearly indicate that this is not the case.

There seems to be a common thread pertaining to retention that is found by examining: (a) the differences in self-reported beliefs between a group of men who remained in the Army and a group of men who departed, and (b) the reasons why the one group departed. The common thread is that the beliefs of these two significantly different groups were compatible with their career decisions. In addition, it was considered that the group of men who remained in the Army was better qualified to cope with the current requirements of the organization.

a. *Self-Reported Beliefs*

(1) The group of 358 individuals who decided to remain in the Army placed a significantly higher value on the following self-reported beliefs:

(a) To believe in moral absolutes.

(b) To accomplish things in a conventional way, and when things are going smoothly, not to make changes which will cause a disruption.

(c) To exert leadership in interpersonal situations and to get results through persuasion or negotiation.

(d) To pursue their own goals when they are in competition with the goals of others.

(e) To counterattack when someone acts towards them in a belligerent or aggressive manner.

(f) To make decisions alone.

(g) To interact with other people.

(h) To plan and supervise the work of other people.

(i) To be actively engaged in work providing a lot of excitement, and a great deal of variety.

(j) To work as a member of a group and not apart from other people.

(k) To conform to the role requirements of society.

(2) The group of 919 individuals who decided to depart from the Army placed a significantly higher value on the following self-reported beliefs:

(a) To have self-confidence.

(b) To withdraw when someone acts toward them in a belligerent or aggressive manner.

(c) To use systematic methodical methods for processing information and reaching decisions.

(d) To analyze problems.

(e) To achieve the status symbols established by their culture.

(f) To obtain the approval of others.

(g) To attain intellectual achievement.

b. *Reasons for Departure* A major reason why many company grade officers depart from the Army is that they feel that their potential for a successful Army career is diminishing. It seems ironic that many of their self-perceived mistakes in performance or in the assignments they receive are not actually relevant. It appears that considerable progress could be made by dispelling many of their imagined career management problems. There is strong evidence to support the view that conditions that increase the actual and self-perceived potential of company grade officers will also tend to increase the retention of these individuals in the Army. Other major reasons why members of this group departed from the Army are as follows:

(1) They did not intend to remain on active duty beyond that time required to fulfill their obligations.

(2) They wanted to avoid repeated tours of duty in Vietnam.

(3) They wanted to consider the desires of their wife and the welfare of their family.

(4) They wanted to complete their education.

(5) They were dissatisfied with current personnel management procedures.

(6) They were dissatisfied with the performance of their leaders.

(7) They felt a conflict of their goals with the requirements of the organization.

c. *Major Goals in Life* While both groups were significantly different in many respects, it is interesting to note that their major goals in life were almost identical. A consolidation of goals for both groups reveals that the most often stated major goal in life is to be successful in their career. This tends to strengthen the above discussion concerning the importance of success in a career. Many other major goals in life that were stated tended to be idealistic and to reflect attitudes of their age group. Measures designed to increase retention should also consider these goals.

5. Comparison of Various Subgroups

The last misperception challenged in this research project concerns the tendency in the current literature for critics of the Army to misjudge the characteristics of various subgroups within the Army. For example, privates, as a group, tend to be viewed as oppressed pawns with a "Beetle Bailey" mentality, and senior officers, as a group, tend to be perceived as manipulators of situations for their own career progression. The findings of this research project do not agree with these misjudgments of the characteristics of various subgroups within the Army. While it was determined that there are major differences in self-reported beliefs between several subgroups of Army personnel, these differences are favorable ones, beneficial to both the individual and the organization.

As a group, for example, Army members of the U.S. Army War College Class of 1972 were found to be optimistic, self-confident, persuasive individuals who have a strong preference for being leaders. While they are aggressive and highly competitive in actions with their peers, they are strongly sensitive to the needs of their subordinates. In arriving at a decision they tend to consider the facts rather than the relative popularity of various courses of action. In cases where the mission conflicts with the approval from others, they place little value in the approval from others. It is interesting to find that these individuals are quite similar to civilian business executives and to Navy War College students.

The responses of six groups of individuals associated with the Army are quite different. (Specific differences were elaborated on in Chapter 7.) Each group with its own set of characteristics is probably best suited for its own particular role.

CONCLUSIONS

1. *Contemporary Literature* The American soldier of the Vietnam War was described unfairly in much of the contemporary literature of that period.

2. *Training* Officer Candidate School training exerts a strong influence on the individuals involved. This training tends to change certain self-reported beliefs in terms of: basic beliefs, activity preferences, personal values, and behavioral styles. These changes can be predicted and are beneficial to both the individual concerned and to the U.S. Army. Years later, those beliefs that are no longer appropriate will tend to change again so that they will be compatible with the individual's new total environment.

Training of the intensity described earlier in this volume can be expanded to include subjects other than officer candidate training. For example, new soldiers in the Army could receive intensive training that molds beliefs concerning such subjects as racial harmony, drugs, crime in the barracks, teamwork, and discipline.

3. *Effects of Combat* The effects of combat on the beliefs of infantrymen returning to civilian life are not detrimental to society. The same group of individuals were more sensitive to the needs of their friends while they were stationed as infantrymen in Vietnam than they were after they returned to the United States.

4. *Retention* There is a significant difference in the self-reported beliefs between groups of individuals who will remain in the Army and groups of individuals who will depart. These differences can be used as indicators to predict, with considerable reliability, whether or not the individual will reenlist. For example, those individuals having the highest probability for remaining in the Army can be identified with considerable accuracy at the time of their initial selection.

A major goal in life most often stated by both those who remain in the Army and those who depart from the Army is to be successful in their career. It is interesting to note that the major reason why many company grade officers depart from the Army is that they consider that their potential for a successful Army career is diminishing.

5. *Comparison of Various Subgroups* There is a tendency in the current literature by critics of the Army to misjudge the characteristics of various subgroups within the Army. While it was determined that there are major differences in self-reported beliefs between several subgroups of Army personnel, these differences are favorable ones, beneficial to both the individual and the organization.

RECOMMENDATIONS

1. *Contemporary Literature* A sincere effort must be made to dispel the misperceptions of the American soldier held by many critics of the Army. This effort should not be in terms of increased publicity but should be directed towards a genuine attempt to solve problems within the Army that tend to generate these misperceptions. Potential solutions for several of these problems will be elaborated in the other recommendations that follow.

2. *Training* Training can have a strong influence on the individual. It is recommended that training similar in intensity to that described in this book be provided to all recruits entering the Army. The scope of this intensive training after concentrating on military subjects would focus on influencing a set of beliefs that would encourage: racial harmony, rejection of experimentation with drugs, rejection of crime in the barracks, and development of a favorable response to both teamwork and discipline. The current four-month training program, consisting of basic and advanced individual training, should be expanded to a six-month program to provide for these new or expanded subjects.

236

The new subjects should be presented to small groups, in a seminar setting, with emphasis on case study methods. Teamwork and discipline would be further encouraged by unit sports, in which all participate, as well as various forms of "adventure" training where small groups of individuals participate in independent rugged expeditions that include such activities as mountaineering and camping.

The overall six-month training program should be challenging and should have high standards. During the first three months of training, the new soldier should have the option of quitting the Army. In addition, those who cannot successfully complete the overall program and those who don't measure up to disciplinary standards should be released from active duty at the end of the six-month training program. The final product of an expanded basic training and advanced individual training program would be a highly motivated, well-disciplined, professional soldier.

Concurrent with centralized training for new soldiers, decentralized training at unit level would reinforce and further develop what the individual learned in his basic and advanced individual training. Emphasis would be placed on training needed for the unique characteristics of the unit. The individual, once trained for a specific career field within a unit, would remain assigned to the same major organization throughout most of his career, commensurate with the availability of opportunities for his own advancement. It would be hoped that the soldier would remain in the same unit for an extended period. It is believed that soldiers given the training as outlined, could easily be formed into cadre for expansion during an emergency.

3. *Effects of Combat* In the selection and training of recruits to become infantrymen, it is recommended that more emphasis be placed on the individual's psychological qualities. Individuals who are not suitable for the infantry should be reassigned elsewhere. If no suitable assignment can be found, the person should be released from the Army.

4. *Retention* It is recommended that current reenlistment programs consider the overall differences in self-reported beliefs between those individuals who tend to remain in the Army and those individuals who tend to depart. It is further recommended that programs of initial recruiting give priority to individuals most likely to reenlist years later. The set of self-reported beliefs applicable to those who tend to remain in the Army is elaborated on in Chapter 6.

It is recommended that existing officer career management programs focus on the retention of exceptionally good individuals who are considering departure from the Army. A major reason for their departure is that they consider that their potential for a successful Army career is diminishing. Often this is not the case, and it appears that considerable progress could be made by dispelling many of their imagined career management problems.

5. *Comparison of Various Subgroups* It is recommended that the differences between various groups associated with the Army be considered when policies and procedures applicable to all of them are developed.

CLOSING REMARKS

An argument in favor of the American soldier of the Vietnam War is that his unique qualities enabled him to perform admirably during a period that lacked major support on the home front for the fighting man. The recommendations of this book are intended to stress an increase in the professionalism of the American soldier. The common thread throughout these recommendations is the need to raise the standards of initial selection and to intensify initial training. A current argument against improved selection and training is that we won't have enough recruits if we raise the entry standards and intensify initial training concurrent with eliminating the draft during times of peace. This may be partly true, but in the long run it is essential that standards for entry into the U.S. Army be raised now, and that the pace and scope of the initial training soldiers currently receive be intensified. By so doing, the nation will have a well-trained force that can be easily and effectively expanded in time of need.

Appendix A

DESCRIPTION OF QUESTIONNAIRE USED THROUGHOUT RESEARCH PROJECT

There were many considerations involved in the selection of the test instrument used in this study. The major factors that facilitated its application were its capability to discriminate between occupational groups and its capability to be administered equally well via mail. In this particular research project, the same individuals were, over a period of time, situated in different occupational groups. Differences in these groups could, in part, be developed by considering the beliefs of their individual members. The Job Analysis and Interest Measurement (JAIM) appeared to be suited to this task. An instrument was needed that would be reliable when utilized on several different occasions, initially in an Army classroom, later in Vietnam, and then again years later via mail. The JAIM satisfied this need. The established self-consistency of the JAIM fulfilled a need for reliability. Prior applications of the JAIM pertaining to the extent to which the instrument measures what it is supposed to measure satisfied the requirement of validity.

The JAIM is a 125–item questionnaire[1] designed to measure certain self-reported beliefs (other than aptitudes, training, or knowledge) which have an influence on job success or failure. Its 125 multiple-choice items are presented in terms of certain self-reported beliefs.

> The Job Analysis and Interest Measurement distributed by the Educational Testing Service for research purposes, is designed to measure the personal qualities of the worker, other than his aptitudes, training, or knowledge, which have an influence on success or failure in a job. It has commonly been observed that failures often result not from lack of specific abilities but from "personality difficulties." Experienced managers know that, while every job requires a minimal level of knowledge and specific ability, after this level has been reached the determinants of job success or failure are intangible and complex. They are often described in such terms as "can't stand pressure," or "intolerant of ambiguity." The JAIM was designed to measure these elements.[2]

[1]Form 864 of the JAIM was used throughout this research project.
[2]Regis H. Walther, *Orientations and Behavioral Styles of Foreign Service Officers* (New York: Carnegie Endowment for International Peace, 1965), pp. 2–3.

It should be recognized that there are no right or wrong answers for this type of test. The instrument[3] is based on the overall concept of the need to have a successful match between the professional requirements of an occupation and the qualities of the individual in that occupation. Thus, for example, it can be conceptualized that the occupation of chief librarian and the occupation of locomotive engineer require considerably different types of individuals. Further, that most chief librarians would probably perform poorly as locomotive engineers and that most locomotive engineers would no doubt perform poorly as chief librarians.

An analysis of the results in this study will provide information relative to both the individual and the nature of his organization. The norms of the test instrument are intended only as a point of departure and are based on a wide variety of occupational groups. The JAIM provides measures for 32 scales.

> The higher the score on a particular scale, the more often the subject has chosen the options for this scale as being descriptive of himself in preference to the options for other scales and has avoided options which are negatively scored for this scale. The lower the score on a particular scale, the less often the subject has chosen the options for this scale as being descriptive of himself in preference to the options for the other scales and the more often he has selected options which are negatively scored for the scale.[4]

BELIEFS

While it is acknowledged that there are many categories of beliefs, the term "beliefs" will refer to the overall set of self-reported beliefs that are associated with the test instrument. Prior studies seem to substantiate that there is a considerable difference in the self-reported beliefs of individuals before and after training. Further, that this difference can be attributed to the conditioning process. In addition, self-reported beliefs tend to change with changes in job position and changes in environment. Empirical observations and the results of prior studies suggest that within this study a portion of an individual's set of beliefs may be categorized as follows: (a) Basic Beliefs, (b) Activity Preferences, (c) Personal Values, and (d) Behavioral Styles.

1. BASIC BELIEFS

> Each of us makes judgments about what we can expect from the world, from ourselves, and from other people. These judgments depend to a large degree, of course, on the situation. Our judgments are also influenced by our basic expectations or beliefs. These beliefs orient us to the world in terms of optimism or pessimism, self-confidence or self-doubt, and trust or suspicion.[5]

[3] A copy of both the JAIM questionnaire and answer sheet are presented in Appendixes B and C.

[4] Regis H. Walther and Shirley D. McCune, *Socialization Principles and Work Styles of the Juvenile Court* (Washington, D.C.: George Washington Univ., 1965), pp. 91–92.

[5] Walther, *The Psychological Dimensions of Work: A Research Approach Through Use of a Self-Report Inventory* (Washington, D.C.: George Washington Univ., 1972).

A person's basic beliefs often influence his response on the job. The nature of this response may considerably affect his performance and the satisfaction he receives from the result of his performance in different work situations.

While it is recognized that there are many basic beliefs, the following basic beliefs will be considered: (a) Extent of Optimism, (b) Degree of Self-Confidence, (c) Belief in Moral Absolutes, and (d) Belief in Slow Change.

a. *Extent of Optimism*—This scale measures the degree to which the individual assumes that the intentions of other people are benevolent and that satisfactions can be expected in the natural course of events. Persons scoring high consider themselves lucky; never or seldom left out of things in group activities; and almost always have had leaders who praised them and gave them credit for work well done.

b. *Degree of Self-Confidence*—This scale measures the degree to which the individual believes that he can, by his own action, influence future events. Persons scoring high on this scale report that they often become enthusiastic over new things or new plans, that their ideas are often considered unusual and imaginative; and that they work well under stress. Individuals scoring low report they get away by themselves when they are troubled; and that they do not perform well under stress.

c. *Belief in Moral Absolutes*—Persons scoring high believe that moral principles come from an outside power higher than man; and that it is most important to have faith in something. Individuals scoring low believe that moral principles are not absolute and unchanging but depend on circumstances.

d. *Belief in Slow Change*—This scale measures the degree to which the individual believes that change should be slow. Persons scoring high say that it is usually best to do things in a conventional way; and that when things are going smoothly it is best not to make changes which will disrupt things.

2. ACTIVITY PREFERENCES

Activity preferences involve the anticipation of intrinsic satisfaction from the performance of certain types of tasks. Some people derive their greatest satisfaction from jobs that involve a challenge; some from jobs that emphasize working with people; and some from jobs that require the competent manipulation of tools and materials. Individuals also appear to differ in the amount of environmental stimulation they require without which boredom influences their satisfaction and perhaps also their performance. [6]

With regard to activity preferences, this research project will focus on the following: (a) Prefers Problem Analysis, (b) Prefers Social Interaction, (c) Prefers Mechanical Activities, (d) Prefers Supervisory Activities, and (e) Prefers Activity Frequent Change.

a. *Prefers Problem Analysis*—This scale measures the degree to which the individual likes to analyze situations and develop ingenious solutions to problems. Persons scoring high prefer to be considered ingenious; like to

[6] *Ibid.*

develop new ideas and approaches to problems and situations; and like a job which permits them to be creative and original.

b. *Prefers Social Interaction*—This scale measures the degree to which the individual likes work involving interactions with people. Persons scoring high attend parties or social gatherings once a week or oftener; do not like to work apart from other people; and frequently entertain groups at home.

c. *Prefers Mechanical Activities*—This scale measures the degree to which the individual likes mechanical activities. Persons scoring high on this scale say they are reasonably skilled craftsmen and enjoy fixing things; like making things with tools; and like hunting and fishing.

d. *Prefers Supervisory Activities*—This scale measures the degree to which the individual likes to plan and supervise the work of other people. Persons scoring high on this scale find that they get along best when they know what they want and work for it; they are generally striving to reach some goal they have established for themselves and like to supervise others in the carrying out of difficult assignments.

e. *Prefers Activity Frequent Change*—This scale measures the degree to which the individual likes to be actively engaged in work providing a lot of excitement, and a great deal of variety. Persons scoring high on this scale say they frequently enjoy taking part in a fight for good causes; sometimes enjoy dangerous situations; work best under a great deal of pressure and tight deadlines; and prefer a job in which there is a great deal of activity and opportunity to make frequent decisions. Persons scoring low like to finish one task before starting another.

3. PERSONAL VALUES

Each of us has a set of standards or values about what is worthwhile and what is not, what we would like to be and what we would not. We use our standards to judge ourselves and our activities. These values are an essential component of our self-concepts and are reflected in the meaning work has for us.[7]

In considering the personal values category, this research project will concentrate on the following: (a) Values Status Attainment, (b) Values Social Service, (c) Values Approval from Others, (d) Values Intellectual Achievement, and (e) Values Role Conformity.

a. *Values Status Attainment*—This scale measures the degree to which the individual values himself by his achievement of the status symbols established by his culture. Persons scoring high on this scale prefer to be considered ambitious and successful; like to have a job which is recognized to be important or desirable; and think that the ideal job is one which shows they were a success and had achieved high status and prestige.

b. *Values Social Service*—This scale measures the degree to which the individual values himself by contributing to social improvement. Persons

[7] *Ibid.*

242

scoring high like to be considered understanding and charitable; consider the social usefulness of the work to be important; and like work which permits them to be helpful to others.

    c.   *Values Approval from Others*—This scale measures the degree to which the individual values himself by obtaining the approval of others. Persons scoring high consider it most important to have congenial peers; to be well-liked; to please others through their work; and to be considered gracious, attractive, and pleasant.

    d.   *Values Intellectual Achievement*—This scale measures the degree to which the individual values himself through his intellectual attainments. Persons scoring high like work which permits them to be creative and original; like to be considered ingenious, imaginative, intelligent, and brilliant; and believe that it is important to be intelligent and resourceful as opposed to having faith in something, or being kind and considerate.

    e.   *Values Role Conformity*—This scale measures the degree to which the individual values himself according to how successfully he has conformed to the role requirements of society. Persons scoring high say that they prefer to be considered reliable, dependable, trustworthy, and industrious.

4. BEHAVIORAL STYLES

> Individuals necessarily develop standard ways for dealing with recurring situations and reserve conscious information processing and decision-making for more significant occasions. This organization gives rise to characteristic types of performance or behavioral styles, conscious and unconscious, in various life situations.[8]

The following behavioral styles are considered pertinent to this research project: (a) Degree of Perseverance, (b) Extent of Orderliness, (c) Prefers to Plan Ahead, (d) Influences by Persuasive Leadership, (e) Influences by Being Self Assertive, (f) Move Toward Aggressor, (g) Move Away from Aggressor, (h) Move Against Aggressor, (i) Prefers Routine, (j) Identifies with Authority, (k) Prefers Independence, (l) Prefers Directive Leadership Style, (m) Prefers Participative Leadership Style, (n) Prefers Delegative Leadership Style, (o) Motivates by Knowledge of Results, (p) Believes in External Controls, (q) Prefers Being Systematic, Methodical, and (r) Prefers Group Participation.

    a.   *Degree of Perseverance*—This scale measures the degree to which the individual keeps at something even when he is not particularly interested in it. Persons scoring high say that when working on a hobby, they concentrate for long periods of time and complete each project they start; that they do not tire easily and can work long and steadily; and that other people seldom find something after they have tried and given up. Individuals scoring low say that when they have something to do that doesn't interest them, they either do it after considerable pressure is put on them or they seldom get around to doing it.

    b.   *Extent of Orderliness*—This scale measures the degree to which the

[8] *Ibid.*

individual has internal standards which he follows. Persons scoring high say that they like work which requires them to be extremely accurate; that they are usually orderly; and that they get up about the same time each morning and do not like to stay in bed later than their getting-up time.

c. *Prefers to Plan Ahead*—This scale measures the degree to which the individual is a self-starter and directs his own activity toward goal achievement. Persons scoring high say that they get best results when they establish long-range goals and follow them as much as they can; and that they are generally striving to reach some goal they have established for themselves.

d. *Influences by Persuasive Leadership*—This scale measures the degree to which the individual exerts leadership in interpersonal situations. Persons scoring high report that they have no difficulty giving a speech or reciting before a large group; that they often take the leadership in groups; and that what they like best in a job is the opportunity to get results through persuasion or negotiation.

e. *Influences by Being Self-Assertive*—This scale measures the degree to which the individual tends to pursue his own goals when they are in competition with the goals of others. Persons scoring high say that it is important to avoid being diverted from doing what is right in order to please someone; that they do better under competition or stress; and that they are proficient in athletic games.

f. *Move Toward Aggressor*—This scale measures the degree to which the individual tries to "pour oil on troubled waters" when someone acts toward him in a belligerent or aggressive manner. Persons scoring high say that when a person behaves toward them in a dictatorial or domineering fashion, they try to win him over.

g. *Move Away from Aggressor*—This scale measures the degree to which the individual withdraws when someone acts toward him in a belligerent or aggressive manner. Persons scoring high say that when a person acts toward them in a dictatorial or domineering fashion, they keep away from him if they can.

h. *Move Against Aggressor*—This scale measures the degree to which the individual counterattacks when someone acts toward him in a belligerent or aggressive manner. Persons scoring high say that when someone crowds ahead of them in line, they do something about it; and if someone acts toward them in a dictatorial or domineering fashion, they seek an occasion to have it out with him.

i. *Prefers Routine*—This scale measures the degree to which the individual likes to have definite procedures available which he can follow. Persons scoring high say they like to have a clear-cut written guideline or manual which tells them clearly what they are supposed to do.

j. *Identifies with Authority*—This scale measures the degree to which the individual identifies with his superior and tries to please him. Persons scoring high say that they like to work closely with, and be of help to, a superior doing important and interesting work; that their leaders, for the most part, have always been helpful and understanding; that they received high grades while in high school; and that they were either obedient toward or tried to please their parents as an adolescent.

k. *Prefers Independence*—This scale measures the degree to which the individual likes to act on his own. Persons scoring high say they were independent toward their parents during adolescence; that they have no fixed pattern for getting up in the morning and sometimes get up early and sometimes sleep late; and that it is most important to teach children to be self-reliant.

l. *Prefers Directive Leadership Style*—This scale measures the degree to which the individual believes that a leader gets the best results by making decisions himself. Persons scoring high say that an effective leader assigns each subordinate a specific job to do and sees that he does it the way it is supposed to be done.

m. *Prefers Participative Leadership Style*—This scale measures the degree to which the individual believes that leaders get best results by having the work group participate in decisionmaking. Persons who score high say that it is most important that a leader develop a strong sense of responsibility in the work group as a whole.

n. *Prefers Delegative Leadership Style*—This scale measures the degree to which the individual believes that the leader gets the best results by delegating decisionmaking authority as much as possible to individual subordinates. Persons scoring high say that to the extent practical, an effective leader permits each subordinate to do the work the way he finds works best for him.

o. *Motivates by Knowledge of Results*—This scale measures the degree to which the individual believes that people are motivated best by knowledge of results (intrinsic motivation). Persons scoring high say that a leader gets the best results from his work group when he shows the employees the importance of their work. Persons scoring low say a leader gets the best results through rewards or punishment (extrinsic motivation).

p. *Believes in External Controls*—This scale measures the degree to which the individual believes that most people require external controls. Individuals scoring high say that most people prefer a leader who tells them clearly what to do; and believe that parents get the best results when they maintain strict discipline.

q. *Prefers Being Systematic, Methodical*—Persons scoring high believe that when they have a difficult decision to make and feel that they have enough facts that it is best to spend considerable time reviewing all possible interpretations of the facts before making a decision; they prefer the opportunity for careful consideration of all aspects of the problem and when they have an important problem to consider, they prefer to think it through alone.

r. *Prefers Group Participation*—This scale measures the degree to which the individual identifies himself with a highly valued group. Persons scoring high say they like best to work as a member of a group and do not like to work apart from other people.

Appendix B

JAIM QUESTIONNAIRE

THE JOB ANALYSIS AND INTEREST MEASUREMENT* FORM 864

Regis Walther, Ph.D.
Center for the Behavioral Sciences
The George Washington University
Washington, D. C.

Distributed for Research Purposes
Educational Testing Services
Princeton, New Jersey

*JAIM questionnaire reprinted with the permission of Dr. Regis H. Walther.

JOB ANALYSIS AND INTEREST MEASUREMENT (JAIM)

Mark the *one* option in each of the following questions which best applies to you. Mark only one in each question. Answer EVERY QUESTION.

1. While in school how often were you an elected officer in an organization?
    a. President or vice president of some organization almost every year.
    b   Often an officer but not usually president.
    c. An officer a few times.
    d. Never an officer of an organization.

2. How often do you write personal letters?
    a. Frequently because you enjoy exchanging letters.
    b. Frequently but as a matter of obligation.
    c. Sometimes.
    d. Seldom.
    e. Almost never.

3. How often do you attend parties or social gatherings?
    a. Several times a week.
    b. About once a week
    c. About once or twice a month.
    d. Several times a year.
    e. Almost never.

4. Which one of the following school or college subjects did you enjoy most?
    a. Social Sciences and/or English.
    b. Shop.
    c. Mathematics, Chemistry, and/or Physics.
    d. Biology and/or Botany.
    e. None of the above.

5. Which of the following best describes your mathematical skill?
    a. You can add and subtract.
    b. You can add, subtract, multiply and divide whole numbers.
    c. You can do arithmetic involving fractions, decimals, and percentages.

d.   You can do ordinary algebraic and geometric problems.
e.   You can do advanced mathematics, such as the differential and integral calculus.

6.   How were your grades in high school?
a.   Excellent.
b.   Good.
c.   Fair.
d.   Failing.
e.   Did not attend high school.

7.   If you went to college, what was your academic standing?
a.   An honor student and awarded commendation.
b.   Above the average of your class.
c.   About the average of your class.
d.   Below the average of your class.
e.   Did not go to college or have just started.

8.   When in school were you
a.   A member of many clubs and organizations.
b.   A member of few clubs and organizations.
c.   Seldom or never a member of any clubs or organizations.

9.   Which of the following do you like best in a job?
a.   Analyzing situations.
b.   Working with other people.
c.   Using skill with tools to make something.

10.   Which one of the following conditions of a job do you dislike *most?*
a.   Working apart from other people.
b.   A great deal of pressure on you.
c.   A poor supervisor.
d.   Detailed and specific instructions.

11.   Which one of the following conditions of a job do you dislike *least?*
a.   Working apart from other people.
b.   A great deal of pressure on you.
c.   A poor supervisor.
d.   Detailed and specific instructions.

12.   The thing you like best in playing cards or similar competitive games is
a.   The competition.
b.   The sociability.
c.   The opportunity to play well.
d.   You do not like competitive games.

252

13. Are you at your best during a written examination?
    a. Yes.
    b. No.
    c. Don't know.

14. As an adolescent you were mostly
    a. Obedient toward your parents or guardians.
    b. Trying to please your parents or guardians.
    c. Independent.
    d. Rebellious.
    e. Resentful.

15. How many friends do you have?
    a. One or two friends.
    b. A few friends, but these are really close friends.
    c. No very close friends, but many casual friends.
    d. Many friends.
    e. No friends.

16. It is most important for a supervisor to
    a. Organize and direct the work so that he gets the most out of each employee.
    b. Give the work group a sense of direction and purpose so that the whole group is motivated.
    c. Make it possible for each individual worker to do his job well.

17. Which of the following is *most* important to you in a job?
    a. Steadiness and permanence of work.
    b. Congenial co-workers.
    c. Promotion opportunities.
    d. Competent co-workers.

18. Which of the following is *least* important to you in a job?
    a. Steadiness and permanence of work.
    b. Congenial co-workers.
    c. Promotion opportunities.
    d. Competent co-workers.

19. When people try to take advantage of you, are you most likely to
    a. Have nothing further to do with them, at least temporarily.
    b. Insist that they stop.
    c. Try to understand them and get them to be reasonable.

20. It is most important for you to be
    a. Independent.

    b.   Successful.
    c.   Well-liked.
    d.   Socially useful.

21.   How lucky do you feel you have been?
    a.   Almost always lucky.
    b.   Usually lucky.
    c.   Neither lucky nor unlucky.
    d.   Somewhat unlucky.
    e.   Very unlucky.

22.   You prefer to be considered
    a.   Successful.
    b.   Ingenious.
    c.   Unselfish.
    d.   Well-liked.
    e.   Reliable.

23.   You get along best when you
    a.   Respect the rights of others.
    b.   Respect the feelings of others.
    c.   Do what has to be done even if it doesn't please everyone.

24.   It would compliment you most to be called
    a.   Brilliant.
    b.   Helpful.
    c.   Industrious.
    d.   Gracious.
    e.   Powerful.

25.   You get along best when you
    a.   Know what you want and work to get it.
    b.   Do what seems to be appropriate in each situation.
    c.   Follow established principles and standards.

26.   Which of the following do you like best in a job?
    a.   To work closely with a superior doing important and interesting work.
    b.   To get results on your own.
    c.   To be a member of a group with high morale and high performance standards.
    d.   To organize and direct the carrying out of an important task.
    e.   None of the above.

27.   When you have something to do that doesn't interest you, you

a. Nearly always do it without delay.
b. Do the things that interest you first.
c. Do it after considerable procrastination.
d. Do it after pressure is put on you.
e. Seldom get around to doing it.

28. If you were asked to be an officer of an organization, you would prefer
a. To be president.
b. To be vice president.
c. To be secretary.
d. To be treasurer.
e. To hold no office.

29. You have been doublecrossed by people
a. Often.
b. Sometimes.
c. Almost never.

30. It is most important for a supervisor to
a. Praise employees for the work they do well.
b. Prod employees for greater effort to get them to work up to capacity.
c. Let employees know the results of their work.

31. People are most likely to be influenced by
a. The fear of punishment.
b. The possibility of rewards.
c. The chance to accomplish something.

32. In your personal habits you consider yourself
a. Unusually orderly
b. More orderly than average.
c. About average in orderliness.
d. Somewhat below average in orderliness.
e. Considerably below average in orderliness.

33. When you have an appointment or have to be somewhere you are
a. Almost always there ahead of time.
b. Almost always on time.
c. Sometimes a little late.
d. Frequently late.
e. Almost always late.

34. It is most important that a supervisor
a. Make definite assignments and insist that deadlines be met.
b. Develop a strong sense of responsibility in the work group as a whole.

c. Encourage each subordinate to do as much as he can on his own and give him help when he needs it.

35. Which type of supervisor do you prefer?
    a. One who makes use of your ability.
    b. One who tells you clearly what is expected of you.
    c. One who expects and permits you to work on your own.

36. As a child the discipline you received was
    a. Very strict.
    b. Strict but not harsh.
    c. Lenient.
    d. Lax.
    e. Strict from one parent and lenient from the other.

37. Which of the following statements best describes how you spend your spare time?
    a. Frequently have trouble finding something to do.
    b. Sometimes have trouble finding something to do.
    c. Almost always have something to do, but don't always enjoy it.
    d. Almost always have something to do that you enjoy.

38. In your work you like to
    a. Be guided by professional standards and practices.
    b. Have definite procedures and written instructions which you can follow.
    c. Help your supervisor with whatever needs to be done.
    d. Decide for yourself what to do and how to do it.

39. You enjoy taking part in a good fight for a good cause
    a. Frequently.
    b. Sometimes.
    c. Almost never.

40. Your associates consider you
    a. Too concerned with details.
    b. Very careful about details.
    c. Somewhat careless about details.
    d. Very careless about details.

41. Have your supervisors or teachers praised you and given you credit for work done well?
    a. Almost always.
    b. Usually.
    c. Seldom.

42. As an adolescent, you *openly* disagreed with one or both of your parents or your guardian on political, religious, social, or other issues
    a. Frequently.
    b. Occasionally.
    c. Rarely or never although you sometimes disagreed with them.
    d. Rarely or never because you almost always agreed with them.

43. Which of the following aspects of a job do you find most desirable?
    a. Using persuasion to get things done.
    b. Helping others deal more successfully with a problem.
    c. Making things through use of tools.
    d. Having a job or position which is recognized to be important or desirable.
    e. None of the above.

44. Which of the following do you like best?
    a. To work as a member of a group engaged in some useful activity.
    b. To develop new ideas and approaches to problems and situations.
    c. To direct and coordinate the efforts of other people.
    d. To get results by overcoming obstacles and resistance.
    e. None of the above.

45. A supervisor gets the best results from his work group when he
    a. Requires a little bit more work than his employees think they can do.
    b. Rewards loyalty and good performance.
    c. Shows employees the importance of their work.

46. When engaged in athletics or physical activities what effect does competition or stress have on your performance?
    a. You do better under competition or stress.
    b. You do better when there is no competition or stress.
    c. Competition or stress does not affect your performance.

47. Which do you like best in a job?
    a. To solve difficult problems on your own through use of ingenuity.
    b. To supervise the carrying out of a difficult assignment.
    c. To use tools to make something.
    d. To work with other people.
    e. None of the above.

48. During your working career your jobs have
    a. Almost always been interesting.
    b. Usually been interesting.
    c. Seldom been interesting.

49. Your supervisors for the most part have
   a. Shown a lack of sympathy and understanding in dealing with you as an employee.
   b. Been for the most part indifferent.
   c. Been friendly but not particularly helpful.
   d. Usually been helpful and understanding.
   e. Almost always been helpful and understanding.

50. Do you complain to the waiter when you are served inferior or poorly prepared food?
   a. Whenever complaint is justified.
   b. Sometimes when complaint is justified.
   c. Almost never.

51. You find you get along best when you
   a. Establish long range plans and goals and follow them as much as you can.
   b. Adapt yourself to the current situation and avoid unrealistic, "ivory tower" plans.
   c. Do what is expected and required of you.

52. When working in your spare time on a hobby or something that interests you, do you
   a. Concentrate for long periods of time and complete each project you start.
   b. Work on a number of things at the same time and complete most of them but not necessarily in the order in which you started them.
   c. Finish those things that continue to interest you and forget about the others.
   d. Start many things but finish only a few.
   e. Seldom finish anything you start in your spare time.

53. An effective supervisor
   a. Assigns each subordinate a specific job to do and sees that he does it the way it is supposed to be done.
   b. To the extent practicable permits members of the work group to decide among themselves how things should be done.
   c. To the extent practicable permits each subordinate to do the work the way he finds works best for him.

54. Do you entertain groups at home?
   a. Frequently.
   b. Occasionally.
   c. Almost never.

55. How do people feel about you?
   a. Almost all of them like you.
   b. Most of them like you.
   c. A few of them like you.
   d. Almost none of them likes you.

56. Your political, religious, and social views are
   a. Almost identical with those of your parents.
   b. Similar to those of your parents.
   c. Different in some important respect from those of your parents.
   d. Very substantially different from those of your parents.
   e. Different in almost every important respect from those of your parents.

57. An effective supervisor
   a. Takes every opportunity to praise employees on their performance.
   b. Only praises employees occasionally or for unusually good work since employees usually know when they are doing well.
   c. Praises employees occasionally but also keeps a careful watch for deficient performance to discipline those who fall below standard.

58. How much energy do you have?
   a. Do not tire easily and can work long and steadily.
   b. Have spurts of energy particularly when working on something interesting.
   c. Work hard for long periods of time but then sometimes suddenly feel great fatigue.
   d. Have about the average amount of energy.
   e. Tire more easily than the average person.

59. When you feel troubled do you
   a. Talk it over with someone.
   b. Get away by yourself.
   c. Get busy and active.

60. Do you feel that laws and social conventions are useless and hamper an individual's personal freedom?
   a. Frequently.
   b. Sometimes.
   c. Seldom.
   d. Never.

61. When a friend or relative makes an obvious grammatical mistake do you
   a. Correct the mistake so that he will know what is right.
   b. Correct the mistake if it has been made a number of times.

c.   Correct the mistake only if you know that he wants to be corrected.
d.   Correct the mistake if it can be done without embarrassing him.
e.   Never correct the mistake.

62.   You prefer to be considered
a.   Intelligent.
b.   Conscientious.
c.   Considerate.
d.   Influential.
e.   Attractive.

63.   Which do you like best?
a.   Working closely with and being of assistance to a supervisor doing important and interesting work.
b.   Working as a member of a group doing important and interesting work.
c.   Working by yourself doing important and interesting work.

64.   When dealing with other people it is most important to
a.   Avoid hurting the feelings of others.
b.   Avoid being diverted from doing what is right in order to please someone.
c.   Avoid unpleasant controversial situations.

65.   If someone crowds ahead of you in a line do you usually?
a.   Pay no attention.
b.   Say nothing, but give him an angry look.
c.   Make a comment to someone else which the offender can hear.
d.   Ask him if he knows he has pushed ahead.
e.   Insist that he go to the proper place in line.

66.   Which of these do you prefer?
a.   To be where there is something going on.
b.   To get away sometimes by yourself and have time for your own thoughts.
c.   Usually to get away by yourself.

67.   Do you feel that you are left out of things, perhaps intentionally, in group activities?
a.   Never.
b.   Seldom.
c.   Sometimes.
d.   Frequently.
e.   Almost always.

68. Which one of the following outside interests appeals to you most?
    a. Plays, concerts, or art exhibits.
    b. Competitive games.
    c. Working with your hands.
    d. Social activities.
    e. None of the above.

69. Which of the these best describes you?
    a. You work best under a great deal of pressure and tight deadlines.
    b. You prefer to work at an even pace, but you are able to work well under pressure.
    c. You prefer not to work under pressure, but you are able to meet most reasonable deadlines.
    d. You do your worst work if unreasonable pressure is put on you.

70. Which do you like best?
    a. Work through which you can influence others.
    b. Work resulting in social improvement.
    c. Work involving the analysis of data.
    d. Steady work without frequent interruptions.
    e. Work through which you can please others.

71. You prefer to be considered
    a. Imaginative.
    b. Ambitious.
    c. Understanding.
    d. Dependable.
    e. Popular.

72. Do you consider your memory for names and faces to be
    a. Above average.
    b. Average.
    c. Below average.

73. Parents get the best results with their children if they
    a. Praise and encourage them.
    b. Praise them sometimes but also maintain strict discipline.
    c. Give them freedom and opportunity to learn from their own experience.

74. People are most likely to be influenced by
    a. Requests from people they like.
    b. Orders from someone in authority.
    c. Opinions of qualified experts.

75. Which of these is most characteristic of you?
    a. You budget your income carefully and follow the budget closely.
    b. You budget your income and follow the budget within reason.
    c. You keep records of personal expenses and check them roughly against what you plan to spend.
    d. You keep no records, but have a rough plan for personal expenditures.

76. Which of the following aspects of a job do you consider most important?
    a. Opportunity to work with a group with high morale and performance standards.
    b. Opportunity for personal accomplishment.
    c. Steady permanent work.
    d. Social usefulness of the work.
    e. None of the above.

77. When you have a difficult decision to make and feel that you have enough facts do you find it
    a. Best to come to a quick decision.
    b. Best to spend considerable time reviewing all the possible interpretations of the facts before making a decision.

78. Which do you like best in a job?
    a. To work closely with and be of help to a supervisor doing important and interesting work.
    b. To have clear-cut written guidelines or manuals which tell you exactly what you are supposed to do.
    c. To have a supervisor who tells you clearly what he expects you to do.
    d. To have a supervisor who expects and permits you to work on your own.

79. Which of the following describes you best?
    a. You get up at about the same time each morning and do not like to stay in bed later than your getting up time.
    b. You usually get off to a slow start in the morning.
    c. You have no fixed pattern and sometimes get up early and sometimes sleep late.

80. Which of the following is most important to you?
    a. Opportunity to understand just how your supervisor expects work to be done.
    b. Freedom in working out your own methods of doing the work.
    c. Opportunity to apply professional standards and skills.

81. When an unpleasant controversy or fight is beginning, you are most likely to

a. Try to "pour oil on troubled waters" and head off the difficulty.
b. Keep from getting involved if you can.
c. Stop the controversy or fight before it gets out of hand.

82. Which of the following types of supervisors do you like *best?*
    a. A supervisor who insists on high performance standards for himself and his subordinates.
    b. A supervisor who gives you clear-cut instructions and is always available for advice.
    c. A supervisor who is considerate and understanding.

83. When procedural changes need to be made, an effective supervisor
    a. Makes a definite decision himself as to what is to be done and how it is to be done.
    b. Tells each subordinate the purpose and to the extent practicable lets each one work out his own methods.
    c. Consults with the work group and encourages them to decide what changes should be made and how they should be put into effect.

84. If a person behaves toward you in a dictatorial or domineering fashion, you
    a. Keep away from him if you can.
    b. Seek an occasion to have it out with him.
    c. Try to understand him and slowly win him over.

85. What responsibility do you think each person has for social improvement?
    a. Each individual should devote some time and effort to improving social conditions.
    b. Each individual should take care of his own responsibilities and avoid "do good" activities.

86. How fast do you drive a car?
    a. Faster than average.
    b. Slower than average.
    c. About average.
    d. You do not drive.

87. Have you found that people break promises which they have made to you?
    a. Frequently.
    b. Sometimes.
    c. Seldom.
    d. Almost never.

88. When watching sports or other competitive activities you usually

263

a. Support the champion or skillful performer.
b. Support the "underdog" or the one who is losing.
c. Do neither, or each about equally.

89. It is most important to
   a. Have faith in something.
   b. Be intelligent and resourceful.
   c. Be kind and considerate.

90. Do you prefer to be considered
   a. Compassionate.
   b. Trustworthy.
   c. Effective.
   d. Pleasant.
   e. Resourceful.

91. Do you take the initiative in planning a party?
   a. Frequently.
   b. Sometimes.
   c. Almost never.

92. Which of these describes your experience with athletic games?
   a. Have received formal recognition of your skill at athletic games.
   b. Enjoy and are or at one time were reasonably good at athletic games.
   c. Enjoy but have never had any particular skill at athletic games.
   d. Do not particularly enjoy athletic games.
   e. Do not like and generally avoid athletic games.

93. What is your ability to fix things around the house?
   a. A reasonably skilled craftsman and enjoy fixing things.
   b. Able to make minor repairs.
   c. Try to fix things only in an emergency.
   d. Almost never try to fix anything.

94. How well do you keep track of your possessions?
   a. Everything is almost always in its place.
   b. Most everything is in its place.
   c. Sometimes things get misplaced.
   d. Frequently things get misplaced.
   e. You have great difficulty keeping track of things.

95. How effective are you at finding lost objects?
   a. Other people seldom find something after you have tried and given up.

b. You are usually able to find things.
c. You sometimes have difficulty finding things.
d. You frequently have to ask for help or else let it go.

96. Do you enjoy trying to solve mathematical or logical puzzles?
a. Yes.
b. No.
c. Sometimes.

97. In what way do you find that you can put your point across best?
a. In writing.
b. Orally.
c. Don't know or it doesn't make much difference.

98. How difficult do you find it to give a speech or to recite before a large group?
a. You have no difficulty.
b. You are a little nervous at first but have no difficulty after getting started.
c. You do not enjoy it but are able to do it adequately when required.
d. You avoid public speaking or reciting whenever possible.

99. Does it bother you to have to give orders to other people?
a. Very much.
b. A little.
c. Not at all.

100. How often do you find yourself taking a position of leadership in a group you are with?
a. Often.
b. Occasionally.
c. Almost never.

101. Which of the following describes you the best?
a. Happy.
b. Ambitious.
c. Cautious.

102. Does it bother you to leave a task unfinished?
a. Almost always.
b. Usually.
c. Seldom.
d. Only if it is very important.

103. The ideal job for you would

a. Enable you to look forward to a stable, secure future.
b. Permit you to be creative and original.
c. Give you an opportunity to be helpful to others.
d. Show that you were a success and had achieved high status and prestige.
e. Provide you with excitement and variety.

Mark the one statement in each of the following pairs which *best* applies to you. Mark only one in each pair. Answer EVERY QUESTION.

104. a. You prefer a great deal of activity and the opportunity to make frequent decisions.
b. You prefer the opportunity for careful consideration of all aspects of a problem or situation.

105. a. You like to work steadily and be busy all the time.
b. You like to work hard when necessary including putting in overtime.

106. a. You like to finish one task before starting another.
b. You like to work on several things at once.

107. a. You like clear-cut guidelines or instructions so you know exactly what is expected of you.
b. You like to decide for yourself how the work should be done.

108. a. You like to be given interesting assignments which you can do yourself.
b. You like to accomplish results through supervising others.

109. a. You believe most people are more inclined to help others.
b. You believe most people are more inclined to look out for themselves.

110. a. You would describe yourself as self-confident.
b. You would describe yourself as cautious.

Mark as many of the following statements as apply. You do *NOT* need to limit yourself to one response.

111. Which of the following statements apply to you?
a. You usually carry through your plans in spite of opposition.
b. You have no difficulty in turning down unreasonable requests.
c. Most people have confidence in your ability.
d. You have no difficulty in maintaining your opinion when other people disagree with you.
e. None of the above applies to you.

266

112. Which of the following statements apply to you?
    a. You believe it is seldom wise to change your plans in the midst of an undertaking.
    b. You try to follow a way of life based on duty.
    c. You have a work and study schedule which you follow carefully.
    d. You are always careful about your manner of dress.
    e. None of the above applies to you.

113. With which of the following statements do you agree?
    a. It is usually best to do things in a conventional way.
    b. It is usually best to change things slowly.
    c. You would rather be a steady and dependable worker than a brilliant but unstable one.
    d. When things are going smoothly it is best not to make changes which will disrupt things.
    e. You do not agree with any of the above.

114. Which of the following statements apply to you?
    a. You have found that people who make quick decisions frequently make poor ones.
    b. You frequently see so many different aspects of a problem or situation that you find it difficult to make a decision.
    c. When you have an important problem to consider, you prefer to think it through alone.
    d. You frequently become so absorbed in what you are doing that you find it difficult to turn your attention to something else.
    e. None of the above applies to you.

115. With which of the following statements do you agree?
    a. Spare the rod and spoil the child.
    b. There are certain types of behavior which are always right, moral, and good.
    c. Moral principles come from an outside power higher than man.
    d. Obedience and respect for authority are among the most important virtues children should learn.
    e. You do not agree with any of the above.

116. Which of the following statements apply to you?
    a. Like to keep going until you have finished a job.
    b. You are thorough in any work you undertake.
    c. You have a reputation for keeping at something after other people have lost interest.
    d. You are generally striving to reach some goal you have established for yourself.
    e. None of the above applies to you.

117. Which of the following apply to you?
    a. When things are dull you frequently like to stir up some excitement.
    b. You frequently like to take a chance rather than play it safe.
    c. You sometimes enjoy a dangerous situation.
    d. You enjoy a race or a game better when you bet on it.
    e. None of the above applies to you.

118. With which of the following statements do you agree?
    a. The best defense is a good offense.
    b. It is more important to be respected than to be liked.
    c. People are more competitive than they are cooperative.
    d. No matter what a superior officer says he should always be obeyed.
    e. You do not agree with any of the above.

119. Which of the following statements apply to you?
    a. You can deal more effectively with words than you can with numbers.
    b. You often depend on overall impressions more than on systematic analysis.
    c. You frequently find it is better to act now rather than to take the extra time needed to plan and think things through carefully.
    d. You believe that moral principles are not absolute and unchanging but depend upon circumstances.
    e. None of the above applies to you.

120. Which of the following statements apply to you?
    a. Your ideas are often considered unusual and imaginative.
    b. It does not disturb you to be different from other people and to do things which are not customary.
    c. You often contribute new ideas to your work.
    d. You often become enthusiastic over new things or new plans.
    e. None of the above applies to you.

121. Which of the following activities do you enjoy a great deal?
    a. Reading nonfiction or serious novels.
    b. Hunting or fishing.
    c. Playing cards.
    d. Making things by using tools.
    e. You do not particularly enjoy any of the above activities.

122. Which of the following sayings have you found frequently to be true?
    a. "It is often necessary to be cruel in order to be kind."
    b. "Give someone an inch and he will take a mile."
    c. "Familiarity breeds contempt."
    d. "Good fences make good neighbors."
    e. You have not found any of the above to be frequently true.

123. Which of the following leisure-time activities interested you in high school?
    a. Doing scientific experiments.
    b. Using tools to build, improve, and repair things.
    c. Playing on a school athletic team.
    d. Participating in social affairs.
    e. None of the above.

124. Which of the following statements describe the attitudes of most people toward their work?
    a. Most people shirk their duties whenever they think they can get away with it.
    b. Most people prefer a supervisor who tells them clearly what to do.
    c. Most people take very little interest in their work.
    d. Most people prefer an easy uninteresting job to a hard interesting one.
    e. None of the above applies to most people.

125. Which of the following statements apply to you?
    a. You frequently like to get away by yourself with your own thoughts.
    b. When you are walking somewhere you are more likely to concentrate on your own thoughts than to notice the things around you.
    c. You are more a theorist than a practical person.
    d. You often find it necessary to stand up for your principles or standards.
    e. None of the above applies to you.

Look over your answer sheet and make sure you have answered every question. There should be only one option checked for questions 1–110. As many options as apply should be checked for questions 111–125.

Appendix C

JAIM ANSWER SHEET

Job Analysis and Interest Measurement (JAIM)

Form 864
JAIM

Name..Date.....................

Current Position... ....

Specialty, if any, in your occupation...

Age.....................Sex...

Questions 1–110 require your choosing only ONE option. Please PRINT a capital letter for your choice (A, or B, or C, or D, or E) on the line following the number of the question. Please make the letter large and distinct. Answer EVERY question.

1.—	20.—	39.—	58.—	77.—	96.—
2.—	21.—	40.—	59.—	78.—	97.—
3.—	22.—	41.—	60.—	79.—	98.—
4.—	23.—	42.—	61.—	80.—	99.—
5.—	24.—	43.—	62.—	81.—	100.—
6.—	25.—	44.—	63.—	82.—	101.—
7.—	26.—	45.—	64.—	83.—	102.—
8.—	27.—	46.—	65.—	84.—	103.—
9.—	28.—	47.—	66.—	85.—	104.—
10.—	29.—	48.—	67.—	86.—	105.—
11.—	30.—	49.—	68.—	87.—	106.—
12.—	31.—	50.—	69.—	88.—	107.—
13.—	32.—	51.—	70.—	89.—	108.—
14.—	33.—	52.—	71.—	90.—	109.—
15.—	34.—	53.—	72.—	91.—	110.—
16.—	35.—	54.—	73.—	92.—	
17.—	36.—	55.—	74.—	93.—	
18.—	37.—	56.—	75.—	94.—	
19.—	38.—	57.—	76.—	95.—	

On the remaining fifteen questions (111–125), you may mark as many options as apply; you need not limit yourself to one. All five responses are therefore listed by the letters (a, b, c, d, e); CIRCLE the option or options which apply.

111. a   b   c   d   e   116. a   b   c   d   e   121. a   b   c   d   e

112. a   b   c   d   e   117. a   b   c   d   e   122. a   b   c   d   e

113. a   b   c   d   e   118. a   b   c   d   e   123. a   b   c   d   e

114. a   b   c   d   e   119. a   b   c   d   e   124. a   b   c   d   e

115. a   b   c   d   e   120. a   b   c   d   e   125. a   b   c   d   e

BIBLIOGRAPHY

1. Argyris, Chris. *Executive Leadership: An Appraisal of a Manager in Action.* New York: Harper & Row Publishers, Inc., 1953.

2. ———. *Integrating the Individual and the Organization.* New York: John Wiley & Sons, Inc., 1964.

3. ———. *Organization and Innovation.* Homewood, Ill.: Richard D. Irwin, Inc., and the Dorsey Press, 1965.

4. *Army War College Leadership Study.* Carlisle Barracks, Pa.: U.S. Army War College, June 30, 1970.

5. Barnes, Peter. *Pawns: The Plight of the Citizen-Soldier.* Also promotional indorsement by Robert Sherrill. New York: Alfred A. Knopf, Inc., 1972.

6. Baumgartner, John S. *The Lonely Warriors: Case for the Military-Industrial Complex.* Los Angeles: Nash Publishing Co., 1970.

7. Bennis, Warren G. "Revisionist Theory of Leadership." *Harvard Business Review,* January–February 1961.

8. Bennis, Warren G.; Benne, Kenneth D.; and Chin, Robert. *The Planning of Change: Readings in the Applied Behavioral Sciences.* New York: Holt, Rinehart and Winston, 1964.

9. Bienvenu, Bernard J. *New Priorities in Training.* American Management Association, 1969.

10. Bieri, J. "Changes in Interpersonal Perceptions Following Social Interaction." *Journal of Abnormal and Social Psychology* 48 (1953).

11. Bletz, Donald F. "After Vietnam: A Professional Challenge." *Military Review* (August 1971).

12. ———. "Military Professionalism: A Conceptual Approach." *Military Review* (May 1971).

13. ———. "Mutual Perceptions: The Academic and the Soldier in Contemporary America." *Parameters* 1, no. 2 (Fall 1971).

14. ———. *The Role of the Military Professional in U.S. Foreign Policy.* New York: Praeger Publishers, 1972.

15. Bossom, J., and Maslow, A. H. "Security of Judges as a Factor in Impressions of Warmth in Others." *Journal of Abnormal and Social Psychology* 55 (1957).

16. Broom, Leonard, and Selznick, Phillip. *Sociology.* New York: Row Petersen and Co., 1958.

17. Bunting, Josiah, Major. *The Lionheads.* New York: George Braziller, Inc., 1972.

18. Burke, R. L., and Bennis, W. G. "Changes in Perception of Self and Others During Human Relations Training." *Human Relations* 2 (1961).

19. Cantril, Hadley, "Perception and Interpersonal Relations." *American Journal of Psychiatry* 114, no. 2 (1957).

20. Chapman, Herschel E. *Officer Candidate School Evaluation and Training.* Fort Benning, Ga.: The Infantry School, June 1956.

21. Chung, Ly Qui. *Between Two Fires: The Unheard Voices of Vietnam.* New York: Praeger Publishers, 1970.

22. Cross, Edward M. "The Behavioral Styles, Work Performances and Values of an Occupational Group: Computer Programmers." Unpublished Doctoral Dissertation. Washington, D.C.: George Washington University, 1970.

23. Dearborn, D. C., and Simon, H. A. "Selective Perception: A Note on the Departmental Identifications of Executives." *Sociometry* 21 (1958).

24. Deutsch, M., and Solomon, L. "Reactions to Evaluations by Others as Influenced by Self-Evaluation." *Sociometry* 22 (1959).

25. Douglas, William O. *International Dissent.* New York: Random House, 1971.

26. Edwards, Allen L. *Statistical Methods for the Behavioral Sciences.* New York: Holt, Rinehart and Winston, 1964.

27. Eichelberger, Robert L. *Our Jungle Road to Tokyo.* New York: The Viking Press, Inc., 1950.

28. Festinger, Leon, *et al.* "The Influence Process in the Presence of Extreme Deviates." *Human Relations* 5 (1952).

29. Finn, James, ed. *A Conflict of Loyalties: The Case for Selective Conscientious Objection.* New York: Western Publishing Co., 1968.

30. ———, ed. *Conscience and Command: Justice and Discipline in the Military.* New York: Random House, 1971.

31. Fitzgerald, Frances. *Fire in the Lake: The Vietnamese and Americans in Vietnam.* Boston: Little, Brown and Company, 1972.

32. Fleishman, Edwin A.; Harris, Edwin F.; and Burtt, Harold E. *Leadership and Supervision in Industry.* Columbus, Ohio: Bureau of Educational Research, Ohio State University, 1955.

33. Getlein, Frank. *Playing Soldier.* New York: Holt, Rinehart and Winston, 1971.

34. Glasser, Ronald J. *365 Days.* New York: George Braziller, Inc., 1971.

35. Glick, Edward B. *Soldiers, Scholars, and Society; The Social Impact of the American Military.* Pacific Palisades, Calif.: Goodyear Publishing Co., Inc., 1971.

36. Gordon, Leonard V., and Medland, Francis F. *Values Associated with Military Career Motivation.* Washington, D.C.: U.S. Department of the Army, 1964.

37. Hamrick, Tom. "Coping with the Boob Image." *Army,* July 1970.

38. Hauser, William L. "Professionalism and the Junior Officer Drain." *Army,* September 1970.

39. Hayes, Thomas L. *American Deserters in Sweden: The Men and Their Challenge.* New York: Association Press, 1971.

40. Herbert, Anthony B. Lt. Col., USA—Ret. with Wooten, James T. *Soldier.* New York: Holt, Rinehart and Winston, 1973.

41. Herzberg, Frederick. "One More Time: How Do You Motivate Employees?" *Harvard Business Review,* January–February 1968.

276

42. Hickman, Martin B. *The Military and American Society.* Beverly Hills, Calif.: Glencoe Press, 1971.

43. Holmen, Milton G., *et al. An Assessment Program for OCS Applicants.* Washington, D.C.: Human Resources Research Office, George Washington University, 1956.

44. Holmen, Milton G., and Katter, Robert V. *Attitude and Information Patterns of OCS Eligibles.* Washington, D.C.: Human Resources Research Office, George Washington University, 1953.

45. Hunt, George P., Managing Editor. "Our Four-Star Military Mess." *Life,* June 18, 1971.

46. Huntington, Samuel P. *The Soldier and the State: The Theory and Policies of Civil-Military Relations.* Cambridge, Mass.: Harvard University Press, 1967.

47. Janowitz, Morris. *The Professional Soldier.* New York: Free Press, 1960, and revised in 1971.

48. Jennings, Eugene E. *The Executive: Autocrat, Bureaucrat, Democrat.* New York: Harper & Row Publishers, Inc., 1962.

49. ———. *The Executive in Crisis.* East Lansing, Mich.: Michigan State University, 1965.

50. Johnson, Haynes, and Wilson, George C. "Army in Anguish." *Washington Post,* September 12, 1971.

51. Johnston, Jerome, and Bachman, Jerald G. *Young Men Look at Military Service.* Ann Arbor, Mich.: Institute for Social Research, University of Michigan, April 1971.

52. Just, Ward. *Military Men.* New York: Alfred A. Knopf, Inc., 1970.

53. ———. "Soldier." *Atlantic,* October 1970.

54. Katz, Daniel, and Kahn, Robert L. *The Social Psychology of Organizations.* New York: John Wiley & Sons, Inc., 1966.

55. Kelley, H. H. "The Warm-Cold Variable in First Impressions of Persons." *Journal of Personality* 18 (1950).

56. Killmer, Richard L.; Lecky, Robert S.; and Wiley, Debrah S. *They Can't Go Home Again.* Philadelphia: Pilgrim Press, 1971.

57. Killmer, Richard L., and Lutz, Charles P. *The Draft and the Rest of Your Life.* Minneapolis: Augsburg Publishing House, 1972.

58. Kirch, J. M. *The Successful Police Educator: A Profile.* Master's Thesis. Washington, D.C.: George Washington University, 1969.

59. Kirkpatrick, D. L. "Techniques for Evaluating Training Programs." *Journal of American Society for Training and Development.* A Series of Four Articles, November 1960–February 1961.

60. Kotula, Leo J., and Haggerty, Helen R. *Research on the Selection of Officer Candidates and Cadets.* U.S. Army Technical Research Report 1146, 1966.

61. Lehner, G. F. J. "Some Relationships Among Personal Adjustment Self-Ratings, Self-Scores, and Assigned 'Average' Scores." *Journal of Psychology* 50 (1960).

62. Leider, Robert. *Why They Leave: Resignations from the USMA Class of* 1966. A study by the U.S. Department of the Army, July 6, 1970.

63. Leonard, R. G. *An Exploratory Study of Executive Personality Patterns Within Selected Private Industry.* Doctoral Dissertation. Washington, D.C.: George Washington University, 1972.

64. Levy, Charles. "The Violent Veterans." *Time,* March 13, 1972.

65. Lieberman, Seymour. "The Effects of Changes in Roles on the Attitudes of Role Occupants." *Human Relations* 9 (1956).

66. Lifton, Robert J. *Home from the War—Vietnam Veterans: Neither Victims nor Executioners.* New York: Simon & Schuster, 1973.

67. Likert, Rensis. *The Human Organization.* New York: McGraw-Hill Book Co., 1967.

68. Lippitt, Gordon L. *Effects of Information About Group Desire for Change on Members of a Group.* Unpublished Doctoral Dissertation. Washington, D.C.: American University, 1959.

69. ———. *Organizational Renewal.* New York: Meredith Corp., 1969.

70. ———. "What Do We Know About Leadership?" *National Education Journal* (December 1955).

71. Lippitt, Gordon L., and Petersen, Peter B. "Development of a Behavioral Style in Leadership Training." *Training and Development Journal* 21, no. 7 (July 1967).

72. ———. *Measuring Changes in Behavioral Styles During a Leadership Program: A Study of an Officer Candidate School.* Unpublished Paper. Washington, D.C.: George Washington University, 1967.

73. Lippitt, G. L.; McCune, S. D.; and Church, L. D. "Attitudes of Training Directors Toward the Application of Research to Training Programs." *Training Director's Journal* 18, no. 3 (March 1964).

74. MacArthur, Douglas. Farewell Address to the Cadets of West Point, May 12, 1962.

75. Mager, Robert F. *Developing Attitude Toward Learning.* Palo Alto, Calif.: Fearon Publishers, 1968.

76. Mayeske, G. W.; Harmon, F. L.; and Glickman, A. S. "What Can Critical Incidents Tell Management?" *Training and Development Journal* 20, no. 4 (April 1966).

77. McCune, Shirley D. *An Exploratory Study of the Measured Behavioral Styles of Students in Five Schools of Social Work.* Doctoral Dissertation. Washington, D.C.: Catholic University, 1966.

78. McCune, S. D., and Mills, E. W. *Continuing Education for Ministers, A Pilot Evaluation of Three Programs.* Washington, D.C.: Ministry Studies Board, 1968.

79. Meckling, William H., Executive Director. *The President's Commission on an All-Volunteer Armed Force.* Washington, D.C.: U.S. Government Printing Office, February 1970.

80. Medland, F. F., and Olans, J. L. *Peer Rating, Stability in Changing Groups.* U.S. Army Technical Research Note 142, April 1964·

278

81. Menzel, Paul. *Moral Argument and the War in Vietnam.* Nashville, Tenn.: Aurora Publishers, Inc., 1971.

82. Miles, Matthew B. "Human Relations Training: Processes and Outcomes." *Journal of Counseling Psychology* 7 (1960).

83. ———. *Learning to Work in Groups.* Teacher's College. New York: Columbia University Press, 1959.

84. Miller, James C. *A Study in Officer Motivation (New View).* Washington, D.C.: U.S. Air Force Studies and Analysis, DCS/Plans and Operations, November 1966.

85. Miller, Robert E., and Creager, John A. *Predicting Achievement of Cadets in Their First Year at the Air Force Academy, Class of 1962.* Texas: Lackland Air Force Base, Personnel Laboratory, 1960.

86. Mosel, James N. *How to Feed Back Performance Results to Trainees.* A paper read before the Employee Training Institute at the Annual Conference of Public Personnel Administration of the Civil Service Assembly. Washington, D.C.: October 9, 1966.

87. Moskos, Charles C., Jr. *The American Enlisted Man.* New York: Russell Sage Foundation, 1970.

88. Murdick, R. G. "Measuring the Profit in Industry Training Programs." *Journal of the American Society of Training Directors* 14, no. 4 (April 1960).

89. Nelson, Paul D. "Similarities and Differences Among Leaders and Followers." *Journal of Social Psychology* 63 (1964).

90. Opinion Research Corporation. *Attitudes and Motivations of Young Men Toward Enlisting in the U.S. Army.* A Study Prepared for N. W. Ayer & Son, Inc., and the U.S. Army. Princeton, N.J.: May 1971.

91. Oppenheimer, Martin, ed. *The American Military.* Chicago, Ill.: Transition Books, Aldine Publishing Co., 1971.

92. ———. *The American Military.* Chicago: Transition Books, Aldine Publishing Co., 1971. Pp. 16–36: "Vietnam: Why Men Fight," by Charles C. Moskos.

93. Osborne, J. K. *I Refuse.* Philadelphia: Westminster Press, 1971.

94. Petersen, Peter B. *The American Soldier of the Vietnam War.* Arlington, Va.: Behavioral Sciences Division, Army Research Office, U.S. Army, June 25, 1971.

95. ———. *Comparison of Behavioral Styles.* Proceedings of Military Testing Association Convention. San Antonio: September 18, 1968.

96. ———. *A Comparison of Behavioral Styles Between Entering and Graduating Students in Officer Candidate School.* Unpublished Master's Thesis. Washington, D.C.: George Washington University, 1967. On file in U.S. Army service school libraries. Available at cost from the National Technical Information Service, U.S. Department of Commerce, Springfield, Virginia 22151 (Document No. AD 644 833). Also for sale by University Microfilms, Ann Arbor, Michigan (Document No. M–1272).

97. ———. *Comparison of Certain Self-Reported Beliefs Between a Group of Men*

Who Remained in the U.S. Army (n = 358) and a Group of Men Who Departed (n = 919). Pending Publication.

98. ————. "Effect and Stability of Leadership Training." *Research in Education.* ERIC Processing and Reference Facility, 4833 Rugby Avenue, Bethesda, Maryland 20014, December 1971. (ED 053 680).

99. ————. *The Effect of OCS Training.* Unpublished Paper. Arlington, Va.: December 1970.

100. ————. *Effects of Combat on the Beliefs of Infantrymen (n = 80).* Pending Publication.

101. ————. *An Exploratory Study of the Psychological Dimensions of Army Students Attending the U.S. Army War College.* Monograph. Carlisle Barracks, Pa.: U.S. Army War College, February 14, 1972.

102. ————. *An Investigation of the Effect and Stability of Training (n = 210).* Pending Publication.

103. ————. *An Investigation of the Effect of Training.* Unpublished Doctoral Dissertation. Washington, D.C.: George Washington University, February 15, 1971. On file in the Library of Congress and in U.S. Army service school libraries. Available at cost from the National Technical Information Service, U.S. Department of Commerce, Springfield, Virginia 22151 (Document No. AD 721 394). Also for sale by University Microfilms, Ann Arbor, Michigan (Document No. 71–14 185).

104. ———. "Leadership Training." *Training and Development Journal* 26, no. 4 (April 1972).

105. ————. *Nonmonetary Factors of Retention Pertinent to a Modern Volunteer Army.* Arlington, Va.: Behavioral Sciences Division, Army Research Office, December 1971.

106. ————. "Psychological Dimensions of Army Students Attending the U.S. Army War College: An Analysis." *Parameters,* Vol. II, No. 1, Carlisle Barracks, Pa.: U.S. Army War College, Spring-Summer 1972.

107. ————. *Reevaluation of the OCS Training Process.* Unpublished Paper. Arlington, Va.: May 17, 1971.

108. ————. *Transition from Vietnam.* Unpublished Paper. Arlington, Va.: May 17, 1971.

109. ————, and Lippitt, Gordon L. "Comparison of Behavioral Styles Between Entering and Graduating Students in Officer Candidate School." *Journal of Applied Psychology* 52, no. 1, pt 1 (February 1968).

110. Polner, Murray. *No Victory Parades: The Return of the Vietnam Veteran.* New York: Holt, Rinehart and Winston, 1971.

111. Porter, Lyman W. "Where Is the Organization Man?" *Harvard Business Review,* November–December 1963.

112. Public Opinion Surveys, Inc. *Attitudes of Adult Civilians Toward the Military Services as a Career.* Prepared for the Office of the Armed Forces Information and Education, Washington, D.C.: U.S. Department of Defense, 1955.

113. Pullen, John J. *Patriotism in America: A Study of Changing Devotions* 1770–1970. New York: American Heritage Press, 1971.

114. Reedy, George E. *Who Will Do the Fighting for Us?* New York: World Publishing Co., 1969.

115. Reeves, Edgar A., Jr. *A Comparative Study of Behavioral Style as Measured by the Job Analysis and Interest Measurement (JAIM) of Retired Adult Participation and Non-Participation in the Institute of Lifetime Learning.* Doctoral Dissertation. Washington, D.C.: George Washington University, 1969.

116. Reimer, David J. *The Relationship Between Childhood Experience and Certain Variables Correlated With Occupational Choice and Performance.* Master's Thesis. Washington, D.C.: George Washington University, 1967.

117. Rensberger, Boyce. "Delayed Trauma in Veterans Cited." *New York Times,* May 3, 1972.

118. Report of Special Commission of Civilian Psychiatrists Covering Psychiatric Policy and Practice in the United States Army Medical Corps, European Theater, April 20–July 8, 1945.

119. Rivkin, Robert S. *GI Rights and Army Justice.* New York: Grove Press Inc., 1970.

120. Robinson, William H., Jr. "An Element of International Affairs—The Military Mind." *Naval War College Review* 23, no. 3 (November 1970).

121. Rodberg, Leonard S., and Shearer, Derek. *The Pentagon Watchers.* Garden City, N.Y.: Doubleday & Co., 1970.

122. Rohr, John A. *Prophets Without Honor.* Nashville: Abingdon Press, 1971.

123. Roth, R. M. *Personal Characteristics of the Overseas Chief School Administrator and the Relationship of These Characteristics to the Type of His School, and Its Geographic Location.* Doctoral Dissertation. Philadelphia: Temple University, 1972.

124. Schein, Edgar H. "Management Development as a Process of Influence." *Industrial Management Review of the School of Industrial Management (MIT)* (May 1961)

125. _____. *Organizational Psychology.* Englewood Cliffs, N.J.: Prentice-Hall, Inc., 1965.

126. Schein, Edgar H.; Schneier, Inga; and Barker, Curtis H. *Coercive Persuasion.* New York: W. W. Norton and Co., Inc., 1961.

127. Shartle, Carroll L. *Executive Performance and Leadership.* Englewood Cliffs, N.J.: Prentice-Hall, Inc., 1956.

128. Sherrill, Robert. *Military Justice Is to Justice as Military Music Is to Music.* New York: Harper and Row Publishers, Inc., 1970.

129. ———. "Some Advice the Pentagon Should Heed." *Washington Post (Book World),* January 9, 1972.

130. Slater, Philip E., and Bennis, Warren G. "Democracy Is Inevitable." *Harvard Business Review,* March–April 1964.

131. Stapp, Andy. *Up Against the Brass.* New York: Simon & Schuster, 1970.

132. Stavins, Ralph; Barnet, Richard J.; and Raskin, Marcus G. *Washington Plans an Aggressive War*. New York: Random House, 1971.

133. Stephenson, R. W.; Erickson, C. E.; and Lehner, G. F. J. *Self-Perception Changes in a Sensitivity Training Laboratory*. Washington, D.C.: National Training Laboratories, National Education Association, No. 5, 1965.

134. Sterner, F. M. "Determining Training Needs: A Method." *Training Director's Journal* 19, no. 9 (September 1965).

135. Stevens, Franklin. *If This Be Treason*. New York: Peter H. Wyden, Inc., 1970.

136. Stouffer, Samuel A., *et al.* "The American Soldier: Adjustment During Army Life," Vol. 1. *Studies in Social Psychology in World War II*. Princeton, N.J.: Princeton University Press, 1949.

137. ———. "The American Soldier: Combat and its Aftermath," Vol. 2. *Studies in Social Psychology in World War II*. Princeton, N.J.: Princeton University Press, 1949.

138. Tannenbaum, R.; Weschler, I. R.; and Massarik, F. *Leadership and Organization*. New York: McGraw-Hill Book Co., 1961.

139. Tauber, Peter. *The Sunshine Soldiers*. New York: Simon & Schuster, 1971.

140. This, Leslie E., and Lippitt, Gordon L. "Learning Theories and Training." *Training and Development Journal* (April–May 1966).

141. Trojanowicz, Robert C. "A Comparison of the Behavioral Styles of Policemen and Social Workers." Unpublished Doctoral Dissertation. East Lansing, Mich.: Michigan State University, 1969.

142. U.S. Army Command and General Staff College. *Leadership RB* 22–1. Fort Leavenworth, Kans.: U.S. Department of the Army, 1952.

143. "U.S. Army War College." *U.S. Army War College Pamphlet*. Carlisle Barracks, Pa.: U.S. Army War College, January 1972.

144. U.S. Congress. House Committee on Appropriations. Subcommittee on Department of Defense. *Department of Defense Appropriations for* 1972. Hearings, 92nd Cong., 1st sess. Washington, D.C.: U.S. Government Printing Office, 1971.

145. U.S. Department of the Army. *Advertising Guidelines From Reenlistment Research*. A study prepared by N. W. Ayer & Son, Inc., Washington, D.C., March 1970.

146. ———. *Department of Army Circular No.* 351–18: *Senior Service College Selection System*. Washington, D.C.: October 26, 1970.

147. ———. *Department of the Army Pamphlet* 601–1: *The OCS Story*. Washington, D.C.: June 1, 1966.

148. ———. *Department of the Army Pamphlet* 601–1: *The OCS Story*. Washington, D.C.: October 1969.

149. ———. *Field Manual* 21–50: *Military Courtesy and Discipline*. Washington, D.C.: War Department, June 15, 1942.

150. ———. *Field Manual* 100–5: *Field Service Regulations-Operations*. Washington, D.C.: February 19, 1962.

151. ———. *Reenlistment Study: An Attitudinal Survey*. A summary of data prepared by Behavior Systems, Inc., Philadelphia: March 1970.

152. Wald, Max. *A Story of Selected Personnel and Behavioral Characteristics of Public School Principals in the Commonwealth of Pennsylvania.* Doctoral Dissertation. Philadelphia: Temple University, 1971.

153. Walther, Regis H. "ASTD Members—Their Perceptions and Training Goals." *Training and Development Journal* (March 1971).

154. ———. "The Functional Occupational Classification Project: A Critical Appraisal." *Personnel Guidance Journal* 38 (1960).

155. ———. *Job Adjustment and Employee Health.* Washington, D.C.: Social Research Group, George Washington University, 1969. Report submitted in connection with Grant No. UI 00447, Public Health Service, U.S. Department of Health, Education and Welfare.

156. ———. "Job Analysis and Interest Measurement." *Education,* 1963.

157. ———. *Job Analysis and Interest Measurement.* Princeton, N.J.: Educational Testing Service, 1964.

158. ———. *Orientations and Behavioral Styles of Foreign Service Officers.* New York: Carnegie Endowment for International Peace, 1965.

159. ———. *Orientations and Behavioral Styles of Public School Officials.* Washington, D.C.: Social Research Group, George Washington University, 1967.

160. ———. *Personality Variables and Career Decisions: A Pilot Study of Law and Social Work Students.* Washington, D.C.: Social Research Group, George Washington University, 1966. Available from the U.S. Office of Education, ERIC Document Reproduction Service (Document No. ED 012 937), National Cash Register, Box 2206, Rockville, Maryland 20852.

161. ———. *The Prediction of Occupational Adjustment Through Measured Behavioral Styles.* Doctoral Dissertation. Washington, D.C.: George Washington University, 1963.

162. ———. *The Psychological Dimensions of Work: A Research Approach Through Use of a Self-Report Inventory.* Washington, D.C.: George Washington University, February 1972.

163. ———. *The Psychological Dimensions of Work: An Experimental Taxonomy of Occupations.* Washington, D.C.: George Washington University, 1964. Available from the U.S. Office of Education, ERIC Document Reproduction Service (Document No. ED 003 075), National Cash Register, Box 2206, Rockville, Maryland 20852.

164. ———. *Relationship Between Self-Description and Occupational Choice.* Master's Thesis. Washington, D.C.: George Washington University, 1960.

165. ———. "Self-Description as a Predictor of Rate of Promotion of Junior Foreign Service Officers." *Journal of Applied Psychology* 46 (1962).

166. ———. "Self-Description as a Predictor of Success or Failure in Foreign Service Clerical Jobs." *Journal of Applied Psychology* 45 (1961).

167. ———., and McCune, Shirley D. "Juvenile Court Judges in the United States, Part II: Working Styles and Characteristics." *Crime and Delinquency,* October 1965.

168. ———. *Socialization Principles and Work Styles of the Juvenile Court.* Washington, D.C.: Center for the Behavioral Sciences, George Washington University, 1965.

169. ———, McCune, Shirley D.: and Petersen, Peter B. *The Shaping of Professional Subcultures: A Study of Student Groups from Five Professions.* Washington, D.C.: Social Research Group, George Washington University, 1968. Available from NCR/EDRS, 4936 Fairmont Avenue, Bethesda, Maryland 20014 (Document No. ED 038904). Also ERIC Processing and Reference Facility, 4833 Rugby Avenue, Bethesda, Maryland 20014 (Document No. ED 038 904).

170. ——— McCune, Shirley D.; and Trojanowicz, Robert C. "The Contrasting Occupational Cultures of Policemen and Social Workers." *Experimental Publication System.* Washington, D.C.: American Psychological Association, December 1970.

171. Waterhouse, Larry G., and Wizard, Mariann G. *Turning the Guns Around.* New York: Praeger Publishers, 1971.

172. Westmoreland, William C., General U.S.A. Speech delivered at Fort Benning, Georgia, September 24, 1971.

173. White, Ralph K., and Lippitt, Ronald O. *Autocracy and Democracy: An Experimental Inquiry.* New York: Harper, 1960.

174. Whyte, William H. *The Organization Man.* New York: Simon & Schuster, 1956.

175. Williams, Roger N. *The New Exiles.* New York: Liveright Publishers, 1971.

176. Woodward, Joan. *Industrial Organization: Theory and Practice.* London: Oxford University Press, 1965.

177. Yarmolinsky, Adam. *The Military Establishment: Its Impact on American Society.* New York: Harper & Row Publishers, Inc., 1971,

178. Zajonc, Robert B., and Wolfe, Donald M. "Cognitive Consequences of a Person's Position in a Formal Organization." *Human Relations* 19, no. 2 (1966).

Index

285

Date Due